COMICS AND THE BODY

STUDIES IN COMICS AND CARTOONS

Jared Gardner and Charles Hatfield, Series Editors

COMICS AND THE BODY

Drawing, Reading, and Vulnerability

ESZTER SZÉP

THE OHIO STATE UNIVERSITY PRESS
COLUMBUS

Library of Congress Cataloging-in-Publication Data

Names: Szép, Eszter, author.

Title: Comics and the body : drawing, reading, and vulnerability / Eszter Szép.

Other titles: Studies in comics and cartoons.

Description: Columbus : The Ohio State University Press, [2020] | Series: Studies in comics and cartoons | Includes bibliographical references and index. | Summary: "Looking at works by Lynda Barry, Ken Dahl, Katie Green, Miriam Katin, and Joe Sacco, presents a new way to see how our bodies read and show up in comics. Emphasizes the discursive, performative, and vulnerable nature of the body"—Provided by publisher.

Identifiers: LCCN 2020023809 | ISBN 9780814214541 (cloth) | ISBN 0814214541 (cloth) | ISBN 9780814280805 (ebook) | ISBN 0814280803 (ebook)

Subjects: LCSH: Comic books, strips, etc.—History and criticism. | Human body in literature.

Classification: LCC PN6714 .S98 2020 | DDC 741.5/9—dc23

LC record available at https://lccn.loc.gov/2020023809

Cover design by Amanda Weiss

Text design by Juliet Williams

Type set in Palatino Linotype

∞ The paper used in this publication meets the minimum requirements of the American National Standard for Information Sciences—Permanence of Paper for Printed Library Materials. ANSI Z39.48-1992.

For Kálmán

CONTENTS

ILLUSTRATIONS

ACKNOWLEDGMENTS

I could not have written this monograph alone. I am indebted to and I would like to thank:

Laurike in 't Veld and Harriet Earle, the "Glamorous Ladies of Comics," for their expertise, insightful advice, sense of humor, encouragement, and friendship. A special thanks to Laurike for her help with my comic;

Balázs Horváth for being the first reader of what are now chapters 1, 2, and 3, and for providing extensive reliable feedback;

Judit Friedrich and Zsófia Bán for their guidance and for the questions they have challenged me with;

Kata Gyuris and Dóra Vecsernyés for their editing advice and for helping me to focus;

Paul Williams for demonstrating research discipline at the Billy Ireland Cartoon Library and for the discussions on all things comics;

the community of comics scholars I have met at events. Your feedback has been great encouragement and inspiration while I was writing and editing this book. I have learned a lot from discussions on drawing and comics with you;

the institutions that have supported my research by being inspiring environments to work in: the Billy Ireland Cartoon Library and Museum, the Fine Arts Library of The Ohio State University, both in Columbus, Ohio, and Central European University Library in Budapest, Hungary;

the institutions that have supported my research with their grants: the European Association of American Studies Travel Grant, the Representations of Violence in Contemporary American Popular Culture research project at the University of Bucharest and project leader Mihaela Precup, Eötvös Loránd University, and the New National Excellence Program in Hungary;

the peer reviewers for their remarks, suggestions, and support on the manuscript of this book;

all the staff at The Ohio State University Press who were involved in the process of preparing this book, and the editors of the Studies in Comics and Cartoons series, Charles Hatfield and Jared Gardner, for making this book possible;

my mother, Eszter Meleg, for having encouraged me to study;

my husband, Kálmán Jelitai, for the support, coffee (the best in the world!), interest, questions, and for reminding me that days off are the best things about writing monographs.

Sections of this book have appeared, in a different form, in the following publications:

Szép, Eszter. "Discourses of Trauma and Representation: Motherhood and Mother Tongue in Miriam Katin's Graphic Memoirs." *Documenting Trauma in Comics: Traumatic Pasts, Embodied Histories, and Graphic Reportage,* edited by Dominic Davies and Candida Rifkind, Palgrave Macmillan, 2020, pp. 243–62.

Szép, Eszter. "Embodied Reading and Performing Vulnerability in Joe Sacco's *The Great War." Representing Acts of Violence in Comics,* edited by Nina Mickwitz, Ian Horton, and Ian Hague, Routledge, 2019, pp. 89–102.

INTRODUCTION

EMBODIMENT, VULNERABILITY, AND COMICS AS DIALOGUE

READING COMICS is not only a performance of our cognitive skills, it is also a performance and interaction of bodies. I remember clearly the morning when I was reading Miriam Katin's autobiographical graphic narrative, *Letting It Go* (2013) in the bathtub: What a charming colorful book of memories and mundane events, what a modern old lady talking to her son via Skype, I thought. The book deals with the everyday activities of a comic book artist called Miriam, and the process of her learning to accept that her son plans to settle in Germany, a country that she still associates with the Holocaust and her childhood traumas. I remember marveling at the courage Katin has in drawing caricatures of herself, showing the character that stands for her in a series of unflattering situations, like freaking out at the sight of cockroaches. Katin representing Miriam occasionally almost as a witch, with ridiculous uncombed hair, big bulging eyes, and in an old-school nightgown. What irony, I thought. The narrative is equally honest and uncompromising about the prejudices of the old hag in a nightie. But I was not prepared to see the naked body of the protagonist of this confessional narrative covered in her own excrement. I winced. The scene is in full color and is long, almost longer than one can bear. Why is this such a challenge to bear? What is happening to my body while I am reading that book, that scene? How does this address by the artist change my approach to the remaining parts of the story? Why is Katin doing this? Was she not afraid to draw herself like that? Is it a unique gesture or is it part of a strategy? How does such a representation relate to the tradition of self-representation in comics and to the ways cartoonists communicate with their readers?

This book was born out of these questions.

•

By focusing on ways in which the activities of the body are crucial to making and reading comics, this book explores comics as a dialogue between artists and readers. At the heart of a dynamic and mediated interaction between artists and readers we find the body: Comics are made by expressive lines that mark the unison of movement and thinking, and they are interpreted not simply visually, but also by and via the reader's body. The chapters of this book explore how this embodied dialogue takes place in contemporary nonfiction comics: These comics usually have a first-person character or narrator, and they assert to reveal someone's personal account or experience of reality. This relationship of nonfiction comics to events of reality, together with the essentially embodied nature of both drawing and reading comics, invites the last keyword of my approach: vulnerability. I show that drawing, reading, and the interaction enabled by nonfiction comics are rooted in, and offer means to find out more about, the experience of being vulnerable.

Via interacting with comics, opportunities are offered for artists and readers to share ideas and experiences: The material object of the comic held in hand creates opportunities for a "dialogical and dialectical engagement"—to borrow Vivian Sobchack's term from phenomenological film theory (23). Sobchack's theory of engagement is based on two viewing subjects who can also be seen—there is no hierarchy between them, and neither holds privileges. She states that "both film and spectator are capable of viewing and of being viewed, both are embodied in the world as the subject of vision and object for vision" (23). The readings of comics I offer in this book are all based on a similar realization that engagement with comics is a dialogue, and that the performance of the body is central to experiencing it either as an artist or as a reader. During dialogical engagement with comics, the possible meanings of comics are performed by the artist and by the reader, whose respective active and embodied participation is organized around the actual material comics that they are making or reading. This book explores the nature of this "dynamic involvement" (13) and why I believe it to be inseparable from the experience of vulnerability.

Naturally, appreciating art in general can be approached as interaction, and mutual involvement is not a special characteristic of comics. Yet, I believe there are specific forms of embodied dialogical engagement unique to comics due to comics being a drawn narrative medium. The following chapters link this very specific embodied engagement with drawing comics as an artistic performance, and a specific embodied engagement with reading comics as a readerly performance, to the experience of vulnerability. In fact, I argue that the experience of vulnerability is at the heart of nonfiction comics partly because of its drawn and embodied nature, and partly because of the special modality in which reality is presented in these comics.

Vulnerability, as it will be discussed in a later section of the introduction, is a condition we share because we inhabit bodies. Human bodies in their diversity are seen and experienced as vulnerable in a number of ways; however, vulnerability is always experienced in a dialogue, because it always elicits a response. The parties taking part in this dialogue might recognize each other's vulnerability and might deny it, and they might response in unpredictable ways: It is a dynamic and open-ended interaction. At this point, I would like to emphasize that vulnerability becomes a central aspect of my approach to comics because I think of interactions with comics as essentially embodied and performative, and the ethics of vulnerability are based on these two cornerstones: embodied presence and performative interaction. I see vulnerability as the most fundamental consequence of our having a body, and it is impossible not to include it in my model of "dynamic involvement" (Sobchack 13) with comics.

As a point of departure, this monograph relies on the reevaluation of the body's role in thinking (Lakoff and Johnson, *Metaphors*; Gallagher), and on the phenomenological perception of the lived-body as the basis for communication (Vivian Sobchack based on Merleau-Ponty, Laura U. Marks). Indeed, due to the results of cognitive neuroscience and following a phenomenologically oriented school of philosophy, the body has been considered as having a pivotal role in thinking. My aim is to look into how comics are made and how comics are read by the "mind-body as an interconnected system, rather than disjointed components" (Shaughnessy 5). George Lakoff and Mark Johnson argue in *Philosophy in the Flesh* (1999) that our cognitive actions and reasoning are embodied—that is, they are enabled and shaped by our bodies. Our reason and cognitive capacities are "shaped crucially by the peculiarities of our human bodies, by the remarkable details of the neural structure of our brains, and by the specifics of our everyday functioning in the world" (4). Lakoff and Johnson, fathers of the influential Conceptual Metaphor Theory (CMT), famously show that "the very properties of concepts are created as a result of the way the brain and body are structured and the way they function in interpersonal relations and in the physical world" (37). Philosopher Shaun Gallagher in *How the Body Shapes the Mind* (2005) emphasizes that the very structures of our thinking are enabled by our bodies and its affordances: "Embodied movement contributes to the shaping of perception, emotional experience, memory, judgement, and the understanding of self and of others" (10). In this book, my aim is to characterize some of the embodied aspects of drawing and of reading comics and to describe possible links between embodied cognition and vulnerability. Vulnerability can be a significant part of the reader's engagement with nonfiction comics not simply because of *what* is shown and narrated—the stories are frequently about injustice, illness, trauma, death, war—but because of the embodied nature of reading and cognition.

Evelyn B. Tribble and John Sutton in "Introduction: Interdisciplinary and Cognitive Approaches to Performance" write about "vigorous debates" (31) around CMT and cite Chris Sinha, who states that narrowed focus on embodied cognition substitutes the mind-body dualism with a dualism between the individual and society (31). In this book I focus on how actions of drawing and reading are performed by an embodied mind and I also study how these performances can take part in a "dynamic involvement" (Sobchack 13) at the heart of which we find the embodied experience of vulnerability communicated by the comic as material object.

The study of how the body is involved in activities around comics is not alien from contemporary investigations in comics studies. Recent comics scholarship, however, focuses either on the body of the artist or on the body of the reader. *Comics and the Body: Drawing, Reading, and Vulnerability* maps out a framework in which the embodied processes of drawing and the embodied processes of interpretation can be related in dialogical engagement. Thus, the basic presumption of this monograph, which will be tested by close readings in the chapters, can be summed up as follows: The ways creators and readers interact with each other via nonfiction comics can be seen as embodied engagement with their own and with others' vulnerability. Engagement with comics takes place, on the one hand, by the involvement of the drawer's and reader's bodies, and on the other hand, by interacting with the materiality of the actual comics that is mediating the interaction. Comics can thus be thought of as a mediated interaction between three bodies: those of the drawer, reader, and object (the actual comic). This conception, again, resembles the way Sobchack speaks about experiencing film.

Because of the involvement of the body, both drawing and reading comics can be regarded as a performance: Meaning is born in situated and embodied interactions. During these performances, the drawer and the reader interact with the material features of comics: The drawer uses pencils, pens, brushes, ink, crayons, erasers, paper, and digital tools; the reader (typically) holds the printed comic in hand. Even though the final comic is printed and mass-produced, the reader feels the drawer's bodily trace in the drawings: As Jared Gardner explains, comics is the only reproduced medium where the original line, the trace of the drawer's hand, is not replaced by typography ("Storylines" 56). The Benjaminian *aura* of works of art needs to be reinterpreted in the case of comics: Even printed works establish an embodied connection with the moment and embodied performance of creation enabled by the drawn line.[1]

The chapters of this book will offer close readings of comics by Lynda Barry, Ken Dahl, Joe Sacco, Miriam Katin, and Katie Green with the aim of identifying specific ways in which the drawer's and reader's "dynamic involvement" (Sobchack 13) and embodied engagement with vulnerability can take place. I start out by focus-

1. Comics is not the only medium that builds on the visibility of the drawer's bodily investment: Handmade artist books are created with a similar attention to bodily performance. Artist books, just like printed comics, emphasize their materiality in the current context of digital textuality and digital image making, when "different genres of paper-based literature are . . . reinventing themselves as *embodied* writing" (Brillenburgh Wurth et al. 94). Digital contexts influence the production and interpretation of comics; the present turn to bodily processes might in fact be a way to come to terms with both the new possibilities and the materiality of the old, paper-based media, in light of, and co-present with, digital environments.

ing on ways in which the drawn line, born out of an embodied engagement, is generative of thought and also facilitates rethinking and reexperiencing vulnerability. For this reason, to refer to the producer of lines and drawings, from now on I will use the simple term "drawer" instead of other terms, such as "artist," "creator," "cartoonist," and "draughtsman," all of which open up connotations and associations in directions this monograph does not wish to examine. Using the term "drawer" allows me to narrow my focus on the engagement enabled by the drawn line. However, chapter 5, which focuses on comics as material objects, will revisit the notion of the drawer, or, rather, the idea(l) of a single person behind a publication, and will complicate the notion of authorship in nonfiction settings by acknowledging the work of designers and other team members responsible for how comics as a three-dimensional printed product looks (see figure 5.6). The first three chapters, however, will study acts of mark making and will refer to the mark maker as "drawer." Similarly, I will simply call the person who is involved in embodied interpretation of published comics "reader." Though "reading" is a term biased toward verbal expression, I prefer it to "receiver" or "onlooker" because, in contrast to these alternatives, the term "reader" has a connection to engagement with comics as a partly textual, nonanimated product.

In the following sections of the introduction, I would like to elaborate on some of the key terms of my model of nonfiction comics as embodied dialogue based on the experience of vulnerability. First, I position vulnerability as the basis of an embodied interaction with comics. Second, I survey comics scholarship in which either the underlying importance of the body or the potential of ethical engagement with comics was studied. Third, in order to provide a context for my focus on vulnerability and embodied dialogue, I discuss some questions that have governed the study of autobiography and reportage, the two kinds of nonfiction comics I focus on. I conclude with an overview of the theoretical approaches on drawing in comics—this last section serves as the theoretical background for chapters 1, 2, and 3.

Concepts: Vulnerability as Embodied Dialogue

Vulnerability is a central idea mobilized by this book because vulnerability, as will be shown shortly, arises as an ethical consequence of the bodily nature of our existence. The concept and ethics of vulnerability are central to the way I think of interaction with comics because of the interpretive and performative processes of the body and also because dialogue and the social nature of the interaction are central to both contemporary feminist conceptions of vulnerability and my approach to nonfiction comics. The comics I study in this monograph can all be related to trauma and are often studied as trauma texts with the help of trauma studies. Relying on the concept, ethics, and performance of vulnerability in artistic and readerly interaction with nonfiction comics allows a new approach. Trauma studies has been a very fruitful approach to comics scholarship; it has influenced works like *Comics, Trauma, and the New Art of War* by Harriet E. H. Earle (2017) and *The Trauma Graphic Novel* by Andrés Romero-Jódar (2017), as well as innumerable journal articles and book chapters on comics like *Maus, In the Shadow of No Towers* (Versluys; Orbán, "Trauma"; Pines; Findley), comics on 9/11 (Dony), and many others. Trauma studies has helped think about the representation and the reception of mediated individual traumatic experience in comics. Dominick LaCapra's concept of empathic unsettlement and secondary witness and Geoffrey Hartman's concept of secondary trauma have helped understanding readerly engagement. In an early article on Miriam Katin, Marjane Satrapi, and Zeina Abirached, I myself have worked with the concept of "allo-identification," or identification "by adoption," which comes from Marianne Hirsch's essay "Marked by Memory" (Szép). Focusing on how the condition of vulnerability can inform embodied acts of creation and interpretation allows me to examine expressions of unsettling and painful moments or narrative elements in the context of lines and marks and the performative practices of bodies.

Choosing an encounter enabled by vulnerability as a framework to approach comics helps the study I undertake in two ways: On the one hand, it allows me to focus on the social and interactive nature of engagement with comics, and on the other hand, it allows me to theorize what Jill Bennett in *Empathic Vision* (2005) called an "affective transaction in terms other than those of the identificatory relationship" (10). Bennett uses the word "transaction" to describe an encounter with a trauma-related work of art that "touches us, but . . . does not necessarily communicate the 'secret' of personal experience" (7). Transaction is a "direct engagement with sensation as it is registered in the work" (7), it is an embodied multisensory experience and not only a visual one (35). Transaction is not emotional identification, as for Bennett, the appreciation of a work of art is affective and intellectual rather than identificatory (12). Bennett's emphasis on affect and on the political nature (13) of trauma-related art is important to me because she, too, starts out from the mind-body as inseparably taking part in interaction with a work of art, when she writes, for example, that "affective imagery promotes a form of thought that arises from the body, that explores the nature of our affective investment, and that ultimately has the potential to take us outside the confines of our character and habitual modes of perception" (44), and because she, too, is interested in interactions with works of art as ethical scenes.

The ethical encounter enabled by the performance of bodies of drawers and readers and by the body of the comic is an "affective transaction" between embodied minds and mindful bodies, and it can transform the participants taking part in the encounter by not only acknowledging but also experiencing the vulnerability of the self and of the Other in interactions with the comic. I also show that acts of movement, trace making, and reading enable ways to relate to the Other in terms other than identification. In certain cases, as in Laura U. Marks's concept of feeling with an abstract line, a concept elaborated in chapter 4, identity itself gets questioned, and the ability of the onlooker to let go of judgments, to allow sensations to affect him or her, and to be moved by the rhythm of the line ("I Feel," 156) and experience kinesthetic empathy (168–69) are emphasized. In the chapters focusing on the act of drawing and on the act of reading, I will approach engagement with comics as possible encounters between embodied agents—that is, between a vulnerable drawer and a vulnerable reader, who have a chance to reflect on their own and the Other's vulnerability in their performances and be transformed, and these encounters will not be based on whether identificatory practices are activated or not.

Though the term "vulnerability" is often associated with weakness, disadvantage, and failure in contemporary sociological and political discourses, and is likewise framed in discussions of climate change, following Judith Butler, Simone Drichel, Rosalyn Diprose, Margrit Shildrick, and other thinkers, I do not think of vulnerability as a negative quality or as a lack. Rather, vulnerability is seen as a shared quality that enables new modes of interaction, or, with Bennett's words, "affective transaction[s]" among embodied subjects. Vulnerability is a shared quality based on the simple fact that we all have bodies, and the experience of vulnerability is inherently related to the needs shared by all bodies: We feel pain and we need to be sustained. In *Precarious Life: The Powers of Mourning and Violence* (2004), Butler emphasizes that "the body implies mortality, vulnerability, agency" (26) and explores vulnerability as a universal condition that "emerges with life itself" (31). To underline the fundamental nature of vulnerability, Mackenzie, Rogers, and Dodds, editors of *Vulnerability: New Essays in Ethics and Feminist Philosophy,* state in the very first sentence of their collection that "human life is conditioned by vulnerability" (1). It must be noted, however, that because of social and political framing, the vulnerability of bodies cannot be equally stated and performed: Not all lives count as grievable. Groups in societies are marked as different and inferior either by being labeled as vulnerable or by denying the possibility of seeing them as vulnerable.

The ties between the bodily nature of our existence and vulnerability have political and ethical consequences, and vulnerability can serve as the ground for a practice of interaction with comics that neither emphasizes differences nor erases them and that neither focuses on the unshareable nature of personal experience nor appropriates them. Rather, in this book the experience of vulnerability is regarded as a force that enables discourse, interaction, and affective transaction. These engagements are based on the realization that "we are, from the start, given over to the other . . . by virtue of bodily requirements" (Butler 31). Vulnerability in this way is a relationship between people: One experiences vulnerability in his or her own body, and one also experiences that this vulnerability needs to be and can be attended to by other people, and that one can attend to the vulnerability of others in meaningful ways or one can do harm. In this way, the social aspect of vulnerability is defining: In interactions with the Other, the vulnerability carried by the body becomes manifest. Vulnerability allows for multidirectional open-ended affective interactions and transactions in which all parties involved can be changed.

Vulnerability allows for an ethical encounter with the Other, and this encounter, I would like to show in this monograph, can also happen via the way embodied practices around comics allow performing vulnerability. "A vulnerability must be perceived and recognized in order to come into play in an ethical encounter, and there is no guarantee that this will happen," says Butler (43). Vulnerability can be a central transformative force in the encounter of equal parties, and when the ethical encounter takes place, "when a vulnerability *is* recognized, that recognition has the power to change the meaning and structure of the vulnerability itself" (43). The significance of the ethical encounter is emphasized by Simone Drichel, editor of the vulnerability issue of *SubStance,* who argues in "Introduction: Reframing Vulnerability" that experiencing vulnerability and taking part in ethical encounters are a prerequisite of the development of morality (12). Drichel quotes Adam Phillips to argue that "helplessness is the precondition for human bonds, for exchange; you have to be a helpless subject in order to be helped, in order to be understood, in order to become a moral creature" (12). Avoiding vulnerability does not make one strong; instead, it results in an inability to feel pleasure:

> Getting helplessness wrong, then, means fleeing from and defending against the very relationality that, to be sure, is always a potential source of pain and wounding, but that is also the condition of possibility for pleasure and satisfaction, and ultimately for ethical life. Without helplessness . . . we deprive ourselves of the conditions of possibility of satisfaction. (Drichel 13)

Getting into a dialogical situation with the Other enabled by the experience of vulnerability is seen here as a prerequisite of an ethical life. I believe that Drichel's approach to vulnerability can be related to Butler's in more than one way: Both authors emphasize the foundational importance of vulnerability and both emphasize the dialogical nature of the concept. Based on Freud, Drichel talks about "original helplessness" (12) to describe that from an early age, we are dependent on and vulnerable to others—this is what Butler calls "primary vulnerability" (31). The idea of dialogue and that vulnerability cannot be defined in negative terms as lack or risk, or cannot be attributed exclusively to the Other, are central to Butler's concept of an ethical encounter and to Drichel's above description of an ethical life.

Margrit Shildrick, whose book on monstrosity and vulnerability will be key to my approach to Ken Dahl's *Monsters* in chapter 2, notes that often, vulnerability is not only perceived as a lack of a positive quality but is also directly attributed to the Other as a negative quality. In this way, vulnerability marks how different the Other is from what is considered to be the norm. In *Embodying the Monster* (2002), a work published two years before Butler's *Precarious Life,* Shildrick defines vulnerability as "an existential state that may belong to any one of us, but which is characterized nonetheless as a negative attribute, a failure of self-protection, that opens the self to the potential of harm" (1). Too often, vulnerability is framed as a dangerous openness or as an exposure to violation against which the individual or the community either has to protect themselves or be protected by a stronger authority. In Simone Drichel's words, "the experience of vulnerability . . . generally results in pursuits of invulnerability, where invulnerability serves the function of restoring a sense of control and mastery over a threatening environment" (5). The problem with positioning vulnerability as a negative quality or as a threat is that possibilities for an "affective transaction" and "ethical encounter," which are at the heart of vulnerability as a dialogue, are missed.

One might say that there is a risk in engaging in a transformative dialogue enabled by experiencing vulnerability. Likewise, a certain amount of risk-taking is necessary to make manifest the experience of vulnerability in making or reading comics. However, the word "risk" is also controversial, as it can be part of the military metaphors that often characterize the discussion of vulnerability. For this reason, I would like to introduce Rosalyn Diprose's approach to vulnerability as a dynamic state that is built on the interrelatedness of people and their environment and sheds a different light on the scope of interaction in which vulnerability is articulated among equal parties. Diprose is critical of the way the discussion of vulnerability often assumes that "the body is normally well-bounded and should remain so" (188), and emphasizes that attention should be directed away from the individual, from a fear of change, and from the possible harm the individual needs to suffer, toward an ethical community. She adds that especially in the social sciences, the underlying premise is that "there are physical indicators of vulnerability that can be quantified, and that standard strategies for resilience can be identified and applied uniformly [with] the aim . . . to prevent injury by outside forces and to enable individuals and communities to return to the status quo after the damage has been done" (188). Because of this context emphasizing the status quo, Diprose welcomes Butler's concept of injury. If focus is shifted from the individual toward a community, an injury means not a threat of a healthy body from the outside but losing relatedness to the world and others (188). I would like to show in this book that relatedness can be expressed and experienced in embodied ways by interactions with comics.

Diprose argues that instead of focusing on "human existence in terms of *life,* whether precarious or resilient" (190), the discourse of vulnerability should consider "corporeal interdependence" (190) on a different, bigger scale, and, based on Heidegger, she proposes to understand human existence as dwelling. Dwelling, which is "place and process" (192), allows for broadening the concept of vulnerability, as it enables discussing engagement not only with human but also with nonhuman and built environments (186). Diprose's theorization of "the role of the *built environment* in human existence" (190), and their being a formative part of our experience of interrelatedness, is not a central aspect of this monograph. However, chapter 5, where I analyze the way the size, texture, and physical properties of comics as objects, as well as the haptic charge of visual images can influence readerly performance, involvement, and interpretation, can be thought of as a study in the role of the environment and nonhuman elements in the experience of interdependence and vulnerability.

Diprose proposes to rethink the scope of vulnerability because dwelling "describes the primordial dispersal of human being into a world of material and meaningful relations" (191), and enables seeing that "the essence of dwelling lies in existence *as potentiality*." (191). Her approach to vulnerability liberates the concept from the language of defense and military metaphors, and also from metaphors of risk. The second feature that, according to Diprose, needs to be emphasized in the discussion of vulnerability and corporeal interdependence when dwelling is its starting point is related to potentiality: "The intercorporeal foundation of human existence means that we are vulnerable to loss and violence for sure, but, on the other side of the ambiguity, it also renders us open to new possibilities for existence. It is the dynamism of existence inherent in intercorporeality that is overlooked" (185). Diprose emphasizes the dynamic nature of dwelling and argues that this dynamism is rooted in the experience of fragility (192). Interdependence and vulnerability in this way are seen to enable experiencing plurality, as well as a dynamic, unpredictable, and unfinished (192) state. If the equilibrium of this state is disturbed, instead of a restoration of the status quo, an open-ended transformation takes place (189).

When dynamism and openness are emphasized, vulnerability cannot be grasped within the binary oppositions of lack and gain, self and other: Something completely different can happen in a dialogue or in what Butler calls the "ethical encounter." Such encounters can, in Shildrick's words, "signal a transformation of the relation between self and other" (1). Vulnerability conceptualized in this way can facilitate change for all parties involved. Recognizing vulnerability "is to solicit a becoming, to instigate a transformation, to petition the future always in relation to the Other," says Butler (44). The concept of transformation is a crucial one in my understanding of embodied engagement with comics as a way of dialogue in which one's and the Other's vulnerability can be experienced and performed: This interaction has the potential to change the parties involved; it can lead to new ways of embodied understanding of not only the subject matter of a given comic but also of the experience of vulnerability. My readings of comics in the following chapters aim at shedding light on some of the ways in which dwelling and an ethical encounter *can* happen, and chapters of this book examine some ways in which vulnerability *can* be performed via either drawing or reading comics: in embodied engagement in drawing lines (chapter 1); in drawing and redrawing one's body (chapter 2); in drawing backgrounds (chapter 3); in embodied acts of looking at bodies, lines, and abject images (chapter 4); and in touching, holding, and interacting with comics as three-dimensional objects (chapter 5). As indicated already, my investigation is made possible by seeing a similarity in the structure of interaction with comics and the structure of vulnerability as encounter: Both are embodied, open, creative, dialogical, and dynamic.

Vulnerability is experienced in a dialogue: The nature of the interaction with me defines how the Other experiences his or her vulnerability—and the nature of the interaction with the Other defines how I experience my vulnerability. Vulnerability creates discursive situations, but it does not prescribe how vulnerability will be responded to in a given situation. Ann Murphy writes in *Violence and the Philosophical Imaginary*: "There is nothing in the experience of vulnerability that necessarily promotes tolerance, restraint, or generosity. Indeed, a reckoning with one's vulnerability is often painful" (66). To put it bluntly, one's vulnerability, which is put forward in this dialogue, can be answered in two ways, either by wounding or by caring (Cavarero qtd. in Drichel 10). How one's vulnerability will be answered cannot be prescribed, just like the way in which a piece of art is interpreted cannot be predicted with certainty. This, according to Simone Drichel, enables reframing the very concept of vulnerability by reinforcing its provocative, ambiguous, and complex nature, and by introducing uncertainty in its discussion: "Vulnerability is marked by a constitutive doubleness: we cannot know in advance whether it will bring us satisfaction or violation" (Drichel 23).

Receiving and giving wounding and caring responses in a dialogue of vulnerability are at the heart of the plots of many contemporary nonfiction comics, which also center around the nonequal distribution of vulnerability. Lynda Barry's stories, studied in chapter 1, center on her life as a child in a neglecting family. Ken Dahl, whose *Monsters* is read in chapter 2, represents his autobiographical avatar as a person wounding others while also being wounded. Joe Sacco's stories from the Bosnian War (chapter 3) and on the Battle of the Somme (chapter 5) show abuse and the trauma of war along with an array of caring responses. Miriam Katin's graphic memoirs expose her traumatic memories as a persecuted child in the Second World War (chapter 4).[2] Finally, Katie Green in *Lighter Than My Shadow,* her memoir on eating disorders and sexual abuse, reveals thoughts by which one can wound oneself both mentally and physically and also narrates the emotionally extremely difficult process of healing after sexual abuse (chapter 5). Some plot elements of these comics can be thought of as discursive situations where engagement with the vulnerability of the Other, as revealed in the stories, can serve as a starting point of a transformation in the reader (and also in the artist, especially if we focus on the healing process enabled by artistic engagement). They also show that it is possible for humans to consider the Other as *not* equally vulnerable, and that in these cases there is absolutely no dialogue and no transformation.

Instead of studying the plots or the characters of comics, in this book I study acts of interactions with comics as material objects in acts of drawing and in acts of reading. These performances can establish new relationships between the self and the Other, and they can be sites of ethical encounters. Ethical encounters are initiated by the drawers of comics autobiography and reportage; invitations are mediated by the drawn line, other traces of the drawer, and the actual printed comics. The following chapters examine potential ways of "affective transaction" (Bennett 10) enabled by engaging with vulnerability artic-

2. Seeing the Other as equally vulnerable is a prerequisite of an array of caring responses and of an unfolding dialogue between self and Other. Comics narratives provide numerous instances where caring responses to vulnerability creates sociability among people: Joe Sacco's *Safe Area Goražde* features caring communities in times of war, and Sacco's reporting work can also be approached as a form of care. However, in this book I do not focus on plot elements of comics addressing the discourse of vulnerability. Instead, I study ways in which vulnerability is manifest in the drawer's and the reader's respective embodied interactions with comics.

ulated in and around comics. In chapters 4 and 5, I turn from studying the drawers' formulations of vulnerability to readers' engagement. Readers' embodied performances of meaning making that build on not only the movement of the eye but an understanding conveyed by the body cannot be predicted with certainty and cannot be measured in quantifiable terms. Moreover, readers may choose not to engage with a specific comic at all. Yet readers' individual embodied interpretive strategies and performative responses (as well as embodied responses and performative interpretive strategies) can be instances of ethical encounters and "transformation of the relation between self and other" (Shildrick 1) enabled by the experience of vulnerability.

In the study of ethical engagement with narrative works of art, empathy and character identification are two often studied readerly responses. I have started this section with offering an alternative to identificatory reading strategies, and now I would like to draw a distinction between empathy and vulnerability. Tim Gauthier, author of *9/11 Fiction, Empathy, and Otherness* (2015), defines empathy, similarly to my approach to vulnerability, as an interaction between self and Other:

> Engaging in empathy is a more reciprocal activity than other attempts at understanding the other, since it also requires self-diagnosis. I must seek to find that which makes me and the other same. This implies the bi-directionality of the empathic gesture, since empathy becomes more than simply a way of assessing and judging the other, but also the means through which the empathizer is exposed to different ways of thinking and feeling. (30)

The self has the potential to change during engagement in empathy, although, as Suzanne Keen shows in *Empathy and the Novel,* invoking empathy is not unproblematic at all. There is no guarantee that the reader feels empathy with a character as a result of reading (72), over time some texts change their capacity to evoke empathy (74), readers might empathize differently than what the author invited (75), and it is not proven that empathy would lead to a changed behavior or altruistic action (16).

Both Gauthier and Keen warn about the danger of empathy becoming a condescending reaction and a means to reinforce the dominant position and even superiority of the privileged (Gauthier 31; Keen 142). The dialogue based on the shared experience of vulnerability is essentially different, because the dialogue is so fundamentally linked to the body. If the realness of the Other is not recognized, if the presence and precarity of the Other is not judged as *equal* to the precarity of the self—of the reader—the dialogue does not take place. Via emphasizing the embodied nature of interaction with comics both in performances of drawing and of reading, and by relying on the embodied nature of the ethical encounter, we can understand the difference between feeling empathy and experiencing vulnerability.

Comics require the reader's openness to the touch of otherness. Actual physical contact and a metaphorical touch—that is, being affected and transformed—are both necessary for comics reading to become part of a dialogue centering on the experience of vulnerability, taking place between artist and reader, mediated by the comic. A comic calls attention to the embodied presence of the drawer in its hand-drawn lines (this will be the organizing idea of chapters 1, 2, and 3). Apart from lines as traces of the movement of the drawer's body, drawing a character based on oneself and posing for other characters all refer to the drawer's embodied experience. In turn, the reader's body interacts with the materiality of the actual comic when it is read, and the body also takes part in interpreting the drawings (see chapters 4 and 5). These aspects require the reader to consider his or her own embodied condition and the embodied nature of thinking. The respective experiences of drawing and reading comics can become parts of a transformative encounter between equally vulnerable parties. Interaction with comics in this way becomes, on the one hand, an immersive experience, and on the other hand, a "mutual transformative experience" (B. Bernstein 91). I borrowed this term from artist Barbara Bernstein's description of art—and not comics specifically—in "Drawing a Breath" to show that the idea of transformation is a keyword not only of Butler's ethics of vulnerability but of a number of models describing interaction with art.

Bernstein calls her model of interaction via art "immersive drawing" (91), but in fact her description does not stop at immersive processes of drawing. For Bernstein, drawing and looking at art are organically connected. She describes both experiences as transformative when she says that "immersive drawing," or immersive interaction with art, "shifts the response-ability of creator and viewer, towards an interfaced, simultaneous, and symbolic relationship of observation *and* participation" (91). Again, the dynamic, mutual, and transformative nature of mediated immersion is emphasized, and immersion is explained as an affective response.

Immersion, especially that of the reader, is one of the most often referred to characteristic of comics. Scott McCloud's positioning of the reader as the artist's "collaborator" in crime and co-creator (65) is possibly the most famous of the theories accounting for the very specific way comics are interpreted. In the next section, I survey comics scholarship for how the immersive work of the drawer and the reader and the role of the body have been theorized. Given my focus on communicating vulnerability in an encounter, I am particularly interested in how ethical concerns and the idea of being transformed appear in comics scholarship.

Contexts: The Body and Ethics in Comics Scholarship

There is an underlying agreement among comics scholars about the unique potential of comics as a medium to invite engagement, and some even connect this unique invitation to engage with the comics form to exploring ethical issues. Kate Polak, for example, states very early in *Ethics in the Gutter: Empathy and Historical Fiction in Comics* (2017) that

> the formal qualities of graphic narratives—including the gutter, the staging of point of view, and the textual-imagistic hybridity—make them uniquely suited to questions relating to how we negotiate representations of extremity because their staging of the gaze and their staging of questions surrounding both how and what we remember prompts readers to consider their emotional and ethical relationships to the text. (2)

I very much agree with Polak in seeing comics as a structure that invites establishing an "ethical relationship" and reflection on our readerly performance. However, whereas Polak's analysis focuses on ways in which point of view complicates the ethical engagement of readers or on ways in which the gutter takes part in situating the reader, the subject of my study is the experience of the drawn line as a drawer and as a reader. Therefore I study an "ethical relationship" enabled by the line (and by the material characteristics of comics as objects in the last chapter), and I connect this to a bodily performance enabled by the experience and embodied understanding of vulnerability as articulated in the comic being read.

Comics has been understood as a collaboration between artist and reader since Scott McCloud's *Understanding Comics*: The concept of closure and the idea that "comics is closure" (67) are some of the most influential theories about how readers engage mentally and visually with comics. McCloud thinks of the reader as the artist's accomplice: The reader connects the gaps or gutters between panels and this way mentally constructs a continuous narrative out of visually distinct units of information. The concept of closure narrows readerly involvement to the visual and mental fields (63), and so do subsequent approaches that emphasize the defining role of the gutter in reading comics. Harriet Earle, for example, says in *Comics, Trauma, and the New Art of War* that "the gutter is the most important aspect of the comics form" (47), because "each type of transition [that is, mental involvement to connect adjacent panels] will alter the way the text is read and the way the reader reacts to the text" (47). Similarly, Hillary Chute, writing on the peculiar relationship between comics and memory, emphasizes the role of the gutter to segment and to connect when she argues that "images in comics appear in fragments, just as they do in actual recollection" (*Graphic Women* 4). Chute sees the significance of the gutter in the way it spatializes time—this is why memory and trauma lend themselves to be subjects of comics so frequently—and in a section devoted to the gutter in *Disaster Drawn*, she reads the gutter as equally a "space of stillness" and a "space of movement" (35). She elaborates this dichotomy: "Comics texts can capture, can textualize, the context of bearing witness to trauma, the context of an articulation that also carries its own inchoate parallel, its own inarticulate shadow" (36).

Kate Polak reinterprets the significance of the gutter by connecting the performance of closure to identification and ethical issues: The gutter is a space that "allows the reader to invest in rapport with the content in the panels" (13). Furthermore, she argues that

> closure as I see it automatically has an ethical dimension; who you are and who you are prompted to identify with, how you are prompted to make inferences about what is and isn't depicted, how you make sense of your own imagination in relation to what is depicted, these are only a few areas in which comics create a *different*

> ethical universe for the reader. For example, identifying with a perpetrator and identifying with a victim are two very different ethical relationships with a text. (15)

The gutter in this interpretation becomes a powerful means, unique to comics, to influence the reader's connection to the story and its characters. In this respect, the gutter is one of many tools and representational strategies, along with focalization, that will be studied in a moment, aimed at influencing readerly empathy and both ethical and critical engagement. Polak departs from the interpretation of the gutter as an actual physical space on the page and emphasizes that the gutter also encapsulates "the choices made by artists and writers to not say and not show" (16); the gutter is a space "of material evidence of how the gaze of the reader is situated in specific ways in relation to what is shown" (16). The gutter can be used to reflect on representation and viewing, and these questions in themselves have ethical consequences. It is because of this ethical connection, which is a departure from the study of point of view, that Polak writes, "I believe that comics should be understood . . . as a form that naturally lends itself to the complexities of our contemporary ethical questions, particularly those surrounding how we narrate and receive history and how we affectively engage with historical atrocity" (1).

McCloud, Earle, Chute, and Polak all start out from the fact that the gutter is a site of the reader's imaginative work. This work is approached in a very different way by Thierry Groensteen, who departs from McCloud's focus on adjacent elements and sequences when he conceptualizes pages, issues, and even series of comics as a network of interconnected elements. Groensteen relies on the reader's visual memory as well as their imaginative involvement: The reader imaginatively connects tabular elements and remote parts of comics, which might even have been printed in different issues. Yet Groensteen's approach still restricts the reader's involvement to the visual and mental fields and minimizes the role of the reader's body in interpretation (Hague 9–33).

The study of how point of view influences the reader's position and identificatory practices is a key undertaking of Polak's book. Point of view is an important question when discussing ethics and empathy, as, contrary to verbal mediums, in the visual-verbal storytelling medium of comics, narratives are not simply filtered through the consciousness of characters of narrators—that is, they are not simply focalized via a character or a narrator. Focalization, which enables "relational identification" and which "directs meaning and opens up the possibility for variance in meaning and mood" (S. Horstkotte and Pedri 351), happens simultaneously verbally or visually (Horstkotte and Pedri 350). Focalization does not simply mean drawing a scene in a comic from a character's point of view—though this technique of ocularization (Fischer and Hatfield 80) is part of the process and is often used by creators to facilitate identification with a character, or, on the contrary, to enhance distance. Graphic focalization is a "communicat[ion of a] subjectivity through pictures" (Fisher and Hatfield 77), and showing an action "in ways consistent with the character's emotional state, while still being presented through an ocular perspective external to the character" (Fisher and Hatfield 78). This way a scene can be focalized from the point of view of the character while that character is also visible. The study of focalization techniques is a fruitful way of approaching the involvement of nonfiction comics in human rights discourse, political questions, or the way empathy is evoked in graphic narratives (Keen, "A Theory of Narrative Empathy"). In this book, however, this direction of study is not pursued; rather, I show that, due to the involvement of the body, the relationship between author, reader, and narrative is different from identification.

For similar reasons, I will not study the gutter in the rest of the book. The gutter is a space designated for projection, mental activity, reflection, and involvement, and I think a focus on structural elements like the gutter or the page contributed greatly to a tendency to theorize the reader's mental—and not bodily—activity prompted by visual clues. Parallel to this, ethical questions have been framed as mental and visual ones. I would like to elaborate on this by claiming that an understanding enabled by the way bodies can be involved in interpreting comics is also essential in the study of ethical questions.

Rebecca Scherr calls attention to the body in interpretation and postulates comics reading as a reciprocal activity in her essay "Shaking Hands with the Other People's Pain." Scherr analyzes actual representations of hands in Joe Sacco's comics, arguing that "truth-telling happens in the exchange between reader and text and is based on a kind of emotional and corporeal form of evidence that occurs through a haptic, visceral engagement with the pain of others" (20). She wittily sums up this maze of metaphorical and physical influences with the phrase "to touch is always, also, to be touched" (22), and concludes that the experience of metaphorical touch (as in being touched by the story of the characters' pain), as well as the reader's actual physical touch, lead to an acknowledgment of the realness of the Other. I find this as a significant statement as seeing the Other as real and as equally vulnerable as the subject who performs the seeing are prerequisites of the "ethical encounter" in Judith Butler's theory of an ethics of vulnerability (43). Scherr also emphasizes that the difference of the Other must be acknowledged: "There is an element of this exchange that reminds us that we are not the other and the other is not us" ("Shaking Hands" 22).

In "Joe Sacco's Comics of Performance" (2015), Scherr continues her study of representing and witnessing pain in comics, and introduces not only the concept of performativity but also the concept of the dialogue between comic and reader (191). I find this essay truly fascinating, because it shares many of my own concerns and interests, but Scherr's train of thought is also different from mine in inspiring ways. First, Scherr, just like me, is influenced by Jared Gardner's theory of the line as the trace of the drawer's labor. I will elaborate this, as well as several other theories on drawing, in the last section of the introduction. Scherr writes,

> The presence of the artist in the process of work, in the laborious process of creation, also makes itself palpable through self-portraiture, framing, sequencing, and the careful juxtaposition of text and image. All of this comes together to perform a dialogue with the reader: it is in this dialogue that stretches from form to content to ethical contemplation that the work and presence of an activating authorial figure is powerfully manifest. ("Joe Sacco's Comics" 191)

She calls comics reading a dialogue because in comics the reader can meet the characters of the represented narrative and can establish an ethical relationship toward them. Scherr analyzes the representation and framing of characters, including that of the avatar, as well as the point of view from which scenes are represented. The first step of comics reading as dialogue is reflection: "Calling attention to self-performance [of Sacco's avatar performing as a journalist] is also a kind of call out to the reader, a request to reflect on what it means to examine people's pain secondhand" (190). Apart from the study of characters, point of view is important, especially if a scene is drawn from the perspective of an eyewitness, as these scenes frame and implicate the reader's body in what is represented in the frames. They create "a pictorial form of empathetic, corporeal address, as we imaginatively become a victim of this violence [due to the eyewitness perspective]. We are being asked to perform victim here, with no redemptive ending; this is no longer a kind of distanced reflection on pain, but a bodily, imaginative encounter with it" (191).

For Scherr, reading Sacco's comics reportage is a kind of witnessing ("Joe Sacco's Comics" 194): Comics possess "transitive potential" (184) and they have an "ability to *do* things, to intervene in a reader's world through properties that go far beyond line drawing" (184). Scherr's analysis is fascinating to me because she, just like me, refers to Judith Butler's notion of "shared precariousness" and states, just like I do, that it can be experienced via comics reading—in a marvelous essay published in the same year I had to submit the first one hundred pages of my PhD dissertation. She writes of panels drawn from the witness's perspective:

> Sacco's deliberate use of framing shortens the distance between reader and the object of vision, and in narrowing this gap we are forcibly led into discovering what Judith Butler calls "shared precariousness," whereby we become aware of our connection to others based on the very human apprehension of the body's frailty, the potential for pain, instability, and loss that always exist as possibilities in this life. ("Joe Sacco's Comics" 191)

Scherr provides a captivating analysis that builds on the reader's bodily and imaginative encounter with what is represented in Sacco's comics, and, focusing on how pain is conveyed with the help of framing and point of view, theorizes comics reading as a dialogue with the object of representation. In contrast to Scherr, this book does not focus on point of view and characters until its last chapter, where I study ways in which Katie Green draws the pain of her avatar and connects the character's body to the published comic as a three-dimensional object. Similarly to Scherr, I also believe that engagement with comics can be the site of "becom[ing] aware of our connection to others" ("Joe Sacco's Comics" 191) and that engagement with comics can be the site of ethical encounters due to the fact that comics can articulate the primary experience of vulnerability by the very lines by which it was drawn.

The experience and performance of the reader's body is a cornerstone of Scherr's approach, and a year before her essay's publication, Ian Hague published an important contribution to exploring the body's role in interpretation by including sense perception into theorizing how comics is read. *Comics and the Senses* (2014) categorizes and lists the ways in which comics can provide sensory input for readers: Readers react to these material characteristics—for example, the size, shape, or weight of the comics, its colors and gloss, its soundtrack—and these sensory influences can have an effect on the reading experience. Hague's approach emphasizes lists and categorizes the material characteristics of comics, which results in an elaborate account of the physical levels of comics as material objects and potential ways to interact with these levels.

I believe that these physical levels, which are engaged by several senses at a time, are interacted with as a result of the reader's meaningful, goal-oriented, and embodied actions to engage with the comic. By goal-oriented I mean that the reader will connect the physical properties of a given comic to its meaning, establishing a relationship between form and content. This connection might be reflected upon or might be unreflected, and it ranges from form and content helping each other to form and content working to undermine each other. My approach foregrounds comics as communication and interaction between the embodied drawer and the embodied reader, and I believe that apart from the physical characteristics listed by Hague, "physical-mental levels" and "imaginative levels" (Polak 7) are also mobilized when the material object of the comic is interacted with in the performance of reading.

The sense of touch in reading is also studied by Katalin Orbán, who writes about the reader's "visuo-haptic processing" of comics ("Language" 171). As the term suggests, Orbán builds on visual and tactile interaction with comics, which are at work in digital and printed comics alike. Orbán has written extensively on reading haptically visual images in comics, a mode of reading addressed by chapters 3 and 5, and by connecting comics reading to hyperreading ("Language" 170), she has proposed new ways to approach the multimodal nature of comics. The fact that senses are connected, and that, for example, one does not need to touch a picture in a comic to have haptic information about is summed up by Shaun Gallagher as the "intermodal communication among sense modalities" (160). In chapters 4 and 5, I rely greatly on both Orbán's and Gallagher's work, elaborating on the fact that "perception is less the result of an internal processing of sense information, and more the result of an interaction between the body and its environment" (Gallagher 172).

The emphasis in my model on the role of the reader's body in the interaction with comics has a further forerunner in film historian Tom Gunning's comparison of comics reading to playing games, an immersive experience in which the whole body takes part. Gunning uses the body as a frame of reference when he writes that navigating irregular page layouts and intricate grids requires "acrobatic skills" (46). These skills are not only metaphorical. Often, as in the case of oversize comics, such as Art Spiegelman's *In the Shadow of No Towers,* or Joe Sacco's *The Great War,* they are also physical. Because of this, the involvement of the body in comics reading can also result in "vertiginious" sensations (Gunning 46). Comics scholar Scott Bukatman also compares reading (and not specifically comics reading) to play. He emphasizes immersion and performance in play and reading when he writes: "Play can serve as an equally valuable concept in thinking about the operations—or performances—of reading and viewing" (*Poetics* 11). Bukatman reaches back to the immersive attention of children at play and makes it clear that immersion is not simply a mental exercise, it is also a bodily practice. The immersive experience that "reader and book are entwined; neither exists without the other" (Bukatman, *Hellboy's World* 3) will be linked to the discourse of vulnerability mediated by comics in chapter 5. Gunning's and Bukatman's language suggests that the body as a whole, and not only vision or specific senses, working in relative isolation, influences comics reading. The body is an active performer of both comics reading and vulnerability.

In chapters 4 and 5, I examine the body's performance in interpretation: I see comics reading as an embodied process, which, in the case of nonfiction modalities, makes it possible for readers to engage with the vulnerability of the Other articulated in the drawn lines. This can happen by immersion in the movement and vitality of the drawn lines, and by the contradictory process of suddenly becoming conscious of one's body's performance while reading comics in order to reflect on one's actual physical and also ethical position in the discourse of vulnerability.

It is important to note that the reader's response to the dialogue of vulnerability initiated in nonfiction comics can also be evasion: Readers are free to stop interacting with the comic any time, and readers can also refrain from the great degree of openness that is a prerequisite of engagement via vulnerability. Suzanne Keen calls evasive reactions "personal distress" (*Empathy* 4) and contrasts this reaction to empathy: While empathy is "other-directed," personal distress centers on the self, and leads to avoidance (*Empathy* 4). Similarly, a caring response to vulnerability and engagement in the transformative dialogue enabled by it are directed toward the Other. Refusal to engage at the point of reading can be caused by personal memories, ideological dispositions, fear, complacency, or misunderstanding.

Materials: Nonfiction Comics

This monograph focuses on contemporary nonfiction comics. My argument assumes that interaction with nonfiction comics is slightly different from interaction with fictional comics, though, naturally, they utilize similar practices as well. Nonfiction comics, particularly genres with a first-person focalizer, claim that they have a special connection to reality. They offer to reveal someone's mediated account or experience of reality, and by various narrative strategies and paratextual elements put great emphasis on the person of the author,[3] who is the key to the credibility of the work. Strategies and processes by which authenticity and credibility can be asserted and by which truth-claims can be performed in nonfiction comics have been widely studied (Chaney; El Refaie; Hatfield; Mickwitz). Nina Mickwitz, for example, says in *Documentary Comics* that nonfiction comics "invite a response of suspended disbelief" (20): Comics that invite the reader to "see/witness" (20) a course of action, and not simply to imagine it, "can be seen as making certain claims for cultural validity" (20). Mickwitz thus finds that a specific "mode of address" (24) distinguishes nonfiction comics from fictional ones:

3. I use the word "author" here, and not "drawer," which I already established as a term to be used in this book. The reason is that comics autobiography and comics journalism are not necessarily written and drawn by the same person. The avatar of the writer can feature in co-created comics; for example, in *Our Cancer Year*, an autobiography written by Harvey Pekar and Joyce Brabner, and drawn by Frank Stack, or in *War Is Boring*, written by David Axe and drawn by Matt Bors.

> So the term "mode of address'" indicates that a text might offer its viewers/readers a particular position and that, in the case of documentary [I use the word "nonfiction" in this meaning], this position invites them to "look to its images as records of the specific, not as envisioning of the possible" (Vaughan, 1999, 154). (Mickwitz 24)

Due to the specific "mode of address," the position of the reader is different in nonfiction comics. Similarly to Mickwitz, Suzanne Keen approaches the difference between fiction and nonfiction based on the reader's relation to what is read. She focuses on fiction and claims that fiction is engaging for readers because it is so different from reality: "For immersed readers, entering fictional worlds allows a refreshing escape from ordinary, everyday pressures and preoccupations" (Keen, *Empathy* xv). Based on Keen's line of argumentation, I would argue that nonfiction is based on precisely the opposite of escape: I show in this book that nonfiction comics offers various opportunities for engagement, immersion, and the study of the relationship of the world of the narrative with an actual reality. This engagement creates the possibility of an ethical encounter and makes a discourse of vulnerability possible.

The nonfiction comics examined in this monograph are marketed the same way as books are, and, with the exception of Joe Sacco's *The Great War,* they all look like books.[4] Until the appearance of the one-shot book-format comic at the end of the 1970s, comics as a medium has been rooted in seriality not only because it consists of sequences of visual units but also because of the rhythm of publication of daily strips, weekend specials, or comic books (Gardner, *Projections;* Hatfield; Sabin). Comics autobiography and reportage, the two genres of nonfiction comics I focus on, became successfully marketable and increasingly visible as books, and not as serialized booklets, around 2000. Naturally, book-format comics, omnibus editions, and trade paperbacks were published before this year in genres of both fiction and nonfiction, but I believe the one-shot long-form comic gained significant cultural space in English-speaking markets roughly after this year. At around this time, the generation of cartoonists inspired by Art Spiegelman's *Maus* started publishing their own nonfiction narratives, and Joe Sacco's comics reportage, *Palestine,* which was initially

4. On the relationship between experimental or unusual formats and the graphic novel, see Crucifix.

published in booklets between 1993 and 1995, was republished as a one-shot volume in 2001 by Fantagraphics, and was given more and more attention by readers and by various media outlets.

Comics is a drawn, interpreted, and subjective narrative medium, in which marks and lines are made and drawn with a specific purpose. Drawing is a goal-directed activity (Grennan 14) that uses the resources of the body (its mass, size, and motion) to make marks (Grennan 17). The undeniably subjective and interpreted nature of drawing as well as the same qualities of narratives are always clearly visible in comics—and comics creators working in autobiographical and journalistic genres, creating memoirs, diaries, travelogues, reportage, case studies, or interviews, do not consider this transparency as a hindrance. Quite the contrary. According to Jared Gardner, the openness about the processes of mediation is what nonfiction comics creators—and in my view, readers as well—find inviting about the medium. Talking about creators of biographical comics, whom Gardner calls "autographers," he writes:

> The split between autographer and subject is etched on every page, and the hand-crafted nature of the images and the "autobifictional" nature of the narrative are undeniable. But it is important that this split is not a casualty or regrettable cost of the autobiographer's chosen form, but is instead precisely what motivates the drive to tell the self in comics form. ("Autography's Biography" 12)

The on-the-spot term "autobifictional," used by Gardner to explain the lure of comics life writing, was mockingly coined by Lynda Barry, whose views on drawing will be explored in chapter 1. The word "autobifictionalography" indicates the difficulty of separating fiction from fact, or memory from imagination, and it first appeared as a joking warning: "Please note: this is a work of autobifictionalography" as part of the front matter collage of Barry's *One! Hundred! Demons!* (2002). This collage is followed by Barry's further musings on the nature of life writing: In two well-known panels, her avatar is shown to be sitting at her desk, with a text in the upper section asking, "Is it autobiography if parts of it are not true? / Is it fiction if parts of it are?"

It is not a coincidence that Justin Green's *Binky Brown Meets the Holy Virgin Mary* (1972), the first autobiographical comic in the US (Gardner, *Projections* 127), brings attention to the embodied and vulnerable nature of making autobiographical comics *on its very first page.* This page addresses readers in its title, "A Confession to My Readers," thereby involving them in the intimacy of the confessional mode. The character to be associated with Green, the author's autobiographical avatar (Gillian Whitlock's term: 971), is drawn naked, hanging facedown over what Gardner calls "an inverted sword of Damocles" (*Projections* 128). His hands are tied behind his back, and he is drawing comics with a pen held between his teeth. With this powerful image, Green shows the very moment when his first-person graphic narrative is born, and significantly to my argument in this book, he depicts this moment as one where the vulnerability of the first-person character is in focus. Furthermore, and supporting my model of embodied interaction with comics, the autographical situation is discursively constructed: Green's avatar is looking out at the readers, addressing and involving them in his literal performance of his graphic confession.

The painful honesty of Green's comic showed the possibilities of the comics medium to go analytical, and autographers[5] following in Green's footsteps confirm the relationship between body, vulnerability, and creating comics. Aline Kominsky-Crumb said: "When I saw Justin's work it gave me permission to or a way to find my voice to talk about my own life" (Gloeckner et al. 89). Similarly, Art Spiegelman, a major influence for the post-2000 generation of autographers, famously said that "without Binky Brown there would be no *Maus*" (qtd. in Gardner, *Projections* 127). Art Spiegelman's Pulitzer Prize–winning *Maus* (1986, 1991), an early first version of which was published in the same year as Green's *Binky Brown,* is a narrative of trauma and post-memory (Hirsch, "Generation") caused by the Holocaust. Significantly, it also engages with the issue of representing the body. It reaches out to the funny animal tradition by Spiegelman's rendering of various nationalities as humans with the heads of mice, cats, pigs, dogs, moths, reindeers, or frogs. These composite bodies can be interpreted as the second-generation Holocaust survivor's reply to the purifying rhetoric and practices distorting, experimenting with, or annihilating the bodies of people considered subhuman by the Nazis and their allies decimating the first generation.

5. A note on terminology: The term "autographer" is used by Jared Gardner to refer to the authors of autobiographical comics ("Autography's Biography"). For life writing in comics, Gardner uses the term "autography," while Whitlock, in an essay published two years earlier, uses the term in the plural, as "autographics."

Maus offers a life narrative of Spiegelman's father, but it is also a record of Spiegelman's life. Cartoonists disagree on the degree to which the plot of autobiographical comics could or should be interpreted as authentic or transparent reformulations of actual life events, expressing that the truth value of nonfiction comics cannot be reduced to factual truth. Phoebe Gloeckner, author of *A Child's Life and Other Stories* (2001), repeatedly claims that she maintains a distance between herself and her cartoon self in her autobiographical comics: "I mean you make a character of yourself. It is not really you. People can feel like it is you, but in a sense it is not" (Gloeckner et al. 93). In contrast, Aline Kominsky-Crumb, creator of *Need More Love* (2007), said in the same conversation: "My character is me. I have no detachment and no control and I can't make up anything" (Gloeckner et al. 93). Comics autobiography is motivated by this tension between distance and identification that is present both in its creation and in the fluctuating reading strategies utilized by its audience. Consequently, identification and authenticity, and the representation of the "complicated nature of identity" (Versaci 49), are among the most often studied topics of academic studies of nonfiction comics.

Having examined influential examples of comics autobiography, I now would like to introduce comics reportage as a special case of nonfiction comics where journalistic intent and an autobiographical angle can be present simultaneously. Comics reportage is discussed in chapter 3, where I study how drawing can mean a connection to other people and argue that drawing styles can have ethical stakes in comics reportage by Joe Sacco, who, according to Duncan et al., "has raised the profile, and the respectability, of journalism in comics form" (22). Reporting about atrocities by means of visual narrative can be traced back to Jacques Callot's (1592–1635) and Francisco Goya's (1746–1828) drawings of atrocities (Sontag, *Regarding*; Chute, *Disaster*). These artists are forerunners to Sacco's comics journalism by articulating painful visual truths in personal ways and by inviting the onlooker to take part in the act of witnessing articulated by the very drawings. Sacco's comics—as well as many contemporary journalistic pieces—are political and can be considered as related to drawn political commentaries in illustrated magazines and newspapers throughout Europe and in the US in the nineteenth century. Constantin Guys's illustrations of Crimean War in the 1850s and Frank Vizetelly's sketches from the front lines of the American Civil War (Duncan et al. 15) are early examples of drawing being the medium for narratives of war and for artists visiting conflicts in person in order to report on them. Consequently, when 150 years later, in the 1990s, Art Spiegelman, cartoon editor of *Details* magazine, sent Peter Kuper to report on the Burning Man festival, he "revived the tradition of sending artists into the field to produce drawn journalism" (20).

The current proliferation of comics journalism,[6] and, more broadly speaking, nonfiction comics, must be understood in the context of digital image making and image manipulation, which are practiced both by news agencies and by individuals. Paradoxically, as Frank Möller and Fred Ritchin show us, Western societies are simultaneously dependent upon digital and edited images and suspicious about the truth value of the same images. Manipulating photographic images can be the practice of news editors, political activists (Jenkins, "Photoshop"), and governments alike (Campbell): The audience in most cases is not even aware if a photograph has been doctored, nor is the audience informed about why, to what end, and by whom. In comics memoirs and in reportage, actual or drawn photographs are used to ascertain the authenticity of the given work, or, on the contrary, to problematize the represented action's relationship to reality. "Fiction . . . is now a fundamental part of each reading of photography, including its most direct and non-subjective documentary uses," warns Jan Baetens ("Guest Editor's Introduction" 94), and this fictionality of the photograph is an important point of departure behind any truth claims made in the visual and drawn genres of nonfiction comics. I would like to depart from regarding photography as a tool that facilitates or hinders authentication, factuality, or remembering, and my intention is to contribute to the study of photography in comics by looking at photographic realism as a stylistic influence. I approach photography as a medium of representation that can inform the drawn line in comics. The contrast of realistically drawn photographs and a nonreferential imaginative style is studied

6. By now, several other comics journalists have joined the field, publishing in book format (e.g., David Axe, Guy Delisle, Sarah Glidden, Ted Rall), in printed periodicals, and online (e.g., Patrick Chappatte's "Inside Death Row" at the website of the *New York Times*). While major print news outlets such as the *Guardian* also occasionally order comics reportage (e.g., "Complacency Kills" by Joe Sacco), several websites have been established to be dedicated to comics journalism, such as The Nib: Political Cartoons and Nonfiction Comics (http://thenib.com) and Cartoon Movement (http://cartoonmovement.com).

in chapter 2, where I show that the deliberate style change from a cartoony style to photographic realism in Ken Dahl's *Monsters* expresses uncertainty about the body and is also used to shock the reader.

In the context of digital image manipulation, comics' transparency about not being transparent, about being an interpretation, can be refreshing. Comics is always open about its artifice and interpreted nature because it is drawn, and it cannot hide that it is the result of someone's (or a team's) interpretation. The structure of the grid or other layout forms of comics also make the editing process visible. Some pieces of online comics journalism are more conscious about revealing their editing practices than others. Dan Archer, for example, in "The Nisoor Square Shootings," re-creates the controversial shooting incident second by second and shows the events from the points of view of several witnesses. Archer's piece incorporates comics, videos, and links and is all about editing. Similarly, "50 Years on, Still Hungry," an online piece on agriculture in Kenya by Victor Ndula, published on the website of *Cartoon Movement,* includes links to the photographs and video clips on which the drawing was based, in this way encouraging critical comparison and also supporting the status of the comic as reportage.

Truthfulness, authenticity, subjectivity, and mediation in framing and storytelling techniques have been major topics of studies of comics journalism in general, and of Sacco's works in particular (Versaci; Woo; Worden). In chapter 3, where I focus on Sacco's reportage on the Bosnian war (1992–1995), my aim is to depart from these concepts and approach Sacco's comics reportage as a means of dynamic engagement with the vulnerability of the Other. Instead of "truthfulness," "authenticity," and "subjectivity," the keyword of my readings will be "presence." Just like memoirs and diaries, Sacco's reportage is imbued by the personal point of view and the presence of the artist in the line. With this in mind, in chapter 3 I turn to the ways in which this embodied presence becomes expressive of the vulnerability of the Other.

Methods: Reading the Drawn Line

The starting point of my approach to comics is its foundation in drawing. The academic study of comics has had a strong focus on comics as narrative structures and how certain topics, such as gender, race, heroes, and memories, are represented in the medium, but there is still a paucity of research on drawing in comics. By investigating questions raised by the drawn line (chapter 1), drawing autobiographical characters (chapter 2), and drawing the background of panels (chapter 3) in nonfiction comics, as well as by studying the reader's perception of the line and of drawn bodies (chapter 4) and the materiality of comics (chapter 5), this monograph wishes to contribute to the study of drawing in comics in general.

Recently, comics scholarship has turned to the study of drawing in comics, but the general reception of works in the medium also changed over time: It has brought about an increased readerly appreciation of the drawn and visual nature of comics. Artistic craft has been recognized as a vital component of the narrative, claim Jan Baetens and Hugo Frey, who point out that "in the early to the mid-1990s, graphic novels were sometimes identified simply as comics created by better writers. In contrast, grosso modo, today's contemporary graphic novel is more associated with visual sophistication" (94). Naturally, this is a generalization, but it describes a tendency that manifests in many ways. For example, trade paperbacks and collections of mainstream comics include sketches, pages before coloring, color variations, and fan art. Or, the strong emphasis on original art in Chris Ware's *Monograph* (2017) also shows an interest in drawing and encourages bending over stages of drawing preceding publication. The oversize volume of *Monograph* also features handmade objects whereby it emphasizes a material culture around Ware's comics and the materiality of comics in general. This publication, as well as many others, reminds us that recognizing the material nature of comics is essential in order to study the artist's and the reader's respective embodied interactions with it.

In chapters 1, 2, and 3, I approach comics by focusing on the drawer's creative thinking, which manifests in drawing and through the movement of the drawer's body. As a result, even in the final printed product, the reader can trace and relate to the imprint of the artist's mark on the pages. The handmade quality of nonfiction comics creates what Hillary Chute calls "intimacy" (*Graphic Women* 10). "Intimacy" is a prevailing embodied presence that the reader can feel despite the processes of editing, finalizing, and printing: "There is an intimacy to reading handwritten marks on the printed page," states Chute, emphasizing that autobiographical comics are emphatically private (*Graphic Women* 10). As a result, drawing is embodied even if it is printed and reproduced. In Simon Grennan's words, "a reproduction of a drawing does not undermine our understanding of it as a drawing" (16).

For the study of drawing, I rely on the questions raised by comics studies as well as the findings and points raised by art history, art theory, and art practice concerning the nature of bodily investment in artistic creation. I believe that approaches coming from the study of art have relevance in the study of comics, and I summarize recent research into drawing in the upcoming four sections. I start out by outlining similarities between associations about drawing in contemporary fine art anthologies and comics studies ("Drawing in Art History and Comics Studies"), then I explore the relationship between drawing and thinking ("Drawing, Thinking, and Embodiment"). The third section collects opinions on whether the drawn line can be seen as a transparent trace of the drawer's personality ("Drawing and Subjectivity"), and the last section enquires into the conventional aspect of drawing and its relationship to the conventionalized system of writing ("Drawing and Writing"). My aim with these summaries of secondary literature is to provide a context for the subsequent chapters: Drawing will be a central point of inquiry in all of them.

Drawing in Art History and Comics Studies

Fine art and comics come from radically different institutional backgrounds, which is possibly the most basic reason for the mutual disregard of the disciplines in how they approach drawing (Miodrag 198). This institutional difference is one of the reasons why comics artists feel that the art world is not open toward them. Comics, "for so much of the twentieth century, [has been] excluded from the canons of art," states Bart Beaty in *Comics Versus Art* (8). Comics can be approached along traditional categories and institutions of art only with difficulty, while the interactions between comics and museums or auction houses as well as the slow processes of canonization have usually reinforced existing differences and obstacles. This situation has led Beaty to argue for considering comics "a distinct field of cultural production" (8). I share Beaty's view that the practices around comics constitute a distinct field, a field that is now actively changing with the popularization of book-format comics and webcomics. However, I also believe that the methodologies relied on in the field of fine art to study representation in general, and drawing in particular, help us theorize the visual aspects of comics.

Studying the position of fine art drawing in relation to its big sister, painting, I argue, sheds new light on the position of comics within cultural production. In "Drawing Is the New Painting" (2011), Karen Kurczynski claims that fine art drawing is currently undergoing reevaluation and reappreciation (95)—just like comics, which has recently been discovered by new groups of readers and cultural gatekeepers.[7] Fine art drawing has been considered as inferior to painting for a long time; it has been seen merely as a step in fine art education[8] and has rarely been considered as an aim or a creative means in itself. This is undergoing a change, and drawing is getting more and more attention as its associations with rawness, immediacy, and self-expression are increasingly valued. Similarly, after decades of judgment and miscomprehension, certain kinds of comics have recently been reappreciated: The popularity of the graphic novel and the cult of superheroes in print and on film have helped comics to come out from below the critical radar.

In *Contemporary Drawing: From the 1960s to Now* (2015), Katherine Stout writes that "although it is no longer contested that drawing can be a primary medium for artists rather than playing a supporting role to painting and sculpture, it continues to elude any fixed classification" (9). The parallel to comics is clear: Comics, too, eludes classification, partly because of its drawn nature. Comics, too, has often been positioned as a supporting medium that helps children learn to read or makes readers like literature and for long was not seen as a valid and serious means of expression or an independent medium.

On the reasons why the status of fine art drawing in relation to other means of expression has changed, Kurczynski writes:

7. As a sign of the change in the appreciation of comics, let me mention that in 2018 the longlist of the Man Booker Prize contained a comic for the first time. Although Nick Drnaso's *Sabrina* (2018) did not make it to the shortlist, its nomination generated constructive debate and an awareness of comics as an awardable storytelling medium.

8. Drawing became an autonomous activity in the second part of the fifteenth century, summarizes Allegra Presenti, pointing out that during the Renaissance drawing was the foundation of artists' education, and that apprentices "were not allowed to even touch a paintbrush before at least 10 years of training as draftsman" (143).

> In the postindustrial economy, drawing's associations with individual expression, accessibility, easy or automatic production, and flexibility, coupled with its newfound economic viability as a commodity, make it uniquely suited both to counterculture and business interest. Drawing now takes full advantage of having it both ways. (98)

I believe that comics, and especially contemporary nonfiction comics, is framed by similar associations to the ones in Kurczynski's list. In fact, in the quote above the word "drawing" could easily be replaced by either "nonfiction comics" or "the graphic novel" (in the sense Baetens and Frey use the term), revealing a diagnosis of the current state of comics:

> In the postindustrial economy, non-fiction comics'/the graphic novel's associations with individual expression, accessibility, easy or automatic production, and flexibility, coupled with its newfound economic viability as a commodity, make it uniquely suited both to counterculture and business interest. Nonfiction comics/the graphic novel now takes full advantage of having it both ways.

The qualities valued in drawing in Kurczynski's list are "individual expression, accessibility, easy or automatic production, and flexibility" (98)—and the same elements can be found in the reception of comics, as will be shown shortly. Interestingly, Kurczynski's list contains the quality of accessibility. Being accessible happens to be one of the most often repeated stereotypes about comics. Comics has been regarded as accessible for children or for people with reading difficulties, because the relationship between words and pictures in comics has been believed to be unproblematic. Another aspect of the premise of accessibility can be seen in the current framing of comics reportage. As mentioned in the previous section, it is often assumed that exploring difficult or controversial subjects in the medium of comics can introduce these topics to those presumed readers who would not read the same content in the form of a longer article or a book. This is believed precisely because comics is more accessible than other mediums of reportage.

In *Contemporary Drawing,* Katherine Stout quotes a list of associations similar to those collected by Kurczynski, detailing why drawing has been reappreciated during the twentieth century: "spontaneity, creative speculation, experimentation, directness, simplicity, abbreviation, expressiveness, immediacy, personal vision, technical diversity, modesty of means, rawness, fragmentation, discontinuity, unfinishedness and open-endedness" (the list was originally assembled by Michael Craig-Martin, qtd. in Stout 10). While all these associations and qualities are important and have their specific historic roots, immediacy seems to stand out because it is key to other art historians' descriptions of drawing, and it is a quality aimed at by several comics artists. For example, immediacy in drawing is emphasized multiple times in the editors' texts of *Drawing Now 2015* (Schröder 6; Lahner 15). Immediacy is key to some of the ideas associated with drawing in both comics studies and art history: It is related to thinking, to performance, and to authenticity. As will be shown, the elements on Kurczynski's and Craig-Martin's lists return in comics scholars' discussions of the line, drawing, and autobiographical comics.

Immediacy, together with intimacy, are key qualities of Vanessa Davis's collection of autobiographical comics and sketches, *Make Me a Woman* (2010). Davis alternates painted comics and short scenes drawn by pencil. In her pencil drawings, Davis imitates the lines of children that aim at drawing a figure or a scene with a single gesture. These lines create figures seemingly without planning, as if the attention of the drawer was always focused on the tip of the pencil without considering where the drawn line would end or where the gesture would take her. In these scenes, the pencil is pushed too hard and the lines are almost etched into the surface, remaining visible even after attempts to erase them. *Make Me a Woman* is haunted by erased but remaining limbs, sentences, and figures, which give the impression of sketchiness, rawness, and an immediate translation of experience to paper (see figure I.1).

However, as Kurczynski argues, what appears to be immediacy in drawing is constructed. Immediacy is not inherent to drawing itself. Kurczynski shows that thinking of drawing as authentic has its roots in historically specific art movements, such as in the conceptual artists' use of drawing and handwriting as criticism of established art in the 1970s (94, 98), or earlier, in the avant-garde's gestures of deskilling, and their favoring the unfinished sketch to a finished drawing (97). The principles of, and yearning for, transparency and authenticity in the current definitions of drawing have been inherited from high modernism: High modernist concepts of art have been applied

FIGURE I.1. Immediacy, lack of finish, and deskilling are among the key aspects of Vanessa Davis's drawings and comics, contributing to their authenticity in *Make Me a Woman.* Copyright Vanessa Davis. Image courtesy Drawn and Quarterly.

to the understanding of contemporary drawing as a more authentic means of expression in a postmodern setting (99).

Kurczynski also points out a temptation in fine art drawing similar to the one we encounter in comics, namely the temptation to "identify the privacy, lack of finish, and visibility of process evident in drawing as sources for . . . authenticity" (99). Exploring the authenticity of comics memoirs and comics reportage has been a major drive of comics scholarship (Hatfield; El Refaie; Kukonnen; Precup), and drawing styles have also been linked to authenticity. The sketchiness, rawness, and lack of finish of the drawing style in Willy Linthout's comics memoir, *Years of the Elephant* (2009), are considered to be authentic expressions of the emotional state of the autobiographically motivated character, whose son has committed suicide. For example, Ian Williams writes in his review: "Linthout's artwork remains deliberately unpolished in this book—the rough pencil drawings uninked, mistakes uncorrected, giving the work an immediacy and rawness that possibly reflects the emotions conveyed in the narrative" ("Years").

The relationship between the line and its drawer is an undertheorized question in current comics scholarship. Can a transparent relationship be postulated between one's lines and personality or message? Can the lines in comics contribute to authenticity? According to Elisabeth El Refaie, authenticity in comics is equally performed by the artist and by the audience: Readers play a decisive role in establishing a work as authentic. The audience evaluates the performative strategies used for authentication in comics and can reject them (138). I will focus on the performative aspect of the drawn line in chapter 2, in my reading of Ken Dahl's memoir, where I examine the relentless redrawing of the autobiographical avatar's body into newer and newer forms.

Authenticity is often associated with lines made by drawers who do not have formal training in visual expression. Lack of artistic training is assumed to be a source of authenticity for those skeptical about schooling, such as Lynda Barry (see chapter 1). This association can be seen in the reception of Miriam Engelberg's witty and painfully honest memoir, *Cancer Made Me a Shallower Person* (2006): "Her untutored, charmingly naive style lends an air of veracity to the work," writes Ian Williams ("Graphic Medicine" 24). Appreciating authenticity in lines drawn by people without artistic training or in uncertain lines is possible because usually each comics page is preceded by drafts and sketches, and the actual drawing is usually completed in at least two stages, penciling and inking. (Digital drawing boards make the transformation of the qualities of an outline much easier, though many artists who draw digitally still prepare hand-drawn drafts and sketches.) Though comics readers and scholars are aware of the stages of production, looking for the trace of the artist's hand in comics can—but not necessarily does—result in psychoanalytical readings of drawings. Such readings attempt to find signs of psychological states, conditions, or traumatic events in lines, which, as Jan Baetens warns, "risk[s] reducing the work to a symptom of self-expression" ("Revealing" 151).[9] As will be elaborated later in detail, Baetens reminds us that the relationship between artist and line is always influenced by a number of choices as well as by artistic schooling, and the line is never as transparent as a symptom.

As Philip Rawson reminds us in his monograph, *Drawing* (1987), "drawing is not seeing" (21). Rawson emphasizes that drawing is neither a mechanical copying of what is seen, nor is it a selective record of reality. Rawson argues:

> The old academic cliché that the draughtsman "selects" aspects of a given "real theme" must be set aside. The draughtsman may indeed "select" in drawing. But he does not select by an act of conscious eclecticism. Nor does he pick items that he can actually see, for he makes up his drawings out of elements no one can see *in* any object. No one ever actually sees a black outline. (21)

Drawing is interpretation; it is a way to *organize* reality. Michael Archer confirms this when he writes in the introduction of *Draw: Conversations around the Legacy of Drawing* (2007) that "what drawing does is not to mirror what exists, but to realise it" (7). In this respect, drawing is partly thinking, and it is also partly performance.

According to Rawson, drawings are affirmative statements conveying visual truths (21): They are statements about the world, made by a specific person in a situation, during an activity. This means that drawing "implies and illustrates the artist's conception of reality" (Rawson 19). This conception of reality is present, for example, in the stylistic and spatial relations within the drawing. Drawing is not seeing but a visualization of what can be real: Ultimately, drawing provides a "visual ontology" (Rawson 19). Inspired by Rawson, Pascal Lefèvre argues that "the artist not only depicts something, but expresses at the same time a visual interpretation of the world, with every drawing style implying an ontology of the representable or visualizable" (16). The reader of comics has no other choice but either to share the visual interpretation of the drawer or to completely reject it by refusing to read on. The reader cannot look at the object of repre-

9. My interpretation of Miriam Katin's energetic and raw lines, almost carved into the surface and made without preliminary sketches, might fall under the category of a psychoanalytical reading in Baetens's eyes—see chapter 4.

sentation in any way other than the ontology suggested by the drawing (Lefèvre 16). In nonfiction comics, a character modelled on the author also often shares the visual ontology of drawing; the implications of drawing oneself as a character are studied in chapter 2.

I agree with Rawson when he claims that drawing creates an ontology. My aim is to show that in nonfiction comics meaning-creation by drawing is inherently connected to exploring one's vulnerability and discursively situating it. Rawson also touches upon this aspect of drawing when he connects it to introspection: "A drawing . . . shows us to ourselves as it were in a mirror at the heart of our own world of truth—truth not of abstract concepts but of visual conviction" (6).

Drawing, Thinking, and Embodiment

Curiosity about the relationship between the line and thinking is a common interest in comics studies and the study of drawing in fine art. For example, in the album *Draw: Conversations around the Legacy of Drawing* (2007), Jennifer Higgie describes Matisse's drawings thus: "Matisse took responsibility for the marks in his drawings, refusing to disguise either his hesitations or victories. Rubbed out or corrected lines are as important as the more exploratory ones; in this sense, *Matisse's drawings are thinking made flesh*" (Higgie 40; emphasis added). In this quote, Higgie reaches back to most associations with drawing as listed by Kurczynski and Craig-Martin, and with her last words she roots these qualities in the close relationship between thinking, drawing, and the body.

According to Elizabeth A. Pegram, editor of *Drawing in the Twenty-First Century* (2015), the presumption that drawing and thinking are more closely related than, say, painting and thinking, is rooted in the practice of making preparatory sketches and quickly recording ideas that are later reworked and the lines finalized. However, Pegram also states that "rooting drawing in mental activity goes beyond the sketch, and . . . can be applied more broadly" (7). What Andrew Hewish, editor of the special issue on the line of the *Journal of Visual Art Practice,* calls the "intersection of the appearance of line with that of mind or presence, both in production and reception" ("Introduction" 1), has currently become a quickly developing subfield of comics studies. Relating drawing and thinking has been, in Pegram's view, a successful strategy to strengthen drawing's institutional position within fine art (7).

From the point of view of institutionalization, it is little surprise that within comics studies, the connection between drawing and thinking has been influentially asserted possibly for the first time in relation to Chris Ware's comics. Ware "occupies the social space that exists between the worlds of comics and art as he . . . has achieved a high degree of credibility in both areas," summarizes Bart Beaty (213), arguing that "Ware is the first American cartoonist to be considered a true visual artist, celebrated for both technical mastery and conceptual brilliance" (213). Ware has called drawing a way of thinking (Ball and Kuhlman xix), and his statement got embraced in the subtitle of Ball and Kuhlman's collection of essays on Ware's work, *The Comics of Chris Ware: Drawing Is a Way of Thinking* (2010). Ware elaborated on the same idea at the Edinburgh International Book Festival in 2013, where he participated in a talk together with Joe Sacco. Ware interpreted and praised Sacco's comics pages as "a product of your hand, of your mind" (Sacco and Ware 14:40). For Ware, the hand cannot be separated from the mind, and comics is a product of both.

The coworking of hand and mind is a subtopic of Nick Sousanis's *Unflattening* (2015), an argumentative work made in the medium of comics. Sousanis demonstrates a kind of thinking that builds on imagination and interconnectedness, and he also considers drawing as a mode of thinking: "We draw not to transcribe ideas from our heads but to generate them in search of greater understanding" (79). Thinking via drawing is multidirectional and multidisciplinary, and it is also related to the body; these claims are demonstrated by Sousanis's intricate page structures on every page of *Unflattening*. The textual layer of *Unflattening* confirms that Sousanis's assertions are close to those of Rawson and Ware, and to those of this very monograph: "Drawing is a way of seeing and thus, a way of knowing, / in which we touch more directly the perceptual and embodied processes underlying thinking" (Sousanis 78).

Sousanis, similarly to Lynda Barry, describes a connection between the drawn line and the movement of the body. For Barry, as will be shown in chapter 1, an almost automatic and continuous movement of the hand is essential for reaching a creative state of mind. Sousanis establishes a different connection between line and movement when he claims that a single drawn line and a more complex image are understandable for the observers because the onlookers translate the relationships between represented elements to their own experiences of their bodies. Relying on one's own bodily experiences while reading will be further explored in chapters 4 and 5, where I turn to the embodied performances of readers and to feeling a kind of empathy with lines in the body. I agree with Sousanis when he writes that the drawn line "carries the marker's expression" (75), which the observers understand because they understand the dynamics and the route of a given line by comparing it to bodily movements that they themselves have experienced making any kinds of movements, including drawing lines.

Drawing and Subjectivity

The drawn line has dual characteristics: It is a performance and a product at the same time. Many theories exist on how this performance and product is related to the person drawing it: Does the line carry the drawer's personality? Or is it rehearsed and learned? I propose placing these approaches along a scale, which I will call the transparency scale. At one end, the drawn line is considered a direct expression of the artist's intention or personality. This perception builds on an immediacy between the drawing agent and the result of the performance of drawing, and postulates a transparent, almost organic relationship between the line and the drawer. The other end of the transparency scale stands for the opposite approach, which considers the line nontransparent, and thinks of it as born out of conventions and conventionalized systems, such as culture, education, and expectation. The drawn line in this view is socially conditioned; institutions, training, and contexts have a decisive role in its expressive possibilities.

I believe no one would maintain a position at either extreme end of the scale, arguing for either a fully personalized or a fully conventionalized approach in determining the nature of the drawn line. I also believe that practices of line making and approaches to it change over time and from context to context within one's artistic and theoretical practice. There are, however, noticeable tendencies in approaches to the line: The different theories can be characterized by the degree of transparency and degree of convention they attribute to the line.

Jared Gardner observes in his seminal article "Storylines" (2011) that every comic page is emphatically embodied due to the act of drawing. The bodily labor of the drawer (or team of artists), which Gardner calls "trace of the hand" (54), is inscribed and felt on every page. This is true for commercial and noncommercial, mainstream and nonmainstream, fiction and nonfiction comics alike. Gardner argues that "the physical labor of storytelling is always visible in graphic narrative, whether the visible marks themselves remain, in a way unique to any mechanically reproduced narrative medium" (65). Despite approaching the line as a physical trace of a physical body, Gardner is skeptical about the existence of the transparent or natural line. On the example of Eddie Campbell's and Art Spiegelman's commercial and autobiographical works, he shows that the line cannot be translated directly to the artist's life and personality. Both Campbell and Spiegelman are known for their characteristic and recognizable visual styles, which they utilize for narrative ends. Regardless of the comic being fiction or nonfiction, both comics artists use their same respective styles and build on the same respective ideas about lines and representation. "The same line that in *From Hell* [a fictional narrative written by Alan Moore and drawn by Campbell] is overworked to create the oppressive atmosphere . . . in the autobiographical stories is handled with a lighter, quicker stroke, underworked to evoke a very different quality of cobweb: the fragile spontaneity of the everyday" (61). In Gardner's argumentation, the line does not necessarily provide access either to the original scene of composition or to the personality of the artist. Like Baetens and Kurczynski, he refuses full transparency. The effect of spontaneity of the artist's line and style is learned; the illusion of spontaneity is the result of practice.

Simon Grennan undertakes a thorough investigation on how subjectivity is expressed and how conventions are manifest in drawing in *A Theory of Narrative Drawing* (2017). Grennan conceptualizes drawing as a socially and historically embedded activity directed at communication in which the drawer and the recipient are present with their goals and points of view—this, by the way, is also my starting point. Grennan's conception of drawing as an intersubjective form of communication that is both cognitive and embodied is very close to how I see comics. Grennan includes a set of his own comics that he made in order to demonstrate and test his approach to subjectivity and convention in narrative drawing. In these drawing demonstrations, Grennan takes the text and narrative of existing comics, such as six pages from Jim Medway's *Teen Witch,* and reinterprets these scenes in the visual style of other comics artists. *Teen Witch,* for example, is redrawn and redesigned in Mike Mignola's style (Grennan 190–91). Grennan aims at adapting the subjectivity and the form of other artists as they are represented in their comics, and he aims to identify and re-create the subjectivity of the panels and lines as faithfully as possible. However, he concludes:

> It is not possible for me to be someone else, to make someone else's trace. . . . The series of subjective relationships embodied in the new drawings in the *Demonstration* are specific to me, communicated through the physical form of *this* expression, the situation of which I'm a part. When Mignola, Ware or Medway express themselves, it is always their self-expression and always their physical trace. (214)

With this, Grennan attests to the subjective nature of drawing: He cannot fully re-create, for example, Mike Mignola's drawings; he will always see the traces of his own subjectivity (and of what Gardner would call "hand") in his presentation (213). In this way, Grennan's book argues for the presence of an inescapable subjectivity in the drawn line.

The line is seen as not only subjective but also autobiographical by Hillary Chute, who has described nonfiction comics as "manuscripts" in her "Comics Form and Narrating Lives" (112). "Comics works are literally manuscripts: they are written by hand. (Comics is a form invested in the *auratic* but an auratic that is divorced from fixed notions of the authentic)" (112). Chute establishes a relationship based on the idea of direct access to the original moment and embodied situation of creation, which is made possible because the starting point of her investigation is the strong relationship between the line and the artist's body. For her, creating comics is "a procedure of embodiment" ("Comics Form" 113). Her remark in parentheses in the quote above hints at a reinterpretation of the Benjaminian aura by taking the mechanical reproduction of the drawn line into consideration: The artist's line is not effaced in print; there is no tension between the original and the reproduced line in terms of access to the bodily mark. In this respect, the line can be thought of as preserving the immediacy of a manuscript.

Furthermore, Chute argues that due to handwriting, *any* handmade and mass-produced comics carries a "trace of autobiography in the mark of its maker" (*Graphic Women* 10). In this way, Chute sees an autobiographical quality in any handmade comic, including fictional works. This idea of linking the line to autobiography is very close to Lynda Barry's theory and practice of the line, elaborated in, for example, *What It Is* and *Syllabus.* Among comics scholars, Chute's view of the line is the closest to the transparent end of the transparency scale. She argues that "handwriting underscores the subjective positionality of the author" (*Graphic Women* 11), and it is from this subjective positionality that nonfiction comics is born. Chute also writes that "the subjective mark of the body is rendered *directly* onto the page and constitutes how we view the page" (11; emphasis added). For Chute, comics *"looks like what it is"* (11). This assertion, however, is not necessarily true, not only because I believe that complete transparency of the line is impossible, but also given the possibilities and existing practices of recoloring[10] or redesigning comics, or simply publishing them in different formats,[11] thereby providing a different material support.

Focusing on the original moment of creating the manuscript and looking for an autobiographical trace in the line can favor the study of only a certain type of comics and may lead to neglecting others. Comics that do not erase the traces of the process by which they were created, like Linthout's already mentioned *Years of the Elephant* or Davis's *Make Me a Woman,* are in fact extraordinary works. Jan Baetens warns that basing theories exclusively on such works can lead to false results, as such works can be "excessive on the graphic plane, because [their approach to comics] lingers over the unfinished, the rough copy, deletion, and overloading" ("Revealing" 153). Though I believe Baetens to be right, it must be noted that the format of the graphic novel, which is typically thought of as the work of a single author or *auteur,* has been recently repositioned at a higher cultural status partly because of its creator's aim at establishing a unique and recognizable style, which often relies on excessive features, dele-

10. Although fictional and not autobiography, Daniel Clowes's *Ghost World* has been recolored, which created a very different atmosphere in the world of the comics.

11. Several nonfiction comics are published in hardback first, and then paperback. Carol Tyler's trilogy on her father was published in three volumes at first, then collected in a single, smaller volume.

tion, and overloading. Characteristic style is one of the aspects by which Baetens and Frey argue for the graphic novel as an independent means of expression (Baetens and Frey 9–10). Recognizable style can incorporate qualities of lack of finish, roughness, or excess, as we see in Davis's work, but these qualities are often at a distance to the immediacy of manuscripts: They are at least partly consciously applied.

The immediacy of drawing verbalized by Chute is relatively rare in comics but is not unheard of. For example, the American graphic memoirist Miriam Katin, whose comics will be studied in chapter 4, occasionally uses the first drafts of comics pages in print without retracing or refining the original ideas and page design. These pages are in this way one step closer to being manuscripts than comics that are reworked several times. In an interview about *We Are On Our Own,* Katin explains that she did not return to images she experienced as traumatic. She says, "The pages I had difficulty describing were left in an almost sketchy way. The reason was that once I almost scratched them into the page, I did not feel like rendering them any more" (Baskind 240).

Though exceptionally raw works can more easily be seen as the "subjective mark of the body . . . rendered directly onto the page" (Chute, *Graphic Women* 11), comics artists who rework and refine their drawings and pages also have personal traits in their lines. The hand of individual artists can easily be recognized by the trained eye. Possibly some of the most remarkable proof for the existence of personal traits in lines even while working in a given uniform style is Carl Bark's establishment as a serious comics artist. Throughout his career, Barks worked within the stylistic restrictions and anonymity of the Walt Disney corporation, yet in the 1960s fans identified his anonymous drawings by identifying individual traits of his style (Beaty 80).

However, linking the hand-drawn nature of comics to autobiography is not the same as being reminded of the embodied actuality from which the line and eventually the comics were born—as theorized by Gardner in "Storylines." In the case of the confessional genre of comics memoirs, it is especially tempting to approach the line as a direct and transparent access to an authentic message or personality, rather than a mere (reproduced) trace of the author's bodily movement. The temptation of enabling direct access to the original autobiographical situation in which the line is born is explicitly represented in many memoirs. Scenes showing the artists themselves sitting at their desks, creating the very comics the reader is holding, are abundant. Lynda Barry, for example, starts *One! Hundred! Demons!* (2002) with a desk scene, carefully labeling all the instruments surrounding her in the moments of creation. Such moments can be interpreted either as access to an original subjectivity via the act of drawing or as visualizations and mediations of the birth of the line. In other words, there is a difference in thinking about the line as an index of the author's subjectivity (most strongly verbalized by Katin, and, as it will be shown, by Barry) or as an index of the author's body or hand.

Drawing and Writing

Even with its inescapable subjectivity, drawing is always conventionalized to some degree. As already hinted, Baetens argues that "graphic representation is a socialized act, involving many codes and constraints" ("Revealing" 152). Grennan concludes his above elaborated investigations into subjectivity in drawing by saying that he feels more confident in imitating a drawing style—that is, in applying a set of conventionalized codes about drawing—than in imitating the expression of a specific individual. To be exact, Grennan claims that it is impossible to draw as someone else, but it is easy to draw in a given style (243). Grennan defines style as a constraint on subjective expression by social consensus and self-observation (239) and says that drawing according to the conventions of a style is not contradictory to subjectivity: "I embodied my own subjectivity . . . albeit in a self-conscious way and with a specific aim" (247).

Baetens compares the conventionalized nature of the drawn line to that of the line used for writing: The line cannot be considered simply as "the mechanical or modified reflection of a personality, a body or an unconscious" as "even if the drawing is very personalized or hyper-individualized, it is still as indirect as the writing itself" ("Revealing" 152). Both kinds of lines are appreciated by a community, and because of this, they are socialized by necessity. The line cannot be fully natural—and fully transparent—without risking its accessibility to its audience. To be interpretable, both writing and drawing need to meet the criteria for common understanding of what communication, writing, and drawing are in a given temporal, geographical, and social context. Training and schooling seem to be the first major step in learning to create a socially embedded written sign.

During the process of being taught to write, that is, to recognize and make the forms of a set of characters, one's handwriting starts out as standardized. Over the years of practice, one's handwriting gradually becomes more and more unique: The handwriting of a six-year-old has fewer personal features than that of a sixteen-year-old. This tendency is true even for Chinese calligraphers, who spend long years by tracing, copying, and reproducing the characters in as perfect resemblance to the template as possible. Yet, at the last stage of their long training, calligraphers are encouraged to disregard the rules learned by their hands and let individual inspiration guide their pens (Ingold 148). In *Lines: A Brief History,* Tim Ingold argues that handwriting is neither as indirect, nor as socialized, as one would expect—and this observation contradicts Baetens's argument in exciting ways. Ingold shows that though the shapes of letters are conventionalized, when they are drawn by hands, they are just as different and unique as drawings. Ingold considers writing as a "special case of drawing" (122) and reminds us that the medium of both drawing and writing is the line (129): "Writing is still drawing. But it is the special case of drawing in which *what is drawn comprises the elements of a notation*" (122). For Ingold and for Lynda Barry, the written and the drawn line belong to a single category. Writing and drawing coexist in Barry's artistic and teaching practice. Both are inseparably present in her assignments to students and readers,[12] and their mutual influence is also expressed by Barry's practice of coloring certain letters from her sentences. This way, and by using the same tool, the sumi brush, to create textual and pictorial parts, Barry emphasizes the visual nature of text (e.g., *What It Is* 81) and the arbitrariness of differentiating lines of drawing and lines of writing.

The idea of *re*uniting textual and pictorial interpretation of lines in our interpretations of comics has been also been expressed by film scholar Tom Gunning. In "The Art of Succession: Reading, Writing, and Watching Comics," Gunning writes that "in order for comics to liberate reading, they must first liberate the act of writing, reuniting the art of calligraphy with the art of making images" (46). Theorizing the relationship of the drawn line and the written line in com-

12. In her diary exercises, for example, apart from having students verbally list what they did and saw that day, she asks them to draw a picture for each day in their diaries (*Syllabus* 182).

ics, Gunning does not speak about simple combinations but argues for their active and mutual influence. This active influence is demonstrated by Barry's work by the intensive and improvisational copresence of written and drawn elements over the pages: Both and either can come out of the drawer's brush (or other tool) in a creative state of mind. In this way Barry offers a reunion of calligraphy with image making, which, as Gunning puts it, is a way to "liberate" both writing and comics reading (46).

Handwriting seems to have a link to the person regardless of the content of what is written: According to Rosemary Sassoon, author of *Handwriting of the Twentieth Century* (1999), handwriting is an "emotive issue" (3). One establishes a deep and emotional connection toward one's handwriting even if one is not entirely satisfied with it, and the emotionally loaded nature of handwriting manifests especially when one's handwriting is criticized by others. Handwriting "is oneself on paper" (Sassoon qtd. in Ingold 146). The praise of one's handwriting reassures the whole person, while the failure of handwriting is considered "as a crisis of the whole person" (Ingold 146). Similarly, one is linked to one's drawing in complicated emotional ways, be it trauma, as in the case of Katin, or a desire to draw well, as in the case of Barry (see figures 4.3 and 1.4).

The above sections demonstrate that the line and the practice of drawing have been approached sometimes in radically different ways. I do not believe that drawing and the line should be looked upon in the same way when discussing different comics or different works of art. However, an awareness of the complexity and the depth of the questions concerning drawing needs to influence the discussion of lines or style when close-reading individual comics.

•

Drawing as a performance of the body and the line as expression of vulnerability in nonfiction comics will be in focus in chapters 1, 2, and 3. Following Jared Gardner, I understand the line as a trace of the drawer's body on paper ("Storylines" 54), but it is also an indexical sign of the drawer's body (Grennan 15). Chapters 1, 2, and 3 consist of case studies and provide interpretations of comics by Lynda Barry, Ken Dahl (Gabby Schulz), and Joe Sacco, respectively. These chapters establish that elements of the practice of drawing comics, such as drawing lines (chapter 1), drawing oneself as a character in comics autobiography (chapter 2), and drawing style (chapter 3), can be seen as expressions of vulnerability and as initiations of an embodied dialogue with the reader around the quality of vulnerability. I agree with Paul Karasik and Mark Newgarden when they state in *How to Read Nancy* (2017) that "in comics, all is ultimately expressed through line" (137), and in the first three chapters I argue that vulnerability can be more than a central topic of nonfiction comics—it can also be seen as a central experience expressed by drawing.

Chapters 4 and 5 change perspective in investigating the expressive potentiality of lines and turn from the study of the drawer's embodied engagement to the study of the reader's engagement and performance. I study the performance of reading in the material interaction with comics, in the reader's habituated reading performance and its sudden disruptions, in relating to drawn lines, in the perception of haptically visual surfaces, and, finally, in relating to drawn bodies. These chapters are linked to the first part by their methodology—the are based on my personal readings of Miriam Katin's and Joe Sacco's comics—and in the attention given to the body. I see the first and the second part of this book as related in their aims of describing interaction with nonfiction comics as embodied, performative, and part of a dialogue.

As I have already said, I believe that some points of my argument are not exclusive to nonfiction comics but are valid in the case of fictional comics, too. Fictional comics, that is, most comics published in the world, can also be seen as part of a dialogue; drawing and reading it can be seen as embodied and as performative. I restricted my examples in the case studies to nonfiction comics as I believe that due to their special and multiple connections to reality, real events, and real people, the link between their embodied and performative nature and vulnerability is easier to see. Nonfiction comics address readers in a different modality than fictional comics, and because of this different kind of address, the drawn nature of nonfiction comics can be interpreted as an invitation for readers to engage in a dialogue on one's own vulnerability and on that of the Other.

Subjectivity and self-expression will be in focus in chapter 1, where I analyze Lynda Barry's conception of the line, showing that for Barry authentic expression cannot be achieved without the coordination of bodily movement, a certain state of mind, and an experience of vulnerability. Following the interdisciplinary approach outlined in the introduction, I read Barry's comics along Paul Klee's classic formulation of drawing as taking a line for a walk, arguing that a key to understanding Barry's ideas on drawing is considering the line a partner, and equal to the drawer.

Chapter 2 turns to the line by which an autobiographical avatar is drawn. By close-reading Ken Dahl's *Monsters,* I approach drawing as a power to transform reality. In focus are Dahl's imaginative and performative lines, drawn in repeated acts of creating the main character's body. By reading *Monsters* along Margrit Shildrick's *Embodying the Monster: Encounters with the Vulnerable Self,* I argue that the creation of the autobiographical avatar's body is a never-ending performative process, during which the body is perceived and visualized as monstrous and vulnerable at the same time.

In chapter 3, I investigate ways in which drawing can be an engagement with the vulnerability of the Other. Whereas Joe Sacco's style has often been described as primarily realistic and has been praised for this quality, I focus on the way he draws abstract backgrounds. Densely crosshatched surfaces around figures or in seemingly not so important parts of the panels are contrasted to figurative representations in Sacco's comics. Reading Sacco's *Safe Area Goražde* and *The Fixer,* I argue that style and technique, as well as the bodily labor of drawing, can constitute a means of dwelling with the vulnerable Other.

Readers' engagement with comics is often discussed as mental and visual participation: Readers connect gaps between panels or pages in individual ways, following the visual and verbal clues in the panels (McCloud 63). In contrast to this view, more and more attention is given to the part the reader's body plays in interpretation, focusing primarily on sensual inputs while reading (e.g., Hague; Scherr; Orbán). Relying on these important studies, my aim in the last two chapters is to establish a model of embodied comics reading that is not based on the isolation of the senses but on their interconnectedness and on the implications of our reliance on the body schema.

Studying body-schematic performances in reading nonfiction comics will be central to both chapter 4 and chapter 5. These performances or series of actions are based on the fact that human beings are innately and unconsciously aware of the positions, feelings, and movements of their bodies. On a practical level, this means that we do not need to look at our hand to perform the series of minute movements required to turn the page and to reflect on the sensations we receive during this performance. In chapter 4, I study multiple ways in which the body understands drawings: In Miriam Katin's graphic memoirs, I examine abstract lines as well as figurative representations of bodies in pain, both of which are interpreted not simply visually, but in terms of our having a body. I study disruptions in the habituated performance of reading, and focusing on abject images, I show that in the context of nonfiction comics, these images can promote reflection on the role of the body in reading and on its vulnerable nature; furthermore, abject images can facilitate reflections on the quality of bodily vulnerability as shared by the reader as well.

In chapter 5, I study graphic narratives published in unusual formats because I believe that strangeness facilitates reflection on both the actual performance of reading and on habituated reading performances. I offer interpretations of Katie Green's unusually thick and heavy graphic narrative, *Lighter Than My Shadow,* and Joe Sacco's *The Great War,* an accordion-format drawn narrative. In these case studies I show that format, material characteristics, and figurative and haptically visual representation can lead to an embodied and performative understanding of and response to the Other's vulnerability articulated in the comic.

Comics and the Body: Drawing, Reading, and Vulnerability concludes with a four-page comic I drew to reflect on and demonstrate by and with drawn lines the ideas on embodied interaction with comics discussed in this book.

ONE

THE AUTHENTIC LINE

Lynda Barry's *What It Is* and *Syllabus*

LYNDA BARRY, the iconic figure of the American alternative comics scene since the 1970s and recipient of the MacArthur Foundation's fellowship in 2019, reveals a unique theory about the line and about drawing comics in her work, namely *What It Is* (2008), *Picture This* (2010), and *Syllabus* (2014). In these works, similarly to other theoreticians of drawing,[1] she emphasizes bodily engagement in thinking and in creation, and unlike the already quoted scholars, she traces the line back to a special state of mind. As will be shown, Barry thinks of the line born out of this special state of mind as uniquely linked to the drawer's personality. Barry's concept of the line can be placed toward the transparent end of the transparency scale, the scale along which I situated approaches on whether the line can be linked to autobiographical, subjective, and personal traits. (For details, please see the introduction.)

In comics scholarship until recently, the line was considered to be the most undertheorized aspect of comics, partly because the line "has no neat equivalent in any other narrative form" (Gardner,

1. See the "Methods: Reading the Line" section of the introduction.

"Storylines" 53), and also because influential studies of comics used concepts borrowed from narratology. By reading two of Barry's educational works, *What It Is* and *Syllabus,* I would like to contribute to this discourse on the line in two ways: First, by exploring Barry's unique approach to the line as authentic and transparent, I study the risky personal and also bodily engagement out of which the authentic line is born, and I discuss some key aspects of Barry's theory and practice of drawing lines, such as the quality of aliveness, the concept of the image, and the practice of unlearning. The second aspect of my contribution to the study of the line is by repositioning the line not as a trace or a product but as an active partner to the vulnerable drawer. Before investigating what Barry says and shows about the line, I would like to briefly introduce the two examined works.

What It Is and *Syllabus* are all about the surface of the page that is to be filled: The chapters alternate between various forms of visual-verbal storytelling, such as the aesthetics of scrapbooks, comics, public announcements, private diaries, notes. The line, the mark and trace of the hand, is an omnipresent element that bridges the aesthetic distance between printed textual inserts and cutout text, on the one hand, and handmade and hand-painted sections, on the other. In this way the books represent an aesthetics where it is not only word and image that coexist on equal levels but also different paper qualities, text sources, and their various authors. The array of word and image relationships mobilized in Barry's works includes hierarchy in illustration, dialogue in comics, facilitation in explaining or demonstrating ideas, ironical commentary, rivalry, reinforcement, ornamentation, and decoration. In her practice, as figure 1.1 demonstrates, textual bits are just as ornamental as the figurative visual elements; both can be decorated and can be used to decorate, or to fill space.

What It Is builds on a rhythmical alternation between full-page montages and short autobiographical comics sequences. The montages pose questions on imagination, memory, and creation, asking, for example: "What is where is your imagination?" (20) or "What are thoughts made of?" (70). The inserted comics address Barry's childhood in a confessional way and contain reflections on her relationship to drawing and comics. The second part of this big and heavy book is designed to address readers and facilitate in them a similar creative state of mind as the one that has been presented in the montages and comics of the first part. The workbook-like structure invites readers

FIGURE 1.1. A page from Lynda Barry's *What It Is*, 106. Copyright Lynda Barry. Used with permission from Drawn & Quarterly.

to take part in creation, thereby introducing an open and dialogical structure after the first part, which was dominated primarily by questions communicated by montages. In the second part, the reader can become a participant, and can share not only the joy of creation but the feelings of vulnerability inherently linked to it.

What It Is is bravely experimental in its treatment of visual elements, which come from the widest range of sources. Barry glues bits of paper—torn or cut up to tiny pieces—to create her collages over ordinary yellow notebook pages. As a result, each page presents an array of surfaces, materialities, and colors (see figure 1.1). The original three-dimensional nature of each multilayered page is clearly felt even in the printed book. This gives the book a very tactile quality: The reader is free to touch the surfaces and trace the irregular lines where two bits of paper meet. For the montages, Barry uses the personal archives of a schoolteacher, Doris Mitchell, and brings the elements of the deceased teacher's books and notebooks into an unexpected, layered, and associative dialogue with each other and with her own drawings.[2] Barry reconstructs phrases by rearranging individual words that have been cut out of aged printed material, such as newspapers, elementary school textbooks, and teaching aids, thereby creating new associations. Figure 1.1, a page from *What It Is,* for example, demonstrates the complexity of a scrapbook page constructed out of handwritten bits that bear the marks of at least two hands. The spaces between these cutouts are filled with drawn elements, while the top and the bottom of the page are framed by rows of printed words cut out of their original contexts (106).

The other book examined in this chapter, *Syllabus,* was published a few years after *What It Is.* It does not build on a structure of collages organized by a central question anymore;[3] instead, as the title suggests, it continues the practice-oriented teaching mode that is dominant in the second part of *What It Is. Syllabus,* however, is not a workbook. It contains Barry's notes and reflections on her teaching practice, assignments, instructions, and students' works from four classes Barry was instructing at the University of Wisconsin–Madison between 2012 and 2014: "The Unthinkable Mind," "What It Is," "Write What You See," and "Making Comics."

In its appearance, design, size, and paper quality, *Syllabus* imitates a composition notebook, but it is equally a scrapbook and a richly illustrated colorful portfolio arguing for Barry's theory of drawing lines and creating drawn narratives as embodied self-expression.

2. Barry dedicates the whole book to Miss Mitchell in the last montage, where she includes a photograph of her as well (210).

3. Though there are exceptions, and we find pages organized around a topic, formulated as a question, in *Syllabus,* too. For example, "Where did you get your imagination?" (34).

However, compared to *What It Is, Syllabus* is more recognizably the work of a single hand, even if the book uses material made by others, especially by Barry's students. *Syllabus,* in accordance with its title, has a clear agenda and a path to follow; it is didactic in its aims, and it focuses on classwork and task descriptions (as can be seen, for example, in figure 1.3). The task descriptions themselves are made by hand by Barry and are richly populated with creatures commenting on the activities to be done by the students at home, in this way transforming a topic as banal as a home assignment into a multilayered narrative. Barry not only provides a theoretical syllabus to a specific university course, but she gives material proof of her practices aimed at relearning and reexperiencing how to bring forward some honest lines that, in her view, almost all of us used to draw as children.

The Image as a Structure of Experience

Barry introduces her ideas on the link between creativity, memory, and bodily movement in *What It Is,* claiming in the form of questions, and demonstrating in the form of montages, that these three are related. "Why do some images come back again and again?" (96) "What is movement? Do thoughts move? Do images have motion?" (83)—these are some of Barry's questions expressing the fluidity of memory and imagination. Visually, these montages feature painted or cutout pictures of animals, such as birds, bunnies, deep-water fish, or plants, as in budding boughs. Some of these figures are linked to permanent and specific associations in Barry's comics. The nearsighted monkey, for example, stands for Barry herself (figure 1.1, top left corner); demons turn up in several of Barry's comics (figure 1.4); and the often-represented octopus even has a name, Magic Cephalopod (figure 1.4). This character is an important figure in a short comic that I will analyze later: It embodies all that Barry has to say about drawing, creativity, spontaneity, and movement. The Magic Cephalopod is "b[orn] when looked upon. Activated by any activity related to the image-world. Guides pens, pencils, and other mark-makers through exercises" (*What* 138).

Barry's montages represent and also ask about aspects of the creative state of creation. A number of montages and creative exercises facilitate reaching "a certain state of mind" (*Syllabus* 22), which does not simply enable working creatively, but is a prerequisite of drawing a deeply personal line. The special state of mind that is key to Barry is called "dream awake" by Dan Chaon (*Syllabus* 128), and it "comes about when we gaze with open attention" (*Syllabus* 22). This dream awake state can be brought about by the mechanical and repetitive movement of the hand. To continuously move the hand and the drawing tool in order to learn to direct attention in it is the aim of many of Barry's exercises, which I will discuss in the next section (see figure 1.2). The creative state of mind facilitates new connections among memories, imagination, and experience. These three, as I will show shortly, are essential components of what Barry calls the image (which is not the same as a picture or a drawing), and they are also the sources of one's creative output.[4]

The creative state of mind has a very special relationship to time. Barry—like Bergson—differentiates measured and felt time: Though measuring time and being aware of how long it takes to draw something are part of the activities in both books, the time of drawing in the creative state of mind is felt rather than measured. In *Syllabus* Barry sums this up in this way: "The drawing seemed to take a long time and then no time at all. Even a minute after I finished it I could hardly remember the beginning stages, and it took on the feeling of having just appeared on its own, somehow making itself come into being" (131). This contemplative state and what I call the meanwhile temporality of drawing cannot be reached at once. Barry shares several exercises, which are to be done in a limited amount of measured time, designed to facilitate reaching the creative state of mind and its meanwhile temporality by making students familiar with the movements of their hands and the materiality of mark making. Drawing a castle or a Batman figure are such exercises designed to learn more about the movement of the hand and the birth of the line: Students draw castles and Batman figures in less and less time, descending

4. Barry discusses her most important concepts and practices of drawing in *Picture This* as well. Though this book was published after *What It Is* and before *Syllabus*, in my opinion it is not as systematic as the other two, and I do not include its longer study in this chapter. It must be noted, however, that the idea that a certain state of mind is required in order to make a drawing is expressed in *Picture This* as well (68, 126, 200, 203, 223). Similarly, Barry discusses her view on spirals (66–69), which will be explored shortly. She asks about the difference between drawing and writing (119, 120, 123), a topic I addressed in the introduction. Finally, she also talks about the vulnerable state of uncertainty in creation (95, 117, 126, 127) in *Picture This* as well, a topic I will discuss in detail in the last section of this chapter.

from as long as three minutes to five seconds (*Syllabus* 94–96). In this way, students experience what a given duration is (*What* 147, 150, 154), which in turn will help them get immersed in the meanwhile temporality of creation.

The line drawn in the right state of mind feels alive and has a special connection to the drawer: It is not simply the product of one's moving hand but is interwoven with thoughts and experience. The aliveness of the line contributes to its authenticity and transparency. Barry uses the word "image" to describe the *experience* of aliveness felt in drawing lines: Images are "alive in the way thinking is not, but experiencing is, made of both memory and imagination, this is the thing we mean by 'an image'" (*What* 14). The image is a dynamic interaction between the individual, his or her memories, and his or her imagination (*What* 34), and it can be expressed on paper in the right state of mind. The image is a structure of personal experience, and not simply a picture. This structure of experience is expressed—in the right state of mind and in the meanwhile temporality of creation—for example, by the montages, such as the one in figure 1.1. Meaning is born out of the coexistence of the various elements over the surface, put there by an embodied mind in a creative state. The image feels alive, on the one hand, because of the associations, memories, the unexpected movements of ideas that the drawer experienced, and, on the other hand, because of the numerous temporal layers that a single image can evoke and incorporate while it is created in the dream awake state of mind.

Explaining what an image is and how it works are returning topics of Barry's educational comics. For example, she emphasizes the transgressive and dynamic nature of images in a full-page montage in which she rhythmically alternates black surfaces and colorful (mainly yellowish) figures, among them the Magic Cephalopod, Barry's returning figure indicating creativity (*What* 30). The questions scattered over the page define the image as experience rather than as a visual entity: "How and why are there images inside of us?"; "After we read a book is it inside of us?"; and "Where is a book before we read it?" (*What* 30). By her word choices, Barry creates unexpected associative connections between the person, his or her environment, and the image. The montages confirm images to be alive, active, and associative, as well as spatial and experiential.

I find Barry's conception of the image very similar to the point made by visual culture theorist W. J. T. Mitchell, who also starts out from the aliveness of images. In *Syllabus* Barry defines the image as follows: "By image I don't mean a visual representation, I mean something that is more like a ghost than a picture; something which feels somehow alive, has no fixed meaning and is contained and transported by something that is not alive—a book, a song, a painting—anything we call an 'art form'" (*Syllabus* 15). In *What Do Pictures Want?* (2005), Mitchell also differentiates the image from the picture: The image is an idea, "the 'intellectual property' that escapes the materiality of the picture when it is copied. The picture is the image plus the support; it is the appearance of the immaterial image in a material medium" (85). Images circulate in human cultural production; they have a "social life" (93) within this circulation. Images influence other images, and they bring forth unforeseen associations, for which reason Mitchell provocatively compares the image to a virus: Neither of them has a life on its own; they both need human participation to be carried or to reproduce (87).

In *What It Is,* images as structures exist and move in space. In this approach, the presented drawings and artwork are not thought of as end products; rather, they are conceptualized as manifestations of the ever moving and living image. This is also the reason why the handmade nature of actions like writing, drawing, tearing, cutting, and gluing is primary for Barry, and why she does not refrain from using—writing on, drawing on, tearing, cutting up, gluing together—drawings or written texts made by others. Both *What It Is* and *Syllabus* are rich in other people's handwriting, and the traces of other people's hands contribute to the final structure of the montages.[5] Individual creativity and expression rely on the work of others in what Schlick described as a democratized creative process (41). The fluid image lives in collaboration, in the reworking, rethinking, and reformulation of works by others.[6]

---

5. This is not simple plagiarism. Barry does not make any attempts to create a unified visual layout in which the work of others would be effaced by the conformity of style. Instead, collaboration is highlighted.

6. The importance of collaboration in Barry's conception of image making and creation can also be seen from the way she changed the title of a chapter in *Syllabus.* An earlier version of "Car and Batman" was published in the "Comics and Media" issue of *Critical Inquiry* (11–19), and a more colorful later version has been incorporated into *Syllabus* (24–33). The most significant difference between the two versions is not the extent to which Barry redesigned, colored, and appropriated the pictures drawn by students. A significant reattribution of authorship has taken shape between the time of publication of the *Critical Inquiry* version, authored by

Images, similarly to what Mitchell has called a "social life," do not stay put in Barry's approach either: Their associations are not fixed, and they require active engagement. In a montage organized around the central question "Where are images found?" (*What* 15), Barry provides the following textual answer: "Images are found by in through action between inside and outside" (*What* 15). Barry's lack of punctuation in her answer emphasizes the spatial multidirectionality and aliveness of the image. Images can be anywhere and can be nowhere at all. For both Barry and Mitchell, the source of the image is in human experience; however, while Mitchell is describing cultural phenomena, Barry keeps to personal involvement with the image and to the expression of personal experience in a certain mental state.

The structure of experience, expressed in the image that feels alive (*What* 202), provides the basic background for the birth of the natural or transparent line. Via its connection to the image and to the dream awake state of mind, the line stems from deeply personal experience, and is expressive of autobiographical content in itself. Though it might seem paradoxical, the aliveness of the image can be found by mechanical exercises like filling the page with parallel lines or copying or coloring other people's drawings. Mechanical manual activities enable entering the right state of mind by making the individual more familiar with the process of mark making and the nature of one's own marks. Furthermore, the exercises facilitate a change in one's attitude toward drawing should one have fears or anxiety about it.

Apart from getting familiar with one's drawn marks, unlearning expectations and associations about them is an important aspect of Barry's exercises. In fact, Barry's aim is to make adults reexperience drawing as a personal and creative activity, and to help them find the aliveness of line that has been lost since childhood by what stops adults from reaching the right state of mind. Many times people who have stopped drawing forget that "there is a way of making lines and shapes that is ours alone, and the more we draw, the clearer it becomes, not just to ourselves, but to others: a style unique and recognizable. . . . The trick is to find a way to keep ourselves from rejecting it before it can fully present itself" (*Syllabus* 70). Learned associations about drawing to be deconstructed include, for exam-

Barry, and the *Syllabus* version, "written by Lynda Barry but drawn by Students" (*Syllabus* 25).

ple, the fear of creating a bad drawing (*Syllabus* 16–17; *What* 123–35), the fear of being judged because of a drawing (*Syllabus* 19), or using drawing skills to become more popular (*Syllabus* 126). These fears block the link between the line and personality and let (real or imaginary) social expectations intervene, as a result of which the right state of mind and the authentic line are never reached.

Instead of judgment, and without the intention to teach drawing techniques, Barry approaches lines drawn by people who have stopped drawing with intense curiosity. She says, "I'm interested in using the drawing that is already there—is *still* there in spite of everything" (*Syllabus* 38). As Barry explains, "people who quit drawing a long time ago make the most incredible drawings when they start up again. Some of the best, most original work I've seen since I've started teaching was made by students who hadn't drawn since they were kids. . . . [T]his kind of picture holds my attention so completely" (*Syllabus* 138).

Unlearning is very much related to exploring hidden and painful areas, which are mapped out in a long process with a complex temporality. One needs to rereach a childhood state in the past (*What* 19), use one's imagination as well as memory (*What* 20, 29–36, 165), and, finally, reexperience the intensity of the present, the temporality of creation. As part of unlearning, one is to reach a state where one is not influenced by judgment. It is only in this state that the originality that Barry is looking for can appear in one's work. Yet when it does, it cannot be defined; rather, it is intuitively felt: "It's unmistakable when it starts to happen. The whole class feels it. A new way of seeing comes about, a new approach to problem-solving and working that extends beyond the limits of our class time into other aspects of daily life" (*Syllabus* 59).

The Line as Movement and Thought on Paper

The textual elements of figure 1.1 explain a central topic of *Syllabus* and *What It Is,* namely that movement is related to thought: The questions "Why write by hand?" and "What is a hand?" are followed by "What is it connected to? What moves it?" and "What happens when we write by hand?" (*What* 106). Not only are movement and thought related, the creative state of mind is in fact presented as born out of their dynamic interaction. "Thinking is a physical act" (*What* 205), which is demonstrated by the parallel lines and spirals in figures 1.2 and 1.3, which will be analyzed in this section. These ideas of Barry echo Chris Ware's proverbial "drawing is a way of thinking" (Ball and Kuhlman xix) and Nick Sousanis's "drawing is a way of seeing and thus, a way of knowing" (Sousanis 78).[7]

In the full-page montage in figure 1.1, Barry ponders about what a body or hand in motion are moved by (*What* 106) and directs attention to what she calls "ordinary motion" and its relationship to thinking. Ordinary motion refers to the automatic activities of the hand, which are mostly not reflected upon, and which are therefore beyond conscious thinking: "There is a state of mind which is not accessible by thinking. It seems to require a participation with something Something physical we move like a pen like a pencil Something which is in motion ordinary motion like writing the alphabet" (*What* 106; figure 1.1). Thinking, when accompanied by moving a pen or pencil in the hand, can bring about a state of mind that is not accessible by thinking alone. Thinking and the movement of the hand can facilitate the expression of an image.

In a relaxed state of mind, and out of the relaxed movement of the body, the line is born. As shown in the previous section, the line for Barry is more clearly a transparent expression of personal experience than for most scholars quoted in the introduction. The line's roots in what Barry calls the image transform drawing lines into an exercise in exploring, enduring, and building on one's vulnerable states. In this way, the stories of comics are linked to vulnerability not only due to their content, such as childhood memories and trauma, but also due to their medium, the line. The line is related to the individual not only as a bodily mark, as Gardner has theorized, but also as a spontaneously born trace of a thought process. Let me illustrate Barry's conceptualization of the line with a page from *Syllabus,* shown in figure 1.2.

In figure 1.2, Barry contemplates whether she as a teacher should ask her students at the University of Wisconsin–Madison to draw a page full of horizontal parallel lines to promote physical and mental immersion in drawing. The montage is filled with lines: A unit of black-gray lines—the result of the planned exercise as performed by the teacher—is placed on the left of the page, taking up the majority of the surface. The lines of various gray shades have possibly been

7. For a discussion of drawing and thinking, see the introduction.

FIGURE 1.2. An exercise of drawing parallel lines from Lynda Barry's *Syllabus*, 72. Copyright Lynda Barry. Used with permission from Drawn & Quarterly.

painted with watercolor: They are not straight, but wavy, and they are not entirely parallel. Their differences in shade provide a rhythm to this insert, yet the white-gray tones are in contrast with the yellow composition notebook page on which it is placed. This yellow notebook page, used as support to the white page with gray lines, is in turn placed on a support of blue striped paper. The resulting blue margin connects this page and the one next to it, while its handmade horizontal lines, this time made by crayon, echo the painted lines on the grayscale insert.

The structure of this page is symptomatic of the way Barry constructs *Syllabus* and *What It Is*: Lines are placed over lines, and at the same time, lines are framed by lines; the context of the line is a network of other lines. This structure gives the book an even rhythm with a feel of spontaneity, but also a strong sense of scale: The even pacing and rhythm of stripes on the yellow composition book pages that regularly come up as support to the montages suggest a constant relation to, and distance from, the human body. In *What It Is,* the reader relies on the horizontal lines as a way of orientation to a greater extent, as here it is not at all difficult to get lost in the richly layered montages of painted colorful surfaces and glued elements. The yellow paper serving as a support of these montages is almost always visible at least in traces, and its printed lines provide a sense of continuity, a sense of scale, and, due to the ordinary nature of the support, a sense of familiarity.

Lines create a layered surface on the page in figure 1.2, providing both context and a structure of frames for other lines. Here Barry uses not only the blue striped second support for framing, but the grayscale insert is also framed by her art made up of geometrical forms. At the top, a horizontal double helix in red is visible against a heavily crosshatched background; on the left, the frame features a vertical formation built on the rhythm of knots and ovals, crosshatched and colored blue; and at the bottom a pattern of rhombuses, with their middles crosshatched, displays all the colors used on the page. The right side of the frame features handwritten notes and a figurative drawing. All in all, the framing emphasizes dynamism by the use of multidirectional lines and color, revealing that ultimately, the whole page is about lines and about the body that has created these lines. Even the seemingly unmotivated figurative element on the right, the elephant-like lady walking on two hind legs while holding an umbrella and a bag (a returning character in *Picture This*), is represented against a heavily crosshatched background.

The whole page is a demonstration of the experience of the line as dynamic movement and the possibilities of play it offers. The textual elements of this page also focus on the line, though the word "line" appears quite late. First, right under the white insert covered in gray lines, Barry includes a typed quote by M. P. Follett from his 1930 book *Creative Experience* on the importance of experience, which says: "Concepts can never be presented to me merely, they must be knitted into the structure of my being, and this can only be done through my own activity" (72). This quote does not mention drawing, nor does the next textual element, the blue sticky note in the top right corner, which speaks further on the experience. Here we read in Barry's capitalized handwriting: "The only way to understand this is by *making* things. Thinking about it, theorizing about it, chatting about it will not get you there" (72). The elephant drawn under the sticky note is a demonstration of the line in the making, while the block of handwritten text under the figure visually completes the frame around the insert of the white page with gray lines.

The unit of handwritten text in the bottom right corner openly calls attention to the line in two ways: first, by asking questions about the time it takes to draw a page full of parallel lines, and second, by contrasting all that the page stands for to "the apparent 'uselessness' of the activity" (72). The central question of the page is how to make the students see that the repetitive activity of drawing lines is useful, parallel to which the page demonstrates how drawing lines becomes part of one's structure of being: The double helix on top immediately gets referenced to the structure of DNA. By the layering of lines and by their intensive coexistence, the page also emphasizes the bodily labor that is a prerequisite to understanding and experiencing the line.

In the gesture of the spiral, Barry unites movement and contemplation, and uses this form to mark physically, on the surface of the page, that the process of image making has begun. The spiral tracks reaching the desired creative state of mind via the movement of the hand. Ultimately, the spiraling line is a visual imprint of the already mentioned temporality of creation, the meanwhile temporality. The spiral is Barry's most frequent and most easily recognizable indicator of thinking through the body, as it is a way to make the hand and the whole body enter the state of mind, where the authentic line can appear. Spiral shapes appear everywhere in *Syllabus*,[8] and concentric circles are also frequently drawn. These are not merely decora-

8. See pages 9, 11, 46, 60, 62, 69, 73, 75, 76–80, 83, 115, 143, 147, 156, 181, 185, 189, and 196, as well as the front and back covers.

FIGURE 1.3. Instructions on how to draw spirals in Lynda Barry's *Syllabus*, 77. Copyright Lynda Barry. Used with permission from Drawn & Quarterly.

tive geometric elements; they are the physical and bodily imprints of thinking and creating.

On pages 76 through 80 of *Syllabus,* Barry encourages students to draw spirals while assignments are read out loud by fellow students or poems are recited by the instructor. As Barry's instructions on how to draw the spiral make very clear, the whole body, and not just the hand holding the pen, takes part in the activity. Her detailed list of parts of the body that are one by one paid attention to has the rhythm of relaxation exercises in yoga (figure 1.3). "While you work on your Spiral put all of your attention on the tip-top of your head . . . then move it to the center of your forehead" (*Syllabus* 77)—she starts tracking the route of attention. The text ignores the preprinted rules of the notebook and is placed under a sketchy drawing. The sketch is drawn partly in non-photo blue pencil, which, according to Barry, is the color of thinking (*Syllabus* 119), and which is usually erased from finished drawings. The black ink that the drawing is traced with comes from the same tool that is used for writing. In the drawing, a character is sitting by a table on which the word "relax" is spelled out by dots. The character is drawing a spiral in a striped composition notebook and his or her hair or brain has the same structure of seemingly concentric circles or a spiral. This way, there are two spirals, one in the head and one produced by the hand.

The drawing in figure 1.3 indicates direct access and communication between the head and the hand. In an immediate flow of relaxed concentration, the image can appear on paper. This direct access and the link of the alive image to personal memory and experience are what make Barry's perception of the line unique. The direct access, as well as the inseparable link between body and thought, are also the reason why, in the next section, I link drawing lines to experiencing and expressing vulnerability.

The Line as Expression of Vulnerability and as Partner

When the authentic line, rooted in the aliveness of the inner image, is born, the students—as Barry is talking in the context of university classes—immediately feel that something has happened. Yet to reach authenticity and originality in the line, one does not simply have to reach the right state of mind, one also has to repeatedly overcome crisis. By my reading of Barry's mini comic about overcoming a mental block, I would like to show how the line is born not only out of movement and out of a state of mind, but also out of exploring one's vulnerability. *What It Is* and *Syllabus* do not simply inspire and motivate; Barry also calls attention to the painful process preceding the creative state. Within this creative process, there is a point where one's vulnerability is experienced in giving up control over the creative process and in giving the lead to the line. First, I examine the way Barry connects the experience of vulnerability to creation, then I turn to the idea of letting the line lead the performance of drawing.

In *The Graphic Novel: An Introduction,* Jan Baetens and Hugo Frey emphasize that often drawing "is an extremely labor-intensive, repetitive, virtually boring, exasperating, and desperately disheartening activity that can lead many artists to extreme states of depression" (138). The authors also acknowledge that drawing can be "mechanical, painful, and dull" (138). Elizabeth A. Pegram, editor of *Drawing in the Twenty-First Century,* notes that though drawing is primarily associated with the present tense and with immediacy (see the introduction for a detailed discussion of associations of drawing), artists can equally experience it as a "painstaking" longer duration (8). Depression and anxiety caused by drawing is one of the topics of Barry's "Two Questions," a short comic in *What It Is* (123–35). The comic represents palpably the painful process of feeling helpless and vulnerable before getting to the point when one reaches the right state of mind and the authentic line can be born. The two questions referred to in the title are "Is this good?" and "Does this suck?" (*What* 123), and the comic explores the expectation to create artwork that can be labeled as good, and the pressure to avoid creating art judged as bad.

"Two Questions" features two characters of autobiographical roots, two Lyndas:[9] a child one and an adult one. Both are constantly engaged in drawing. They put on paper the mocking and encouraging demons who stand for the pressure of expectations and fear: They came alive from the tips of the Lyndas' brushes. Initially, there are two demons. One of them is constantly smiling and expects the Lyndas to create only good art; the other one has "you suck!" written over its body and communicates the worthlessness of what is being created. As the comic progresses, the number of creatures embodying either positive or negative judgment increases, and they occupy more and more space on the pages. While on page 128 the creatures only talk to the young Lynda as she is drawing at her desk, commenting, for example, "What the *#@* is that s'posta be?" and "Be great!," by the next page they are making it completely impossible for the adult Lynda to create (figure 1.4). Not only has their number multiplied, their bodies and their comments completely fracture the

9. In the chapters of this book, I will call the autobiographical character or avatar by the given name of the comics artist it is modeled after, and I will refer to the drawer by his or her family name.

surface: They devour the space for creation. With this panel, the aesthetic principle that the comic has been building on so far is broken down. So far, the structure has been based on the balance of alternating, well-distinguishable blocks of words and images against a cross-hatched background. Now the encouraging and skeptical comments are everywhere, causing chaos not only in the artist's head, but also in the logic of representation (figure 1.4).

At this point, the story narrows down to the grown-up Lynda's complete inability to create. Her mind is blocked, and she cannot tell if what is being drawn is good or bad: "The Two Questions held that part of me hostage" (*What* 130), says the first-person narrator from the present. As a visual expression of the hostage metaphor, in the second part of the story an angular shape is redrawn multiple times in various roles and functions, all of which convey the experience of being held hostage. When it shows up on page 130, it is a tiny package on the demons' table. It has been kidnapped by the demons, and the angry one is shouting at Lynda over the phone, "You'll get it [the box, the hostage] back when you can tell me what the *@#% it is, and give me one good reason—besides the fact that it's yours—that I should give it back to you. / Oh— and you suck" (*What* 130). In the meantime, the encouraging, smiling demon is also an active agent of the hostage situation, saying, "Hee hee I love this riddle!" and "You're great!" (*What* 130). In this first variation on the angular shape as hostage metaphor, the package stands for the lost capability to create, and the ransom is to name what has been taken.

The next pages show that Lynda cannot find the reason why she cannot create. The package is reinterpreted as Pandora's box (*What* 131), and in the next three pages the box becomes literally a prison as the ribbons transform into prison bars. Behind the bars we find two characters: the squeezed Magic Cephalopod, who is Barry's symbol of creativity, and her own surrogate, the nearsighted monkey (*What* 132). Soon enough, the adult Lynda is seen behind the bars reading an oversize book called "On not being able to paint" (*What* 133). The next prison box holds the Magic Cephalopod again, this time begging Lynda to "Give up! Give up!" and repeating, "Don't know! Don't know!" (*What* 134), while Lynda is shown bent under feelings of despair. The Magic Cephalopod's words, as we will find out with Lynda at the end of the story, are the answer that would help Lynda to create. It is only by admitting and accepting that she is unable to answer either question ("Is this good? Does this suck?"),

FIGURE 1.4. A page from "Two Questions," from Lynda Barry's *What It Is*, 129. Copyright Lynda Barry. Used with permission from Drawn & Quarterly.

and by admitting that she does not know what has been taken from her, that she will find peace. This comic shows that being able to accept one's vulnerable state is a necessary step on the way to creation. The answer that makes the demons go away is "unthinkable" (*What* 131): Instead of a single correct and verbal answer, the solution is to live through a cycle of experience that is rooted in vulnerability. When Lynda admits that she gives up trying and does not know the answer, the demons immediately disappear.

It is only by admitting and accepting the idea of not knowing what is good and what is bad, and, more importantly, by giving up volition to control what is being created that Lynda will be able to create again. When she embraces her vulnerability and makes it part of the experience that governs drawing, Lynda experiences the creative state of mind and has a connection to the alive image again. As the narrator says, "That strange floating feeling of being there and not being there came back. One line led to another and a story slowly formed under my hands. / To be able to stand not knowing long enough to let something alive take shape!" (*What* 135). The images on the last page of the story show the adult Lynda being embraced by the Magic Cephalopod, who, as described already, has the solution, "Don' know," written over its body. Lynda and the Magic Cephalopod are holding the brush together, spelling out "abracadabra" over an empty page.

The magic of creation and the connection with the image are born out of facing one's inability to consciously answer and approach creation, and equally, they are born out of the painful process of accepting that one does not control creation, a process during which one is completely vulnerable to one's own anxiety. Furthermore, Barry also makes clear that one cannot escape from this experience of helplessness: It is the nature of creativity to experience vulnerability in cycles; this realization has happened before, and is bound to happen again (*What* 134). Vulnerability is not a singular experience in creation; it is part of the birth of the authentic line.

Creation and reaching originality via the line are never controllable and predictable processes for Barry. During creation, be it the phases when one experiences one's vulnerability or the state of creative flow, one can never know what exactly is going to come out of one's brush or pen. While in the previous example Barry compared the vulnerability inherent in the phase before creation to being imprisoned, in another example she compares drawing to getting lost: "To follow a wandering mind means having to get lost. Can you stand being lost?" (*What* 49). Not wanting to hasten the achievement of a goal and being able to stay in uncertainty open the creative process to experiences of vulnerability. The montage the above quote is part of features seemingly unrelated elements, like a cat wearing an octopus outfit, an eyeball-like structure, a human figure upside down, flowers made of paper and flowers made of lace, and a red theatrical curtain framing the page, as if visual focus was lost already. I would like to emphasize elements that resonate—for me—with the textual invitation of exposing oneself to the experience of getting lost. By painted waves and textual references to water in this montage, Barry utilizes the metaphor of traveling by the sea. In due course, at the bottom of the page we find the nearsighted monkey and a demon crossing water in a boat. They have undertaken the crossing in order to follow the wandering mind and to stand not knowing where they would go. The direction and the outcome of the journey are not clear yet, but its dangerous nature is suggested by dark colors and a pterodactyl hovering in menacing gloom (*What* 49).

Getting lost and experiencing one's vulnerable states repeatedly cannot be spared, even if it seems to be the longer path to creation. In another example from her teaching practice, Barry describes an occasion when she forgot about the significance of getting lost and wanted to save time for her students (*Syllabus* 86–92). She gave them too-specific instructions about how to use crayons, a new material in the class, and with these instructions, she also communicated her preconceptions about crayons. As a result, the class ended up not liking this technique. In her reflection on what happened, Barry concludes that she took away the chance to experiment, explore, get lost, undertake risk, and ask their own questions with their coloring. Getting lost and experiencing one's limits leads to building a personal relationship with the materiality and process of drawing as well as with the image.

Barry thinks of both drawing and writing lines as risky spontaneous "picturing" (*Syllabus* 136) that one cannot lead or direct: "It's a kind of picturing that is formed by our own activity, one line suggesting the next. We have a general direction but can't see where we are until we let ourselves take a step, and then another, and then we move on to the third" (136). Entering the right state of mind and having the ability to stand vulnerable and not knowing have been important precisely because it is via these experiences that one can yield to the spontaneously flowing line. In fact, Barry's conception of the active and unpredictable line resembles Paul Klee's theory of the line as a stroll.

Paul Klee thinks about the line as a walk or stroll in his *Pedagogical Sketchbook* (1925, in English 1953): "An active line on a walk, moving freely, without goal. A walk for a walk's sake. The mobility agent, is a point, shifting its position forward" (Klee 16). Klee approaches the line as a structure of experience or as a process that necessarily has a direction ("forward") but does not have a goal. Importantly, the line possesses equal agency as the artist. As Andrew Hewish emphasizes, the canonical English interpretation of Klee's German original as "taking the line for a walk" results in a false hierarchy that is not part of Klee's model: The drawer has the power to take the line, which, in turn, can be taken, for a walk ("Line" 3). For Klee, as well as for Barry, the line is emphatically active: It is a loaded possibility that can take any direction any time, and at any single point of which any alternate possibilities might appear (Hewish, "Line" 13) and get embodied.

Comics are created via this unpredictable gesture of engaging with an active line. As Barry explains: "You know where the story begins and ends—and you know two things happening in the middle—if you are drawing it in four panels. But you don't know what your drawings will be like until you draw them with this kind of picturing in our mind that moves your hand. The trick is just that: let it move your hand" (*Syllabus* 137). Wandering, encountering something, and getting lost are not at all pleasant experiences; they show the self's essential helplessness or vulnerability before, and also in, the creative flow. The experience of letting go of control can be a painful one, and through it drawing becomes a risky business: Demons can come out of one's brush, just like the ones in "Two Questions." They spontaneously appear to force the drawer to face them. In probably her most famous autobiographical work, *One! Hundred! Demons!,* all the chapters are structured around the spontaneity of the active line to unexpectedly bring forth demons.[10]

The line coming out of Barry's brush can take the shape of a demon any time—and, naturally, demons are not simple creatures but complex structures of experience, that is, they are connected to Barry's understanding of images. The line drawn by the sumi brush can

---

10. These demons embody associations and recollections of Barry's childhood, and they are named in the title of each chapter. In *One! Hundred! Demons!,* each chapter title names a demon—for example, "resilience," "the visitor," "magic lanterns," "cicadas," "dogs"—and elaborates a childhood memory associated with this central traumatic element. Sometimes, as in the case of the mythological *aswang,* cultural heritage merges with personal heritage (see de Jesus 7–12). The demons literally take shape and their black shapes populate the pages of the introduction, which shows the artist in the moment of creation with brush in hand.

FIGURE 1.5. "Rolling forward along in time," a one-page story from Lynda Barry's *What It Is*, 157. Copyright Lynda Barry. Used with permission from Drawn & Quarterly.

equally draw one of Barry's avatars or write the narratorial text. In *What It Is*, the character of the child Lynda is often called forth from Barry's brush suddenly and unexpectedly. It is as if this girl, as well as the demons, manifested involuntarily from the line drawn by Barry's hand.

The dark-tone one-pager "Rolling forward along in time," published in *What It Is* (157), also expresses the dangerous spontaneity of drawing the line and the vulnerability inherent in considering the line as a free-moving active agent (figure 1.5). In this comic, lines put on paper lead thoughts: The drawer must remain passive and has to stand not knowing what direction the line will take so that the line can manifest. Drawing requires an openness to what is to come, even if what comes is painful: "Something happens to my thinking when I start to draw / it becomes more like listening than formulating" (*What* 157), Barry writes in "Rolling forward along in time" about the experience of giving up control. The title of the story records the indeterminate direction and dynamism of thinking and creation. In the panels themselves, we see various heavily crosshatched figures: the young Lynda, a cat, a demon, a robot, and in the final, silent panels, a deep-sea fish and a tapir (figure 1.5). This is a comic about how making marks brings forth and records a spontaneous inner dialogue between memories and thoughts that one has not considered to be interacting. The deep-sea fish is an easily understandable metaphor for the unconscious element in creation, but what stands out for me is how unusually dark the whole page is: The comic is inserted in a black-brown frame reminiscent of dried vegetation, and the panels are dominated by blue wash and heavy crosshatching. The figures are especially heavily crosshatched compared to other pages and characters in *What It Is.* It is as if these characters came into being not because of but despite the lines. The shape of the very pensive cat in panel 4 is born out of the density of lines covering the surface of the panel as if by accident.

In this comic, lines going in all directions make the differentiation of character and background ambiguous and difficult and threaten to deface the characters themselves. Barry depicts the young Lynda in two panels at the beginning: The first one resembles a classical portrait with Lynda looking directly at the reader, addressing us with inexpressive eyes, not smiling. Lynda's face is almost scarred by the hatches; her hair is more easily accessible and recognizable than her face. In the next portrait, Lynda is shown reading a book, with her face in darkness and her hair almost black. While we look at these heavily crosshatched figures, the narrator encourages reading this comic as an illustrated recording of the process of its own spontaneous creation: "While I move my pen, I hear sentences, like this one for example" (*What* 157), says one of the metatexts in the captions.

Both the face scarred with lines and the comics' focus on creation suggest that the overabundance of lines is in fact a materialization of the thought process, which is always on the verge of becoming inaccessible to others. Creative thought is always in danger of becoming illegible to the public, and here it is even shown to be on the verge of being differentiated as a form against a background.

As always, the text encourages a linear interpretation of the page, as it connects panels into a linear narrative. When we follow the direction of reading, the last panel, the endpoint of the story, seems to be different from the previous panels. It shows a crosshatched tapir against an unusually white background. It is now easy to differentiate figure and background, as if a form has emerged out of the materiality of thinking. The last panel reveals that the lines and the thoughts they are connected to have been tamed: They no longer scratch the surface and they are not means of effacement anymore. Whereas in the penultimate panel a prominent role is given to the energetic, freely flowing line, in the last panel the lines are contained by the figure.

"Rolling forward along in time" records the unpredictability of both thought and line, and it conceptualizes making comics as a risky open-ended activity. No wonder that Lynda as a returning character is abandoned early on and is replaced by a series of other creatures. Instead of a returning character, the true hero of this one-page comic is the spontaneous and authentic line. This line is a forever-changing active agent born out of a dream awake state of mind and of personal experience. It is a companion, which is not *taken* for a walk, but has its very own ideas about walking.

So far, I have argued that the line for Barry is a means of authentic self-expression and is equally the product of the mind and of the movement of the body. However, the line is not a simple product of thinking or movement, nor is it a product of successfully connecting to the image or being able to stand the vulnerable states of creation. Instead, the line is a *partner* of the drawer: It is a partner of the mind and the body. The line becomes authentic when one lets go of the desire to control it and when one undergoes the vulnerable states of not knowing. Facing vulnerability is a part of genuine expression and of the creative process: It is part of the active and dynamic partnership with the line. The line's spontaneity is born out of a mindset that allows dwelling with the complex image that one would like to represent. At the same time, the line is produced by an ease about, and consciousness of, the movements of the body. The line is not controlled by the mind or the body. In giving up the lead, artistic self-expression becomes linked to experiencing one's helplessness. In this way, drawing itself stems from embracing one's vulnerability and from a partnership with the line.

TWO

CARTOON BODIES AND TRANSFORMATIVE LINES

Ken Dahl's *Monsters*

HAVING EXAMINED the line as linked to subjective experience and vulnerability in Lynda Barry's metacomics on creation, in this chapter I turn to the representation of characters who have a reference to the actual biological/historical person of the drawer. Following Gillian Whitlock, I call this character the autobiographical avatar (971). Comics offers a perfect medium for autobiographers to express the complexities of identity, subjectivity, or their relationship to their bodies, as the medium builds on the visualization of these questions with a simultaneous visualization of the drawer's attitudes toward them. Comics inevitably makes a set of complex ideas and relationships visible on the page, and the array of visual elements in drawing all work together conveying meaning and ultimately show the drawer's conception of life in the drawing itself. This is what Rawson called the visual ontology of the drawing (*Drawing* 19; see the introduction). Visual ontology, or in Michael Archer's formulation, the fact that "what drawing does is not to mirror what exists, but to realise it" (7), is a key concept helping to understand the performative nature of the line that is being drawn to create the body of the autobiographical avatar (repeatedly, from panel to panel).

In this chapter, I focus on the dynamic visualizations of the avatar's body in Ken Dahl's *Monsters* (2009). In this comic, the avatar's body is constantly drawn and redrawn in newer and newer forms, which clearly shows the performative potential of the line in narrative drawing. My reading examines the morphing of the avatar from one form to the other, which, I argue, can be read as an articulation of not only monstrosity (see the title of the comic) but also of vulnerability. The experiences of vulnerability and monstrosity were first connected by Margrit Shildrick, whose *Embodying the Monster: Encounters with the Vulnerable Self* (2002) serves as the major theoretical foundation of this chapter.

Monsters is a three-part semi-autobiography published in one volume in 2009 by a New York–based publisher, Secret Acres. The comic appeared under the pen name Ken Dahl, but on the last page the author's real name is revealed to be Gabby Schulz. *Monsters* is about facing and learning to live with the burden of an incurable sexually transmitted disease, herpes. Herpes manifests as a skin condition, but in *Monsters* it is not simply skin that undergoes transformation, but the avatar's whole body. In the first and longest part, possessing a dangerous and monstrous body is visualized in inventive ways, and the character's body image is shown to be in a constant flux. The narrative focuses on evading the moral questions and consequences of whether Ken has infected his sexual partner(s) with the virus of herpes. The second part shows Ken, now self-identified as a monster, as a social misfit, trying to control the symptoms of his illness and blaming society for his condition. In the final part, Ken makes some uncertain steps toward building an honest and infection-conscious relationship with his new partner. In the analysis, in order to differentiate character from cartoonist, I will refer to the author as Dahl and his avatar as Ken.

As hinted already, my interpretation of *Monsters* is based on Margrit Shildrick's approach to vulnerability and the body. In *Embodying the Monster,* Shildrick examines various cultural and bodily forms of monstrosity and otherness that have been considered as inferior to the normal body. She explains that throughout history, attempts have been made to confine the quality of monstrosity and vulnerability to people whose bodies "disrupt [the] morphological expectations" (2) exemplified by a white male body—for example, people with disabilities or women. However, despite these attempts, vulnerability cannot be attributed to someone but needs to be acknowledged as a defining characteristic of all bodies: It is "also our own" (6). Shildrick deconstructs the idea that opposes a normative body to a monstrous one, and also deconstructs the "boundaries of the modernist subject" (7), which, in my reading, is precisely what Dahl does in *Monsters.*

Shildrick, just like Judith Butler, thinks of vulnerability as universal. Shildrick claims that vulnerability is "a quality of the self in the encounter with the other" (7). This means that vulnerability manifests and can be recognized in acts of communication and interaction, and because of this, it is truly everywhere. Drawing on Levinas's ethics of encounter, she writes: "In encountering the stranger-neighbour, I may be *called back* to the ethical from my immersion in the ontological; I may be interrupted in my being. Whatever the status of my initial response, then, violent or welcoming, it is the move to responsibility that matters" (91). At this point, I would like to expand Shildrick's argument to the world of drawing nonfiction and autobiographical comics: Drawing one's avatar in comics is based on encounters with the Other within the self, and because of this, it is inseparable from experiencing and expressing vulnerability. As will be shown, the drawing of one's avatar is based on introspection and visualization, and I aim to show that vulnerability is a quality of the self that gets seen and represented in the alienating encounter with oneself as it happens in autobiography, and, in the specific case of comics, in drawing.

As the plural in the title *Monsters* promises, monstrosity is a multiplied experience that manifests in the multiple forms of the shapeshifting main character, Ken, and also in the personified forms of the herpes virus, who happens to be Ken's most faithful companion. Ultimately, Dahl's book is a visual exploration of the interrelated experiences of vulnerability and monstrosity, which manifest both in the experience of carrying a sexually transmitted virus and in the most basic experience of all autobiographical ventures, namely in encountering oneself as Other in the autobiographical look. In this chapter I show two different manifestations of vulnerability in *Monsters,* arguing that the character is vulnerable, on the one hand, to what he will be turned into by the transformative power of the virus within the world of the story. On the level of the story, the first lesson Ken has to learn is the admission of his own vulnerability, experiencing, in Shildrick's words, that "the monstrous cannot be confined in the place of the other" (4). On the other hand, the avatar's body is vulnerable to the twisting logic of metamorphoses, actualized by the drawn line. Ken's body can be transformed into many forms in the performance of drawing, as the ontology of drawing in this comic denies a stable and constant form with which the avatar could be associated. Ken's body is constantly redrawn; it is morphing on and on under the hands of a creative and playful graphiateur[1] or drawing agent.

The aim of my analysis is to examine the performance of the line in creating Ken's ever-changing character in relation to the vulnerability involved in creating a cartoon self of oneself. I believe that the potential to be transformed via drawing also means a certain openness to the grotesque: Playful and caricatural qualities characterize cartoon bodies in the tradition of comics autobiographies, as the grotesque has always offered means to explore and experiment with power and vulnerability. The relationship between the grotesque and transformation via drawing is also noted by Ian Williams, founder of the *Graphic Medicine* blog and movement, who writes in his review: "Herpes, obviously, isn't funny, but Ken[2] is funny, his drawings are funny, the way his characters morph into dogs, viruses and monsters is funny and his observational humour is spot on" ("Monsters"). I will show in this chapter that it is in the acts of redrawing, which make all forms of the body uncertain, where *Monsters* challenges the division of bodies into categories of monstrous and normal, vulnerable and stable. Finally, in the last section of the chapter, I turn to instances where the morphing of the body is accompanied by a change of style. I show that Dahl's ironic take on the visual clarity of infographics and his incorporation of realistically drawn photographs can be interpreted as further visual ways to undermine the illusionary stability of the normative body. This section on style links to chapter 3, which is fully devoted to the study of style and vulnerability.

Dahl is very clear in visualizing his avatar's body as alien and othered, fluid and monstrous, vulnerable and multiple: Both Ken's body and Ken's relationship to himself are constantly being transformed, so that no form can be considered the final one. In *Monsters,* experiencing vulnerability and presenting it in an entertaining way are

1. This is Philippe Marion's term, introduced in Jan Baetens's "Revealing Traces: A New Theory of Graphic Enunciation" (147). The graphiateur is the agent responsible for "the graphic and narrative enunciations of the comics," which Marion calls "graphiation" (147).

2. Williams here is referring to the author, Ken Dahl, not the character whom I have been calling Ken in this chapter.

provocatively matched: Vulnerability and wit are framed as Ken's central characteristics. With this, Dahl breaks away from associations of vulnerability with femininity, weakness, and postcolonial subjects, which have prevailed until the rethinking of this concept by Butler, Shildrick, and others. Dahl demonstrates the universality and the potential of the constant becoming that his experience of vulnerability is tied with. In *Monsters,* a heterosexual white male protagonist loses control of his bodily experience and literally of his body image, to the extent that by the end of the narrative, the possibility of a normal or stable body gets questioned.

Transforming and retransforming the avatar's body offers creative ways for Dahl not only to find visual expressions of complex feelings and experiences but also to testify to the endlessness of pictorial embodiment itself. Pictorial embodiment, a term coined by Elisabeth El Refaie to describe "the process of engaging with one's own identity through multiple self-portraits" (51), is a potentially infinite creative process: There is no end to drawing avatars that express some aspects of one's identity. Moreover, in autobiographical comics, the avatar's body is repeated and redrawn from scene to scene in a repetition that is a necessary and also practical aspect of pictorial embodiment. However, the constant redrawing of one's avatar can be part of a process of continuous self-definition. We can see this clearly not only in Dahl's *Monsters* but in comics by artists who play with the ways their avatars are drawn: Julie Doucet imagines herself a man in her "If I was a man" series (*My Most Secret Desire*), and Daniel Clowes playfully keeps on changing the appearance of his avatar in "Just Another Day." I consider pictorial embodiment a form of performative metamorphosis to keep the avatar in a "constant condition of becoming" (Shildrick 1), which is a particularly vulnerable situation.

During drawing the character based on oneself, the drawer or "comics autographer" (Gardner, "Autography's Biography" 3) reinscribes versions of himself or herself in the scenes of his or her life. The autobiographical avatar is born out of the study, interpretation, and representation of one's subjectivity and physical features. Rather than pursuing factual realism in representing one's bodily features, drawing an avatar aims at a truthfulness in expressing the understanding born out of the objectification of oneself (Hatfield 114–27; El Refaie 147). Drawing oneself as a comics character builds on the play between closeness and distance, between being the object of study and the subject of one's art—mirrors, therefore, frequently appear in comics autobiographies. Dahl's *Monsters* is no exception: He uses the trope of the mirror to reveal the arbitrariness of what seems to be natural and conventional. Dahl transforms the bodies drawn for his avatar freely. Because of this, central concerns of *Monsters* are, on the one hand, the potentially never-ending process of self-study, self-objectification, and recognizing oneself as monstrous and vulnerable, and on the other hand, the artist's skill and imagination in representing versions of this constantly changing body.

As an illness narrative, *Monsters* is obsessed with the various symptoms and signs of the body, more precisely on the skin. The comic is preoccupied with skin as a legible and threatening surface and also as a boundary. As will be shown in the next section, the visual reinterpretations of skin reveal that the actual threat is not coming from the outside; rather, its source is inside the body. In his narrative about a sexually transmitted disease, Dahl addresses bodily taboos[3] and puts a lot at risk when he offers up his autobiographical avatar's body for the judgment of the reader. He builds on the potential of the comics medium to "intervene against a culture of invisibility by taking the risk of representation" (Chute and DeKoven 772) and represents life with a sexually transmitted disease, risking judgment and stigma (Sontag, *AIDS*). Dahl as graphiateur or drawing agent enjoys the reader's shock or laughter caused by sudden changes of bodily forms, and many of the visual puns draw on the proximity of what Bakhtin called the grotesque to the carnivalesque (Koch 155).

Negotiating the Boundaries of the Body

Dahl's work uses striking visual metaphors for the representation of emotional states and the fluctuating ways the protagonist relates to his medical condition. The graphic memoir one immediately associates with the keenness to present illness with visual associations and fluidly transforming bodies is David B's *Epileptic* (originally serialized in six volumes in French between 1996 and 2003; published in English in 2005). "This book is ultimately about art, representation, and creative energy as much as about epilepsy," summarizes Hillary Chute, emphasizing the creative force of David B's visual world

3. Shildrick writes on bodily taboos that "the disruption of corporeal integrity and the open display of bodily vulnerability is always a moment for anxiety and very often hostility" (53).

("Review" 425). I consider the statement to be equally valid in the case of *Monsters*: Dahl's comic is about testing the flexibility of representing the human body in various styles and about transforming the avatar.

Engagement with monstrous bodies is a topic *Epileptic* and *Monsters* have in common. In David B's work, the brother's epilepsy is made manifest as a monster, or as horse, mountain, and bird-snake, while in *Monsters,* Ken's own body is abstracted and made monstrous, dangerous, alienated, and other. Furthermore, just like in *Epileptic,* illness is materialized and personified: It does not only exist inside the avatar's body, but also outside it, as a character. Sometimes Ken and the embodied and personified virus are roommates and best friends, and occasionally they even behave like a couple sharing the same bed (154, 180). The virus-buddy fulfills Ken's emotional needs by expecting him home or telling him off when he comes home late (153). The virus-buddy can change its size from a small, cute, yet annoying pet (125) to an enormous, menacing presence (124). The virus-buddy, apart from being a friend, also acts as a predator and as an embodiment of temptation, trying to persuade Ken to engage in sexual relationships with women without informing them about the details of his medical condition (125). The personified virus is the only being Ken can discuss his infection and his anxiety with. He is the only one who can understand Ken, because the virus-buddy's body visually stands for the fullness of the same monstrous qualities that characterize Ken's body in various degrees. The body of the virus-buddy is fully abject.

The most often returning representation of the virus-buddy—that is, of the personified and embodied monster of herpes—is a jelly-like body that has no head or limbs. It has a transparent, spiky skin that covers the swirling, dark mass inside. Ken in his monster form also looks like this (figure 2.2). To describe the monstrous body, one can easily adapt Kristeva's depiction of the abject as "a massive and sudden emergence of uncanniness, which, familiar as it might have been in an opaque and forgotten life, now harries me as radically separate, loathsome" (2). Kristeva's theory of abjection will be discussed shortly; at this point, I just would like to note the amazing literariness with which the virus-buddy and Ken's infected body visualize Kristeva's description. Furthermore, the transparent body of the virus, in which the outside reveals the inside, visually recalls what Shildrick calls the "confused and essentially fluid corporeality of monsters"

(48). The form's literal fluidity contributes greatly to its abject associations. The monstrous form in its fullness, to which Ken's white, heterosexual, male character has to find meaningful ways to relate, has no sense organs: It possesses only a mouth. The mouth, apart from giving the virus-buddy the ability to speak, also reveals the dotted, uneven, fluid materiality of its inside. In finding ways to relate to this form, Ken is undertaking no less than attempting to redefine the boundary between the autonomous human subject, who has a normative, "integrated and fully functioning body" (Shildrick 50), and the very fluid and monstrous body against which Western cultural traditions have pinpointed their norms.

In *Monsters,* a consequent opposition between the monstrous body and the normative body cannot be maintained. Although early on in the story, Ken is very judgmental about people with herpes, labeling them "disgusting" (6), he has to experience living with an infected and contagious body that embodies the same monstrous qualities as the body of the virus-buddy. Furthermore, Ken is further alienated from his body by the dynamic changes of its form. In Ken's experience, the "openness towards the monstrous other" (Shildrick 3) by which the binary opposition between monstrous and normal will ultimately get undermined, and the experience of finding monstrosity within, are painful. Gradually, as the mirror scene in figure 2.2 shows, Ken arrives from attributing threatening monstrosity to his surroundings to realizing that this quality is also found in him. This process of relocating monstrosity from the outside to the inside goes hand in hand with the realization that his body is vulnerable.

Before the character of the virus-buddy enters the story (quite late, on page 69), and before Ken realizes the monstrous and vulnerable potentialities of his own body (54; figure 2.2), the virus is represented as a dangerous mass dwelling near the characters, threatening with coming too close and making the body disappear. In the first part of *Monsters,* monstrosity is the characteristic of Ken and his girlfriend's surroundings: Monstrous particles fill the most banal actions with an unknown danger, looming near everyday objects, threatening to multiply endlessly. For example, the depth of the earth over which the unsuspecting but already infected girlfriend, Rory, is cycling is made up of monstrous forms (21), just like Rory's thoughts a few pages later (29). In the scene where Ken is told the news that his girlfriend has herpes, tiny bits of the virus-monster overrun and overwhelm the speechless man's body (23–24; figure 2.1). In this two-page sequence,

FIGURE 2.1. Ken finding out Rory is infected, from Ken Dahl's *Monsters*, 23. Courtesy of the artist.

the viral forms are originally the pieces of dough Ken has been working with at his workplace. At this point of the narrative, Ken's condemnatory attitude based on stereotypes about herpes is clear, as well as his perception of his own body as whole and healthy. The virus attacks him, and two times four panels are devoted to representing the swift process during which the viral forms swirl all over his body, cover it completely, and drag it down to the floor behind the table. His body disappears under the spiky forms, but it is not influenced by them: They do not transgress the boundary of his body, and neither does he transform from the inside.

The major marker of qualities of monstrosity, abjection, and vulnerability in *Monsters* is, as at many times in human history, the quality of the skin. The already described viral skin, the skin of the virus-buddy and Ken in his fully monstrous form, is rough and shiny at the same time. With its spikes and opaqueness, it is a truly uninviting, abject surface. Monstrous bodies "disrupt both internal and external order" (Shildrick 4), and indeed it is the disruption and reorganization of external and internal that Dahl is undertaking in the narrative of *Monsters.* The first step of the disruption of internal and external is making skin, the boundary between inside and outside, the primary marker of abjection. The prominence of skin-related imagery can easily be reasoned with the fact that the actual symptoms of the medical condition of herpes also affect the skin. *Monsters,* however, also uses the representations of abject skin to characterize the relationship between the character and society. Skin "negotiates and re-distributes the relation between inside and outside," argue Elsaesser and Hagener (111), and in *Monsters* skin simultaneously becomes the outward expression of the monstrosity and vulnerability inside Ken and a visual marker of Ken's body as contagious. It is the skin that marks and identifies the subject as monstrous and marks Ken as an outcast because the skin is the display of symptoms coming from within the body itself. Monstrous skin marks Ken as repulsive, while it is also a boundary that is crossed from time to time as Ken engages in guilt-ridden sexual relationships with women.

Given the emphasis on skin as a marker of vulnerability and monstrosity, it is no surprise that touch is the sense most often referred to in the narrative. Ken is often featured touching his skin and his infection outbreaks in acts of self-inspection, preventive medication, or masturbation. The opening sequence of the comics jokingly presents scenes of a life where any form of touching, such as kissing, sharing food, or sharing a toothbrush, carries a dangerous potentiality of infection. Yet the last panel of the sequence breaks the relaxed atmosphere not only by the dominance of its black background but also by suddenly representing a person with abject, infection-ridden skin (1–3). This person is in fact the same girl who has been kissed on the first page of the comics. Her return and transformation is unexpected: The sequence uses the structure of a joke with preparation and punchline (or, in this case, punchpanel) to convey a bodily experience of monstrosity and vulnerability that is anything but funny.

The importance of the sense of touch is also alluded to by the most often used way to express the monstrosity and vulnerability of Ken's body: a second layer of monstrous skin drawn over and around his human form (63–67, 78–79, 83, 91–92, 151–52). This state, which I call semi-monstrous form, visually balances between the fully monstrous form and the standard representation of Ken with a normal human body. In this form, the spiky and transparent skin covers Ken's human body like a shell or spacesuit, isolating him from the people around him and imprisoning him in his wounded state. It is in this semi-monstrous form that Ken most heavily experiences social vulnerability: He feels rejected and in turn he sees everyone through his monstrous skin. The semi-monstrous form calls attention to the interconnectedness of bodies by visualizing isolation as part of one's own body.

The semi-monstrous form freezes the in-between stage of Ken's body constantly oscillating between a stage of becoming a monster and a stage of maintaining his human character. This form visualizes the constant state of becoming, theorized by Shildrick, which in turn indicates the interconnectedness of monstrosity and vulnerability. Here, again, Dahl's comics visually supports Shildrick's arguments that "neither vulnerability nor the monstrous is fully containable within the binary structure of the western logos" and that "the strange is not a discrete event but the constant condition of becoming" (1). The semi-monstrous form is an expression of Ken's experience of fluctuating boundaries between self and Other, which, as the narrative progresses, will be completely redefined.

As the narrative continues, monstrosity gradually becomes a defining experience of Ken's body, revealing that his body "has been unstable all along" (Shildrick 4). By the middle of the book, an ambivalent relationship is established toward all forms of Ken's body: The monstrous forms and the semi-monstrous skin are alien but are also recognized as Ken's own. This duality of rejection and possession is the exact description of one's relationship to the abject according to Kristeva. Kristeva aptly portrays the conflict represented by Dahl when she introduces her *Powers of Horror* (1982) with the following description of abjection:

> There looms, within abjection, one of those violent, dark revolts of being, directed against a threat that seems to emanate from an exorbitant outside or inside, ejected beyond the scope of the possible, the tolerable, the thinkable. It lies there, quite close, but it cannot be assimilated. . . . But simultaneously, just the same, that impetus, that spasm, that leap is drawn toward an elsewhere as tempting as it is

FIGURE 2.2. Ken turning into a monster while looking in the mirror in Ken Dahl's *Monsters,* 54. Courtesy of the artist.

> condemned. Unflaggingly, like an inescapable boomerang, a vortex of summons and repulsions places the one haunted by it literally beside itself. (1)[4]

Ken sees his skin and his body as abject, and the book is in fact about the gradual unlearning of contrasting and measuring his body against that of others.

The mirror scene where Ken establishes a relationship between the virus and his body, thereby acknowledging for the first time its monstrous and vulnerable qualities (figure 2.2), is a regular four-panel sequence that is structured similarly to the one showing Ken's

4. Abjection is connected here to the representation of characters. In chapter 4, I will revisit the topic by asking different questions: I will examine how readers of comics can relate to abject images.

first encounter with the virus (figure 2.1). In both scenes, Ken's body is represented frontally, standing behind a flat surface (a sink and a table). But while in the scene at the workplace the body is overwhelmed by virus, in the scene at the bathroom it is transformed into an abject body completely made of tiny viral forms.

The mirror scene shows the moment of Ken's self-identification as a monster, and it is a significant step in recognizing and representing the vulnerability of his body (figure 2.2). In the first panel, three tiny virus bubbles are lurking behind Ken, who is inspecting a sore in his mouth. Just like in figure 2.1, the particles are separate entities; there is no physical connection between them and Ken's body. In the next panel, the viral forms jump on Ken while he is standing impassively, having lowered his hand from his lip. Ken is giving out inarticulate sounds, while a form seems to be coming out of his mouth, indicating that the forms were not only outside but have also been inside his body. However, as the direction of movement is actually not indicated, an equally valid reading of this panel is that the virus is in the process of entering Ken's body, acting out what, in Shildrick's view, counts as the greatest threat associated with the monstrous: "The issue is not so much that monsters threaten to overrun the boundaries of the proper, as that they promise to dissolve them" (11). The forms completely cover Ken's body in the third panel, and the monstrous form coming out of, or entering, Ken's mouth is bigger: The cold sore that is in fact the herpes itself has a life on its own. The process is complete by the last panel, where the virus transforms Ken's body into a single huge, humanoid, spiky, jelly-like form of a monster, with his arms and hands transformed into useless barbed chunks (54) and his eye sockets dark and empty.

As Ken has been transformed into the virus in the mirror scene (54), the next page can be considered as the first time he verbally identifies himself as a monster (55). Dahl utilizes the topos of the mirror as a means by which insight can be gained, and he uses the frame of an actual mirror in which Ken is inspecting himself as a frame for the panel. The mirror frame and the panel frame are identical, which emphasizes the intimacy of this scene of bodily transformation into a monster and gaining self-knowledge (figure 2.2).

The scene of recognizing oneself as a monster is a spectacular example of the process of comics autobiography's plastic rendering of hidden inward processes, during which "the inward vision takes on an outward form" (Hatfield 114). Turning oneself into a character involves reflections on the physicality of one's body and also means that the appearance of the character visualizes the personality and emotions of the actual person (El Refaie 60). The body that is scrutinized becomes othered and appears strange and dysfunctional. Elizabeth El Refaie uses the term (borrowed from Drew Leder) "dys-appearance" to describe this process when everyday associations of the body cease to work (62). The scene of self-study in the mirror represents one moment of the endlessly repeated basic structure of creating autobiography in the comics medium: namely, finding adequate visual forms by which a change in one's mental or emotional state—that is, moments of dys-appearance—can be made manifest. The starting point of the realization is looking at oneself in the mirror, a situation to which Dahl returns later as well (73, 126), and that is further emphasized by showing Ken's mirror image in the moment of self-inspecting on the cover of the comic.

Self-study in the mirror brings dangerous insight and, in two cases out of the three (54, 73), results in Ken's complete bodily transformation into a monster. In these scenes, the instability of the body image is connected to the necessary moments of scrutiny and self-reflection needed to create autobiographical avatars. As mentioned already, establishing distance to visually formulate and express personal knowledge of oneself is the basis of drawing an autobiographical avatar. As an obvious outcome of the ongoing scrutiny and drawing, the avatar is not to be understood as a transparent, unbiased expression of the whole truth about the self and its relation to the world. Quite on the contrary, it is the visual expression of the limitations and the personal nature, as well as the situated quality, of such knowledge about oneself. Ken's shape-shifting is also expressive of the dynamic nature of this knowledge: Drawing an avatar is, following Mark Johnson's description of artistic practice, "a form of experiential inquiry and knowing" (101).

Transforming the Body by Drawing

In the mirror scene Ken identified himself, and Dahl framed his avatar (doubly by the mirror and by the panel), as a monster (figure 2.2), and the following page shows imaginary scenarios of interaction between the monster-self and the world (55). First, Ken, in the form of the monster, is shown embracing a woman while talking inarticulately. Then he starts to devour her: Her face is absorbed by Ken the monster, his grip around her is tightened. The final image shows two monsters standing next to each other without any bodily contact: The woman has been transformed, and this time it is she who is uttering the same sequence of inarticulate sounds that was leaving the freshly transformed Ken's mouth at the beginning of the scene. By now, Ken identifies with the virus, and sees himself defined only in terms of its contagiousness. The captions state: "Let's face it: / nobody wants to fuck a monster . . . / . . . and become monsters themselves" (55). The pictures illustrate exactly what nobody wants: The woman has become a monster. Monstrosity is shown here as a threat that transforms the whole body, not only the skin, and the source of this transgressive danger is Ken's body.

After the first, threatening transformation, Ken's body can turn into a virus-monster or other kinds of monsters quite of a sudden any time, indicating that the body of the cartoon self has become unstable. This, thanks to Dahl's visual inventiveness, is shown to be funny and tragic at the same time. For example, expanding on the topic of isolation, a woman (not the same as the one who has been transformed into a monster) is shown running away in terror from the virus-monster that Ken has become on page 55, only to find refuge on the next page in the persons of two armed macho heroes. It is important to emphasize that the reader needs to turn the page between flight and rescue. During the short hiatus while the page is turned, the monstrosity of Ken's body has been wittily recontextualized and it has been given a new form (56). It is now represented as a new kind of monster and an outcast from society, a vampire (56–58). Recontextualization and the redrawing of the monstrous form happens invisibly, between two pages. On the first page, the reader is made to believe that the woman is terrified by Ken's fully monstrous form, as this is the body that the character was represented in. The second page reveals retrospectively that she has been escaping from the form of the vampire, a newly introduced monstrous body. Playing with what is shown and what is implied calls the reader's attention to the challenge that self-representation poses for the artist. This challenge, which is also a source of inspiration, is usually hidden by the relatively constant way in which characters are represented, although the self-study and self-objectification that lead Dahl to change the form of his character do not ever end in either case.

When drawing their memoirs, autographers face the challenge of re-representing themselves in a consistent way from panel to panel. However, in *Monsters* the morphing of the cartoon self does not seem to stop. During the process of pictorial embodiment, Ken's body becomes an easily transformable shape-shifter that is equally abject and vulnerable in each of its forms, and it is also vulnerable *because of* its many forms. The graphiateur really enjoys the multiplicity of bodies attributed to his avatar. Apart from the viral forms (the completely monstrous form and the semi-monstrous form), Ken's character is drawn as a vampire (56–58), a dog drawn in a cartoony style (69–72), or it becomes a person without a face for several scenes after his face has been smashed by the giant index finger of the virus, imitating God's index finger (97–106). Furthermore, Ken's body transforms into a dragon-like monster of fury without recognizable traces of human body parts (104), while earlier, the guilt felt over not being able to talk honestly about his medical condition to his new girlfriend was shown as a hole in Ken's stomach (87–93). The latest example shows the graphiateur's tendency to connect each form to a specific emotion. Similarly, becoming a dog expresses lust for women and being driven by instinct.

For drawers, creating multiple forms for their avatar's body allows for exercising some degree of control over the represented events. It enables autographers to literally become observers of their cartoon selves. In this way, comics enables autographers to revisit and redraw the sites of memories, which, especially in the case of trauma narratives, helps in restoring a sense of agency. "Paradoxically, playing with one's image can be a way of asserting the irreducibility of the self as agent," claims Hatfield (115), connecting redrawings of the cartoon body with artistic control. The metamorphoses of Ken's cartoon body under Dahl's hands can be interpreted, following Hatfield, as the autographer's repeated acts of asserting agency and taking control of the cartoon form of his body. Simultaneously, the various body forms testify to the transformative and performative abilities of Dahl's line: The line enables and performs the morphing of the cartoon body.

We can regard the whole narrative of *Monsters* to be driven by the performative potential of the line: The story is not pushed forward exclusively by its plot, but also by the line's visual performance. My argument, which I would like to elaborate in the rest of the section, supports Jan Baetens and Hugo Frey's observation that it is the logic of representation rather than a temporally evolving plot that comics build on. Baetens and Frey claim that the graphic novel is "no longer based on plot and action but on the narrative potential of drawing itself" (182), which is demonstrated by the continuous transformations of Ken's body. *Monsters* clearly builds on the narrative potential of the line by foregrounding the fluidity of the drawn line and its performative potential. The morphing of Ken's drawn body, naturally, has its functions in the narrative: It stems from the already mentioned experience of bodily dys-appearance by the autographical look, and it initiates coming to terms with the body's essential vulnerability.

As an example for the performative power of the line, let me cite the sequence where a giant index finger—covered with monstrous skin—crushes Ken's face (97–106), and Ken walks around faceless from that moment on. In these scenes, Ken can no longer evade the consequences of his irresponsible sexual relationship with his unsuspecting new girlfriend, Megan. When the gigantic index finger strikes and crushes Ken's face in a one-page panel, the picture with the sound effect "putsch" (97) expresses the sudden shock and guilt-ridden annihilation that Ken feels. On the next page, however, the scene is transformed into a gag: Ken does not seem to realize that he does not have a face anymore and pours alcohol over his face where his mouth used to be (98). The captions on the next page ("the next day" and "soon"; 99) indicate Ken's complete disregard of his changed bodily conditions over an extended period of time. The panels show Ken doing his morning routine with a black hole over the area where his eyes and nose used to be, with a protruding jaw and some remaining teeth. Dahl then maintains this form of his avatar for the next, longer scene of confrontation with friends, where Ken's losing face becomes a fact in the narrative itself, not only a visual joke—so much so that on page 103, the transformation of the self-defensive Ken continues and proceeds from his face to disfiguring his hands, fingers, and body (figure 2.3). Finally, on page 104, he turns into a gigantic, furious dragon.

Having lost his anthropomorphic attributes, the dragon-Ken in the last panel of figure 2.3 is floating among herpes particles, and his speech is rendered with a jokingly menacing font. But the morphing still does not stop here; the huge dragon turns into a tiny and limbless worm, whose insignificance is enhanced by its past of being a huge dragon. It is sitting in the grass, gaping: "Please let me pretend I'm normal and clean just a little longer . . ." (104). The irony and the joke are on Ken, who still does not get his human form back, and

FIGURE 2.3. The faceless Ken is transforming into a dragon in Ken Dahl's *Monsters*, 103. Courtesy of the artist.

after being briefly given a worm's body, he is represented in his faceless form again (105–6). While the graphiateur frames these metamorphoses as funny, the transformation itself stems from the experience of living in an utterly vulnerable and monstrous body that is partially effaced by (the finger of) the virus and changes uncontrollably under the pencil of the graphiateur. This sequence demonstrates qualities that permeate the whole comics—namely, that the associative and creative drive of drawing pushes the narrative forward in unpredictable directions, and that, simultaneously, the transformative potential of representation is inherently connected to Ken's experiencing multiple vulnerabilities.

On the level of the visual representation of the avatar, the transformations of the body suggest innovation, joke, playfulness, and the fluidity of the cartoon self. In contrast, the textual component of

Monsters is not so easygoing about acknowledging the monstrous and vulnerable qualities of the autobiographical avatar. It seems that on a textual level, Ken is revolting against his condition and goes through phases of denial, as well as feelings of helplessness and optimism.[5] In contrast, on the level of representation, where the character's embodied form manifests, the dynamism of these feelings motivates morphing, and a greater degree of ease is present about the monstrous and vulnerable qualities within. The textual components—what Ken is saying as a character, and the texts of the narrator that accompany the action—verbalize the difficulty of coming to terms with the apparent and uncontrollable morphing of one's body, and the isolation that accompanies monstrosity. They also address the impossible condition of living with an incurable and contagious disease, which makes the monstrosity of the body visible, and which is transferred by sexual intimacy. It seems that whereas the visual layer agrees with Shildrick in valorizing the transgressive qualities of the monstrous, and in acknowledging the vulnerability of both the self and the Other (3), the first-person commentary (of Ken the character or the narrator) channels discomfort and suffering felt precisely because of this very transgressive nature of the monstrous body.

Shildrick in her study of monstrosity and vulnerability shows that monsters are disturbing because of the very difficulties the textual parts in Dahl's comic express: Monsters are "neither good nor evil, inside nor outside, not self or other. On the contrary, they are always liminal, refusing to stay in place, transgressive and transformative. They disrupt internal and external order and overturn the distinctions that set out the limits of the human subject" (4). As has been shown, liminality and transgression are simultaneously a source of humor and self-invention, which are expressed visually, and are a burden. The burden is expressed by the verbal layer, for example in the following narratorial commentary: "Still it seemed like the harder I tried to get rid of my disease, / the further it embedded itself into my life. / I carried it everywhere I went" (Dahl 131). In the interactions of textual and visual elements, Dahl captures the true complexity of the experience of vulnerability, and due to the visual nature of comics, the dialogue of text and image literally shows that finding the vulnerable and the monstrous within, as advocated by Shildrick, are

5. Ken's journey toward redefining himself resembles the five (nonlinear) stages of grief: denial, anger, bargaining, depression, and acceptance (Kübler-Ross and Kessler).

long processes requiring introspection. In this respect, the introspection needed for the heterosexual white male to explore his vulnerability is mirrored by the introspection required by autographers.

Visual Discourses on the Vulnerable Body

The first part of *Monsters* finishes with a longer section, entitled "Herpes. A Brief and Confusing Introduction" (110–19), explaining the medical background of the herpes simplex virus. Dahl engages verbal medical discourse and medical illustration to address the discrepancy between verbal and visual expressions of vulnerability and monstrosity. Instead of creating an illustrated medical text or visualized data, Dahl's innovative vision mocks the visually clear style of infographics, which builds on visualizing relationships, processes, and hierarchies in an accessible and memorable way.

Dahl's comic is not the only graphic narrative that reflects on medical image making and medical representations of the body. Brian Fies's influential illness narrative, *Mom's Cancer* (2006), evokes infographics to explain stages of the illness. David Small's memoir, *Stitches* (2009), contrasts X-ray images of the inside of the hero's mouth, where the threat of cancer is located, with imaginative representations in order to call attention to the contrast between the experience of the body and medical images made about it. Una's autobiography and manifesto about women's rights, *Becoming Unbecoming* (2015), uses infographics to represent data on sexual violence as a way to provide context and convey complicated relationships. For Una, as well as for Ken Dahl, infographics is a way of storytelling—and this is precisely how designers of visualized data define the aim of their projects (Borkin; Groeger; Nussbaumer Knaflic; Smiciklas 22).

Interestingly, and in contrast to other illness memoirs, Dahl does not rely on or refer to what historian of science Peter Galison calls the "expertly produced image" (Galison and Paglen 36). The expertly produced image is produced by a machine, for example an MRI scanner, a PET-CT scanner, or an X-ray, and its interpretation requires a trained person. These image-making technologies, used in various branches of science, increasingly depart from the scale of the body, and they also often produce images of the body bordering on abstraction and intelligibility for an untrained spectator (Elkins, *Object* 60). Such images represent the body from what Galison calls "*nonhuman* points of view" (Galison and Paglen 38), and their discussion is necessary at this point because Dahl makes fun of both such technologies and the language accompanying them by maintaining the subjectivity of his work when reproducing expertly produced images.

The creative flow that transforms Ken's body into various forms pervades even the pages devoted to conveying encyclopedic knowledge about herpes, and this greatly contributes to the confusion promised in the title. On the first page of "Herpes. A Brief and Confusing Introduction," Ken plunges into the blackness of the unknown, and then guides the reader to a greater factual understanding of herpes while navigating among floating chunks of text and enlarged close-up images of infected genitals. The arrangement of word and image, as will be discussed shortly, is deliberately disturbing, while factual information on the types of herpes simplex virus (HSV) and its cycle is merged with Ken's opinion and comments.

"Herpes. A Brief and Confusing Introduction" is visually distinguished from the rest of the book in several ways. Dahl diverges from the usual lettering of *Monsters* and uses his handwritten imitation of a font for playfully appropriating the style of printed documents or medical information booklets (figure 2.4). Moreover, the body drawn to visually demonstrate the explanatory text in each page is recognizably Ken's own cartoon body. Arrows point from the textual chunks toward the illustration of Ken's facial nerves (112) and Ken's own infected body (114). Arrows, as a means to organize knowledge, are possibly the most frequently used elements from the tool kit of infographics on these pages. They come in all shapes, sizes, and trajectories: All of them are unique. In this section, *Monsters* breaks with the way illness and the ill body are usually conceptualized, discussed, and represented in contemporary Western culture in terms of military metaphors of attack and defeat (Sontag, *AIDS* 11) by letting the autobiographical avatar's own cartoon body undergo the medical gaze, and by simultaneously showing the impossibilities of an impersonal scientific discourse.

Another feature that makes this section stand out is Dahl's altered perception of the page. Dahl builds on black surfaces, which depart from the generally used layout of the work. He abandons the structure of the grid, and as a result, textual and figurative bits coexist and freely fill the surface of the page. The text, represented in chunks of clouds, floats among penises and mouths with outbreaks (113) or is inserted between naked bodies of a man and a woman (116).

The most serious undermining of medical discourse happens especially by Dahl's placement of text in between drawings of genitals. As visual objects, genitals are impossible to see, argues James Elkins, based on Georges Bataille. Elkins finds that pictures of genitalia interfere with one's attention; they cannot be impartially observed. One becomes conscious of oneself looking, and one is either drawn to look away, or, on the contrary, one is drawn to stare (*Object* 105). Therefore, it is impossible to see genitals the same way as one sees another body part, or an inanimate object. In *Monsters,* Dahl provokes and challenges the reader with creating a situation where long textual bits are placed among drawn genitalia, and the reader is expected to maintain a context of information transfer while reading these sentences.

The images of genitals do not only influence eye movements; they also influence thoughts. "The sight of genitals often impels us to *act,* not just to see," claims Elkins (*Object* 106), arguing that such images make the onlooker "aware that it [genitalia] belongs in a sequence of sights and feelings that lead toward or away from sex, and I sense . . . that it means something has to be done" (107). The instantaneous reaction of either attraction or escape makes the scientific appreciation of Dahl's pages almost impossible. However, at this point, the reader is shown stylized images in the well-defined context of knowledge transfer. As will be shown shortly, Dahl's realistic renderings of genitals raise a number of further questions.

The page that uses visual means of organizing information in the most traditional way is page 115 (figure 2.4), which shows Ken's naked body infected with HSV at all the places a body can possibly be infected with the virus. Explanatory text is linked to the appropriate part of the body with unusually long, snakelike arrows. By this solution, the body, which suffers under the experience of infection, is distanced from the text of explanation. In each instance, a textual unit contains the Latin name of the specific virus that can infect that body part and a brief, opinion-ridden description of the illness, for example: "Herpes meningitis In the membranes of your brain & spinal cord. Rare, and not usually as bad as it sounds" (115). The page is distanced from the clarity and factuality of infographics in several ways, and the use of what at first seem to be tiny decorative elements emphasizes the painful personal experience of living with a deformed and monstrous body. The most conspicuous element subverting medical discourse, due to its size and also because arrows

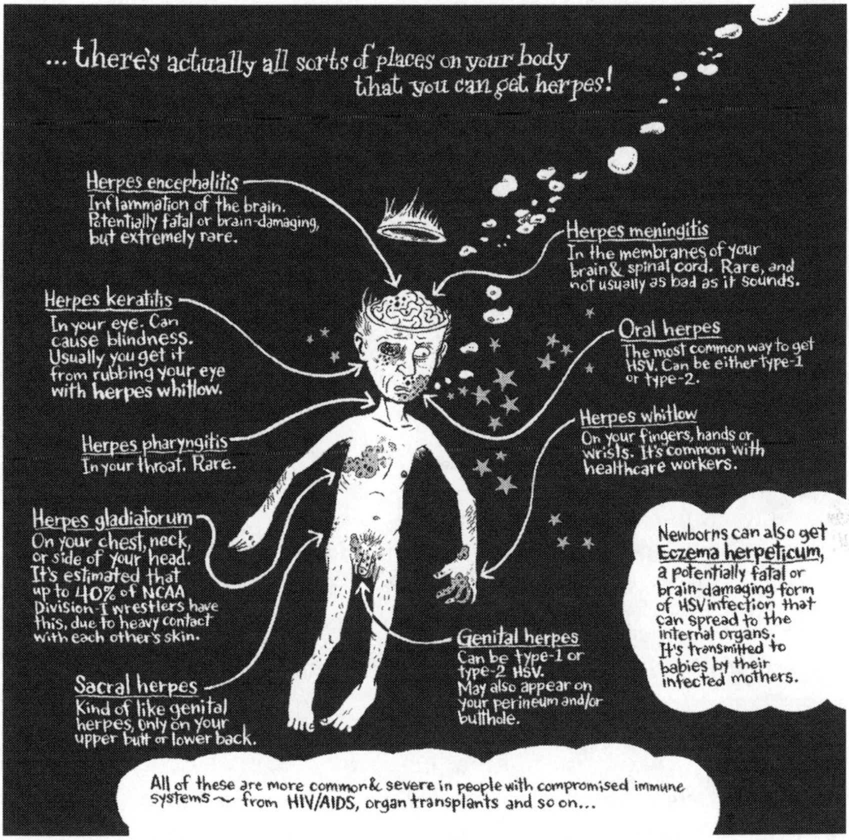

FIGURE 2.4. Infographics in Ken Dahl's *Monsters,* 115. Courtesy of the artist.

direct attention to it, is the posture of the figure in the middle of the page. With his arms at strange angles and legs visibly not supporting the weight of his body, he looks like he is floating in an abstract black space. The figure's face also expresses the experience of inhabiting this body: His scalp has even been removed to reveal his HSV-infected brain, while the text explains how easy it is to get the virus.

The blackness in which the figure is floating might be outer space, as suggested by the stars, but the figure might also float underwater, which is implied by the bubbles streaming from the head to the top right corner. But blackness is expressive of Ken's illness, too, as shown in the opening page of the sequence (110), where Ken, having tiptoed around a crater symbolizing his illness (107–9), dived into the sea of the virus. If we think of the black background as an expression of the illness that transforms the body and creates a monster out of it, the stars get reinterpreted as indicators of bodily pain and the bubbles as virus particles. Indeed, the next page (116) features a swirl of these infectious particles that replace the bubbles in their dynamic vectoring between genitals and text.

References to medical discourse are inserted into a surreal and dreamlike setting, which in turn expresses the lived experience of the body. Representation and commentary both undermine the objectivity associated with scientific discourse: This most medically engaged part of the book refuses the look and illusion of transparency and objectivity that is associated with hard science. Dahl's imaginative style pervades medical illustration, directing attention to the main theme of the comics, the experience of the body as vulnerable and monstrous. Parallel to this, the verbal commentary disrupts the idea that the vulnerability of Ken's body is unique, and extends this vulnerability, and the accompanying monstrosity, to the majority of the population. This way, again, Dahl questions the notions of the normatively able body and shows the vulnerable and monstrous condition of the body as a common one.

In *Monsters,* the acknowledgment of the monstrous and vulnerable aspects of one's condition and body runs parallel to a gradual redefinition of the category of the normal. Later in the story, Dahl makes Ken (141–42) and another character (187) talk about what has been listed as statistical data in "Herpes. A Brief and Confusing Introduction," namely that the majority of the population already carries a form of the herpes virus in their blood. Here, the verbal layer explicitly states what has been happening visually with Ken's body through its shape-shifting: the deconstruction of the notion of the normal body, and the advocation of a perception of the body as complicated, experienced, and distanced at the same time, and, above all, vulnerable. The normative, healthy body gets redefined as a vulnerable one, or, if we look at the other side of the same coin, vulnerability and monstrosity, in their various forms, are redefined as common characteristics of everyone.

Having approached how Dahl's appropriation of infographics and medical discourse engages the ideas of normalcy and vulnerability, in the last part of this chapter I would like to turn to another well-definable segment of *Monsters* where reflection on the vulnerable and monstrous human body happens by change of style. In a two-page sequence (51–52), Dahl redraws eight photographs showing close-ups of faces and genitalia with serious outbreaks of the

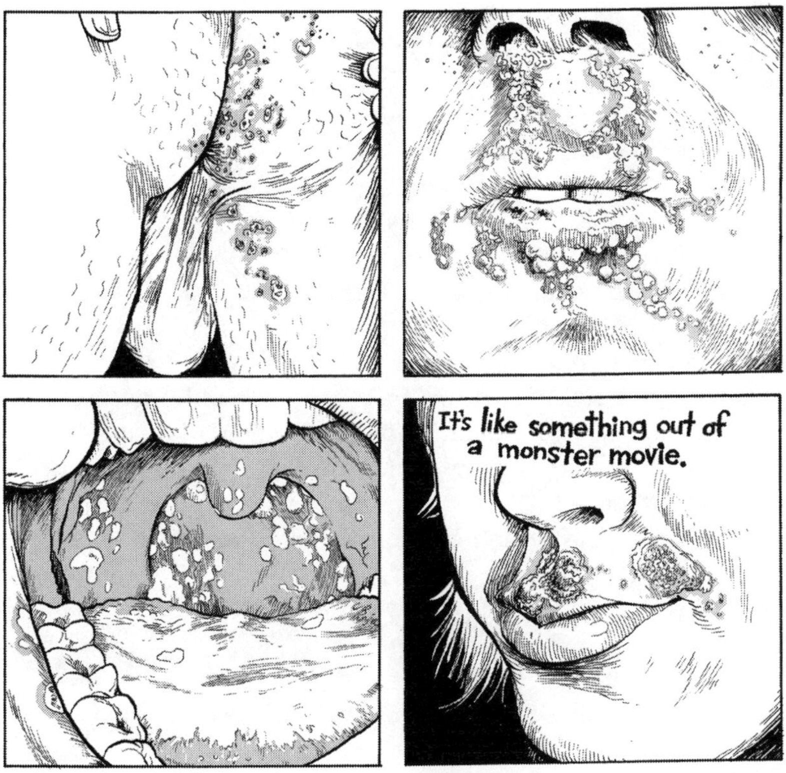

FIGURE 2.5. Photographic references in Ken Dahl's *Monsters,* 52. Courtesy of the artist.

herpes virus, all drawn in a realistic style (figure 2.5). The sudden change to stylistic realism reveals the degree to which the representation of the illness is personified and stylized in the rest of the comics. These images meet current social expectations of how realism is to be marked in a drawing in terms of detail, proportion, and depth (El Refaie 153), as well as with shading, toning, and perspective. The text on these pages constitutes a question-answer sequence: "Have you ever done an image search for 'herpes'?" (51)—"It's like something out of a monster movie" (52). The question connects the drawn images to photographic picture making, to the idea of objectivity it is associated with, and to an existing referent in reality (Galison and Paglen 39). The answer casts doubt upon the freshly evoked associations of objectivity and referentiality by referring to a movie genre—and, in a parallel contradictory move, it also connects stylistic realism with monstrosity (figure 2.5).

The change of style in the drawn photos (51–52) is especially radical if we compare them to the contemplative and intimate pages immediately preceding them (49–50). The preceding pages show Ken and his by now ex-partner Rory reflecting on their lives. Page 49 is a one-panel page showing an empty desert: Ken and Rory are standing naked and speechless under a dark sky; little stars of pain are visible next to both of them. They turn their backs to the reader and are facing what is either the moon or the sun in the form of a viral cell (49), drawn with transparent and spiky abject skin. This page takes the reader to an abstract place, a timeless contemplative situation, suggesting isolation, emptiness, and aimlessness. The next page (50), shown in figure 2.6, breaks up the vast space of the desert and the undivided surface into smaller panels, creating a bridge to the drawn photos shown on pages 51 and 52 (figure 2.5). The page transitions from the abstract to the photographically realistic: The first panel of figure 2.6 keeps the setting of the previous page and shows Ken's lonely figure walking in the desert. Ken looks up at the sky, and the panels show the stars turning into, or their place being taken by, viral cells and then by actual rashes of herpes.

The process happens in three steps: The first panel of the second tier shows stars; the second panel, which is identical in shape, size, and in the positioning of its elements to the first one, replaces the stars with tiny units of viral cells. Both panels show isolated forms against a black background, which, at least initially, under the influence of the previous panels and the previous page, is interpreted as dark desert sky. However, while supporting the interpretation of the background as sky, the second panel also invites its recontextualization: The virus particles can equally float in the sky (as seen on page 49) or in blood. The last panel reinterprets the elements for the third time: By creating a sudden break in the style and logic of representation, the viral forms are now rendered as actual sores on the human skin, drawn in a realistic fashion by shading, allusion to depth, and attention to proportions. Abstract elements of the first two panels have been redrawn as very specific, very human, and very abject surfaces and disfigurations.

The progress from abstraction to realism from the first panel to the third one in the second tier of figure 2.6 is comprehensible only in the light of the realism of the drawn photographs on the following page (51). It is after having looked at realistically drawn images of people with outbreaks of HSV that the third panel in figure 2.6

FIGURE 2.6. Degrees of abstraction in Ken Dahl's *Monsters*, 50. Courtesy of the artist.

suddenly gets actual bodily referents. The background of the third panel can now be recognized as an actual material context, human skin with some hair among the sores. James Elkins lists five criteria for an onlooker to recognize a drawn or painted surface as skin: If the surface changes color uniformly; if it has a coherent texture; if it has a relatively constant degree of tension; if it can be described by topological complexity, that is, it has folds, creases, wrinkles, and macroscopic lines; and, finally, if it is unbroken and continuous, then the surface is seen as skin (*Pictures* 55–61). In figure 2.6, however, skin cannot be recognized without the belated revealing of the context of the body, conveyed by the drawn photos. The drawn photos as referents provide not only a surface for the reader's mental projections but also a scale for them (Elkins, *Pictures* 19).

The slow, silent, and abstract sequence gives way to realistic representations of infected skin and genitals in an unannounced change.

The drawn photographs (figure 2.5) shock the onlooker, and they also evoke the disinterested medical look at the body, which does not recognize shame or privacy (Elkins, *Object* 27). In contrast to the section of infographics, which recalls the language of science ("herpes simplex virus," "mucosal linings," "DNA," "nucleus," "symptom," "infection," and Latin names are visible in figure 2.3) but evades the scientific look at the body (110–19), here the reader is addressed directly and informally in the textual part, but the visual layer establishes a distance.

Furthermore, the images do not show the *whole* body, only fragments. These fragments show the skin in its infected and abject state. The drawings of nostrils, mouths, and exposed female and male genitalia reveal with great poignancy how dubious it is to maintain a boundary between inside and outside. The two pages of drawn photographs zoom in on the very body parts where the meeting of inside and outside is dubious and uncertain. The close-ups question the very definition of skin as a boundary, and they deconstruct the opposition between inside and outside. These drawn photographs demonstrate that "from the point of view of the skin, the world is a series of invaginations and pockets, with no meaningful way to distinguish what is inside from what is outside" (Elkins, *Pictures* 44). In this way, this sequence of realistically drawn body parts doubly deconstructs not only the boundary between inside and outside but the notion of the body as wholeness: first, by the fragmentary look they provide instead of an overview, and second, by their topic of orifices or invaginations and of dubious territories where one cannot decide where one entity begins and where another ends.

While it seems that monstrosity has been defined in terms of the skin, and at the first glance the realistically drawn images seem to add information about the actual nature of the skin condition of herpes, what happens here, in fact, is the questioning of the concept of the body as a whole. The representation reveals that the very concept of the body, either as monstrous or as healthy, is unstable. Dahl is disrupting in this sequence the notion of the body as a given, and he visualizes the body's inescapable vulnerability. These two pages challenge the binary opposition between normal and monstrous bodies and establish the vulnerability of the body as a quality in common in all bodies.

The stylistic change from a lighthearted, cartoony style to the realism of the drawn photograph points to the inherent vulnerability revealed in representation itself. Ken's cartoon body is transformed into newer and newer shapes due to the performance of the line: It is constantly becoming a new and different form. Naturally, the morphing of Ken's body is also connected to his illness, and consequently illness is a prominent topic of the narrative. I believe, however, that the body of autobiographical characters is never stable. Looking at oneself as another is required by all autobiographical genres, but this self-alienating way of looking is also visualized in comics: The avatar is born out of this objectification of the self and of the actual body. The avatar visualizes the complexities of one's identity—here, for example, an extra layer is added by personifying the virus and making it a separate character—and an undertone of Dahl's comics is the narrative about finding oneself monstrous during the objectifying autobiographical look at oneself. The playfulness in Dahl's style does not hide the vulnerability that arises from facing and representing one's monstrosity. On the contrary, playfulness directs the reader's attention to the incredible performative power of drawing.

THREE

STYLE AS ENGAGEMENT

Joe Sacco's *Safe Area Goražde* and *The Fixer*

HAVING EXAMINED how Lynda Barry connects the birth of the autonomous line to bodily movement, a state of mind, a structure of experience, and the ability to face one's uncertainties and vulnerabilities in order to be a partner to the line, and having looked at the ways the creation of the character based on oneself is related to encountering oneself as vulnerable, in this section I turn to nonfiction comics that narrate and document the painful experience of other people. Comics journalism has most often been approached in terms of its authenticity (e.g., Weber and Rall), and Joe Sacco's comics have been frequently analyzed in terms of their framing strategies and journalistic ethic (Lunsford and Rosenblatt; Scherr "Shaking"; Woo). Building on but also departing from these readings, in this chapter I explore the capability of drawing style and technique to express engagement and compassion with the pain and vulnerability of others. In my discussion of Joe Sacco's reportage on the Bosnian war, I argue that Sacco has a compulsive relationship to drawing, which supersedes his often-mentioned meticulous attention to detail. I show that compulsion is present in Sacco's crosshatching, and this laborious technique serves as a means of ethical engagement with the vulnerabilities of the subjects of his stories. Broadly speaking, my aim is to connect drawing style with ethical engagement, and I would like to show that apart from figurative representation, framing, and storytelling techniques, the choice of style also influences the ethical stakes of a given graphic narrative.

Sacco's comics are sometimes difficult to look at and to read: Not only are they text heavy, they also show unsettling scenes about the realities of war, poverty, life, and death. Sacco's images of violence engage with the ethical questions concerning visualizing and watching violent action happening to other people, and they contribute to the discourse about showing and looking at images of violence. Ultimately, Hillary Chute rightly notes that Sacco presents "the complex and ethical plentitude of the visual" (*Disaster* 201), questions inherited notions of what is perceived as realistic representation, and considers what can be achieved by drawing. Sacco's reportage has often been studied in ethical frameworks, and in this respect, my approach has inspiring forerunners. On the one hand, Sacco's topics engage with human rights discourse, and on the other hand, he also comments on journalistic ethic and practice. Sacco has often talked about his journalistic ethic, and scholars and critics have written on the subjective framing of Sacco's reportage and on his constant foregrounding of his own role as a journalist in filtering, interpreting, and framing events (Chute, *Disaster*; Sacco and Mitchell 61; Scherr, "Framing"; Singer; Woo).[1] Sacco represents himself as an audience to testimonies or shows himself as a journalist with a notebook in hand, which contributes to the authenticity and the subjective nature of his work.

A further aspect of the engagement of comics journalism with ethical questions is the practice of bringing characters back to the original sites of trauma and providing an opportunity to trace and redraw the original traumatic event and the traumatized self (Chute, "Texture" 93). The retracing work of comics has been explored in comics autobiography, where the reader is invited to find connections between the narrator, the graphiateur, the autobiographical avatar, and the name on the cover of the comics. A similarly well-studied aspect of Sacco's journalism, related to both retracing and emphasizing his role as a journalist, is his practice of showing the usually hid-

1. For a more detailed discussion of Sacco's journalistic ethos and practice, see the section "Materials: Nonfiction Comics" in the introduction.

den work of those who help him as a journalist, a collective of secret players behind the faces of the news industry and its ethos of objectivity: fixers, friends, interpreters, other journalists, and editors (e.g., Chute, *Disaster*; Dong; Macdonald; Rosenblatt and Lunsford; Scherr, "Framing"; Woo). As Benjamin Woo writes in one of the first discussions of Sacco's reportage: "Sacco never promises or hides behind a false sense of immediacy, allowing the play of subjectivity to reach the audience on an experiential and affective level" (175).

Sacco's comics contribute to human rights discourse by engaging with topics such as displacement, the status of minorities, torture, or war, and his narratives have played important parts in revealing the complexities of armed conflicts for a Western readership. His comics journalism offers points of engagement in the current age of collaborative witnessing and disaster tourism (Orbán, "Mediating" 122), and it has been described as "an ethical attempt to represent intimately those ignored in the world arena" (Chute, *Disaster* 201). The most often repeated promise and premise of comics journalism is that it can reach a different audience than traditional forms of reportage and can engage disinterested readers. This promise is also emphasized by Patrick Chappatte, a Lebanese-Swiss comics journalist working for (among others) the *New York Times,* when he says in his TED Talk entitled "Revealing the Humanity behind the News" that "you might not pay attention to an article about South Ossetia, but an illustrated story, maybe. It can take you to places where you wouldn't go." Here Chappatte is referring to his own piece of comics reportage on the war in South Ossetia in 2008, which is projected in the background during this part of his talk. Chappatte also explains that in his opinion, the drawn nature of reportage can help readers connect to stories of distant people. I share this latter statement; moreover, I also claim that the drawn nature of comics is essential to establishing a dialogue around the experience of vulnerability between drawer and reader, but so far I have not found any studies examining the premise that people would turn to a piece of reportage on a topic they knew little about because it was drawn. The hope that comics journalism—and particularly Sacco's work—can entice involvement in readers is often expressed in comics scholarship (Dunn; Stafford; Scherr, "Joe Sacco's Comics"; Vågnes): It can be used to raise awareness of and shift opinions on a problem, and it can (or can be used to) mobilize for a cause. However, the assumptions that comics journalism has a greater appeal to readers than written journalism, or that readers of comics would turn to the medium (in noneducational settings) to get information are yet to be proven.

In this chapter, I explore a new direction in the ethical readings of Sacco's works by mapping out Sacco's compulsion in drawing, which results in creating heavily crosshatched haptic surfaces and backgrounds. These surfaces offer an opportunity for both artist and reader to dwell with the victims and witnesses of atrocities. I show that crosshatched backgrounds in Sacco's comics create a different temporality for both the artist and the reader: the temporality of dwelling. Dwelling is a dynamic, attentive, spontaneous, and unfinished activity that was connected to the concept of vulnerability by Rosalyn Diprose in "Corporeal Interdependence: From Vulnerability to Dwelling in Ethical Community" (192). She calls dwelling "an ontology of interdependence" (191), as dwelling is a relationship among people and their surroundings based on recognizing the shared nature of vulnerability. This recognized mutual vulnerability is loaded with potentialities for activities: For Diprose, dwelling is an ethical encounter that enables caring, dynamic, and creative interaction between the parties involved. I connect Sacco's heavily crosshatched haptic surfaces and backgrounds to the ethical quality of dwelling, as the slow and laborious technique of crosshatching enables the drawer to dwell with those whose stories are being drawn and to dwell in community with the nonhuman environment that is also key in Sacco's reportage.

The technique of crosshatching, which is primarily present in Sacco's backgrounds (figures 3.1, 3.2, and 3.3), emphasizes the drawer's embodied presence in his art. I would like to show that it also emphasizes the drawer's embodied dwelling with the subjects of drawing. This kind of drawing not only enables the drawer and reader to enter what Diprose calls the "creative dynamism of dwelling" (191), in which the vulnerability of the Other as well as the fundamental connections to a vulnerable built and natural environment are acknowledged, but also enables being transformed both during and after the activity of drawing or viewing (191). I approach the intensive embodied engagement with the materials used for drawing and, more importantly, with the Other being drawn, with the help of art historian Norman Bryson's theory on temporal relations with art, as well as with film critic Laura U. Marks's now-classic investigation of haptic visuality. My aim, as hinted already, is to show that drawing technique, and not only the choice of topic (humanitarian issues) or the nature of narratives (revealing how news reporting operates), can be used as a means to engage with ethical issues and with the vulnerability of others.

In the analysis, I focus on two comics by Sacco that are related in terms of their stylistic features and storytelling technique, *Safe Area Goražde* (2000) and *The Fixer: A Story from Sarajevo* (2003). These are also related thematically, as both are about the Bosnian War (1992–1995), both build on the testimony of the locals, and both provide insight into journalistic work. The narratives use multiple temporal layers and multiple narrators: In both books, a temporal layer is devoted to the representation of personal memories of witnesses of the Bosnian War, while there is a second narrative thread taking place in the present, in the time of Sacco's visit in 1995. *The Fixer,* which also uses a third temporal layer taking place in 2001, focuses on one person's roles in the conflict. This person is Neven, an army veteran of Serbian origin, who was fighting with the Bosnians against the Serbian Chetniks in the war. In 1995, Neven was earning his living by being a fixer to foreign journalists—that is, being a source of information and contacts, and a supplier of practically anything the journalists might need. In contrast to *The Fixer*'s emphasis on one person's life and experience, *Safe Area Goražde* features the testimonies of various people, such as Sacco's friends, witnesses, and experts. The portrayal of the witnesses and the representation of the content of their testimonies shows Sacco's engagement not only with the war but also with questions on the possible ways of representing trauma, pain, and death.

The present analysis relies on an understanding of vulnerability not as a negative quality or a lack but as a universal condition. Following Judith Butler, I consider vulnerability as shared by everyone, because we all live in bodies that feel pain, that can die, and that take part in social interactions (29). In Butler's words, vulnerability "emerges with life itself" (31), and it is always acted out in what Butler calls ethical encounters with the Other (43). As discussed in the introduction, I believe that one's vulnerability is experienced in dialogical situations and in interaction with someone else. Yet, sadly, the vulnerability of the Other is often disregarded or disputed: In discourses of aggression and war, not all lives are considered precarious to the same degree. Sacco's comics show vulnerability-denying political and cultural mechanisms at work, and his representations of pain and death show the extreme consequences of what happens when an ethnic group gets designated as the radically different Other and subsequently gets repositioned as the enemy.

Safe Area Goražde and *The Fixer* draw attention to the ways in which the Bosnian Muslim community gets isolated and elaborate the ways in which the needs of Bosnian Muslims are denied even before the outbreak of the armed conflict. Parallel to the focus on the community, Sacco maps ways in which the vulnerabilities of the individuals have been negatively responded to: This ranges from representing emotional and mental pain to sometimes very naturalistic representations of bodily pain. I believe, and Sacco's comics also illustrate, that the vulnerability of a community or of the individual is an ever-present given, a condition that does not necessarily lead to abuse and war. Rather, aggression is only one of the range of responses that can be given to vulnerability (Drichel 10). Sacco's embodied engagement, brought about by the technique he chose to work with, is another kind of response to the vulnerability of others. Sacco's mode of representation can be considered as a positive response offering care and attention while dwelling with the vulnerable Other. Here I do not mean the caring attention of the empathic listener (Lunsford and Rosenblatt 138) or the committed journalist (Sacco, "Preface"), but the meticulous attention of the drawer. The drawer's attention is different in kind from that of the listener and offers different possibilities and positions for engagement.

Drawing and Knowledge of the Body

Joe Sacco's comics journalism is special because of the visual attention he devotes to his subjects. His characters and locations are researched; his comics are rich in realistic detail and also in signs that convey the physical labor of drawing. In this section, I would like to write about a widespread practice among artists, namely posing for characters in their comics, and its ethical consequence in the context of comics journalism. To be able to get the poses right, cartoonists often model for their pictures in the making and use their bodies as reference for other bodies. In this way, drawing can create an embodied link between drawer and subject.

This practice has been explored in the works of Alison Bechdel (Chute, *Graphic Women* 193), and since then it has been connected to her name in academia. However, I would like to emphasize that using one's own body as a reference for drawn bodies is an obvious and common artistic practice. The drawer's own body can be involved to varying degrees, from observing it in certain positions to posing as a character and taking photos of this pose. This practice of bodily self-referencing entails that a diversity of represented bodies, body parts, and positions contain references to the drawer's body, and that allusions to the drawer's body appear repeatedly on the pages.

The drawer's body can be the model for bodies in a wide range of situations. A complicated mental process accompanies physically experiencing how the body of a character, and, by implication, the body of the person on whom the character is modeled, was acting. One does not need to be an actual model for a body or an action to be entangled in this mental process, as drawing and physical impersonation both require cognitive and emotional investment and an understanding of, and even identification with, the characters. This identification is indiscriminate; one has to build a connection with perpetrators, victims, and bystanders alike in order to be able to draw their bodies truthfully.

Sacco frequently speaks about the challenges and the mental and emotional difficulties that drawing, retracing, and even physically posing for characters of violent scenes means (e.g., Sacco and Ware; Sacco and Mitchell). He says,

> It is much easier to hear the stories than to draw them. Drawing you actually have to really picture it or try to picture it and, as I said before, inhabit things. So you have to inhabit other peoples' pain or other peoples' aggression. You are thinking in those terms. I mean, it comes down to what does the shoulder do when someone is lifting a club. You are looking at yourself in the mirror trying to think of how that works, you know? So you are there in it. And that's much more difficult. (Sacco and Mitchell 65)

According to Sacco, it is a necessity to inhabit everything he draws and find reference to poses in his own body, because this contributes to a truthful representation of people and events: "The thing about drawing is you have to think about, 'How do people walk in mud?' You begin to think about balance and the way people are avoiding things and how that shifts the body. It makes you kind of inhabit everything you draw" (Sacco and Mitchell 60). Drawing this way is an elaborate and intimate engagement with the subjects: One embodies them in various situations by modeling gestures and reactions. The drawer has to understand clearly what is happening to the bodies of his or her characters. He or she needs to know how that body feels and also needs to know what the characters are thinking. Sacco explains: "You have to put yourself in everyone's shoes that you draw, whether it's a soldier or a civilian. You have to think about what it's like: What are they thinking?" (Chute, *Outside* 146).[2]

Naturally, the drawer's body can be a reference in both fictional comics and comics nonfiction. However, the experience is more poignant in the case of drawing violence in nonfiction settings. Sacco has a joking name for this emotional difficulty, the "Joe Sacco Trauma Syndrome" (Chute, *Outside* 146). He admits,

> I like to draw, generally, but it was not a pleasure [to draw *Footnotes in Gaza* (2009)]. I did not want to go to the drawing table. But I knew, OK, just keep going, just keep doing it. It felt like an incredible chore. After I finished the book, I think it caught up with me. When you're in the middle of it, you don't like doing it, but it's your job. You know you have to get through it, you have to show this. You made that decision to show it. But afterward I was a little repulsed by the whole thing. (Chute, *Outside* 146–47)

In representation—and it must be remembered that completing such a comics project takes years of intensive work—the vulnerability of the victims, as well as the aggression of the perpetrators, are shared by the bodily engagement of the drawer in the performance of drawing. It must be noted at this point that bodily self-referencing does not lead to the appropriation of the position, suffering, or feelings of the victims. The drawer does not replace one body with the other, only provides a reference for it. Nor does the drawer relativize individual experience and pain. Sacco explains, "I think really getting inside someone's pain, that's a matter of fiction. That's where fiction works. And I think that's where fiction can take over" (Sacco and Mitchell 65).

---

2. A conscious attempt to avoid the habitation of the other's body can be observed in comics co-created by Aline Kominsky-Crumb and Robert Crumb. In their comics, the two authors have full control over the representation of their own avatars by drawing themselves and writing their own texts in each panel. The stories resulting from this dialogical and performative drawing process are collected in *Drawn Together.*

Fiction and emotional investment by the artist, paradoxically, lead to the communication of actual vulnerabilities of other subjects.[3] However, in a sense, Sacco's whole project of representing traumatic memories and unrecorded aspects of historical events is fictitious: His comics are, by necessity, imaginary reproductions by a third party, himself, even if they have been drawn with a maximum degree of attention to the details of the testimony. The limit to inhabiting the Other's pain is further acknowledged by giving over the right to narrate to the witnesses, who are shown frontally, statically, while the represented action, which is Sacco's reconstruction, is shown from all points of view.

Crosshatching as Compulsion

The drawer's bodily engagement with the precarious Other is not only present in the practice of using one's body as reference. The activities of drawing also offer ways for establishing a mental, emotional, ethical, and embodied companionship with what is being drawn. Whereas the practice of bodily self-referencing is more often used in realistic drawing styles, which have been typically associated with Sacco, in this section and the next one I depart from realism and the representation of characters and focus on Sacco's backgrounds.

In *The Fixer,* two prologues (1–4 and 5–6) introduce Neven's account of his life during the Bosnian War. These prologues present the two basic angles of Sacco's comics that I would like to connect to vulnerability: The first prologue shows a multitude of bodies, and the second prologue introduces the reader to haptically charged backgrounds. These prologues articulate two approaches to the topic of bodily interconnectedness and vulnerability by their respective focus on bodies and background, and they demonstrate the different routes of engagement enabled by haptically charged surfaces and human bodies. However, I believe these two greatly influence each other.

In the first prologue of *The Fixer* (1–4), Sacco is shown looking for Neven first in a park, then in the busy streets of Sarajevo in 2001. A crowd of people walk about with averted gazes, refusing to meet

3. This process is somewhat similar to the processes of ironic authentication in comics autobiographies, where the admission of artifice in the narrative creates a sense of honesty and authenticity (Hatfield 125).

the look of either Sacco's lonely character or the reader: They completely disregard being looked at. As a result, the reader can scan, contemplate, and follow the movements of the bodies in these first scenes freely. There is no risk in the voyeuristic look or in the free movement of the reader's eyes: The framing in *The Fixer*'s first prologue lulls all suspicion in the reader. It communicates ease and comfort, building up to surprise and the abrupt arrest of the reader's look when Neven is suddenly staring at us directly in the first panel of the second prologue (*The Fixer* 5; figure 3.1), which takes place in 1995, at the time when Neven and Sacco first meet.

Neven challenges both the averted gaze of the Sarajevan crowd and the inspecting gaze of the unsuspecting reader. After pages where the reader's gaze was not returned by any of the represented characters, Neven now anchors the reader's gaze and attention, forcing us to face him. The first panel shows a close-up of his face, lit with harsh light: After his absence in the first prologue, when Sacco was looking for Neven in vain, suddenly he has come very close. He addresses us silently from this closeness without intimacy (figure 3.1). This almost hostile arrest makes it impossible to follow the narrator's instruction in the caption: "Put yourself in Neven's shoes" (5). The frontal position of Neven's face, which seemed so prominent and close at first, now signals an almost unbridgeable emotional distance via its impassiveness. Empathy or allo-identification—that is, identification with someone's pain and trauma by adoption (Hirsch, "Marked" 86–87)—are made impossible by this presentation of Neven as frozen in the frontal position. The two-page second prologue keeps to this frontal pose and confronts the reader and the impassive Neven. Neven's body is never revealed in this prologue: His coat and a table hide it, and only parts and details (of especially his hands and mouth) are revealed, as he is sitting in silence.

The way Neven's address of the readers is framed is significant, as it denaturalizes the relations among the bodies of the artist, the character, and the reader. Neven's look challenges the hierarchy among these three agents, making the reader feel a little uncomfortable. Yet the panel is about more than Neven's eyes; significantly, it brings the body of the artist into the game. The frame in which Neven appears starts a discussion on the possibilities of drawing as compassion, as ethical commitment. Neven's face occupies the left side of a horizontal panel (5), making the right side empty of figures. However, this empty background is just as important to look at as Neven's face is

FIGURE 3.1. Neven faces the reader in Joe Sacco's *The Fixer: A Story from Sarajevo*, 5

and as the Sarajevan bodies have been. It reveals well in advance that there is another body that will share the position of the protagonist of Sacco's work: the laboring body of the drawer who is creating these surfaces. Jared Gardner reminds us that the body of the artist is forever present in a work's lines and marks ("Storylines" 62), and the arrangement of the first panel, by relegating half of its surface to the nonfigurative lines of the artist, brings these seemingly aimless or decorative lines of background to the foreground of our attention. The panel emphasizes the importance of the hand that is drawing the story: The geometry of the tightly interwoven thin lines creates a dark texture that is not only visually appealing but also tactile. This surface is just as engaging as are Neven's eyes next to it, creating an address of another kind: The texture of the lines brings back the mobility of our gaze that has been arrested by the direct address of Neven's look. These lines, I would like to argue, also initiate a discourse on ethics and a caring engagement with the Other via an extensive amount of involvement of the artist's body, the traces of which are present in the abundance of lines.

Quite different ways of seeing are required from the reader by Neven's eyes, on the one hand, and the tactile surface of lines, on the other. While Neven addresses and holds the reader's attention and forces him or her to focus, the surface of the background is looked at in order to be skimmed or to follow the direction of the movement of the line. When looking at the right side of the panel, a different concept of visuality is utilized: haptic vision. Haptic vision is a mode of visual perception that is synesthetic in nature: It connects tactile and kinesthetic sensibilities with vision without actual acts of touch. "The eyes themselves function like organs of touch," explains Laura U. Marks in *The Skin of the Film: Intercultural Cinema, Embodiment, and the Senses* (2000; 162), but it needs to be noted that what is normally perceived or thought of as a monosensory experience is in fact a "cross-modal fusion" that comes in "a dominant experiential key," for example, vision (Massumi 195).

Compared to optical visuality, an obvious example for which is the way Neven is represented in the examined panel, we find that haptic vision does not rely on establishing a distance between the viewing subject and the object that is looked at. Instead of focusing at a certain element from a certain point of view, haptic vision "move[s] over the surface of its object" (Marks, *Skin* 162). It is a mobile look that moves along the outside rather than giving in to the illusions of perspective: Haptic vision "is more inclined to graze than to gaze" (Marks, *Skin* 162). In the analyzed panel of *The Fixer,* the haptic charge of the background, which takes up 50 percent of the panel, invites the reader to come close and no longer think of half of the panel as empty. When haptic vision is utilized, the rich surface on the right side of the panel starts telling a story; it testifies to the presence and embodied investment of the artist.

The haptic and the optical modes of representation and vision coexist in the above single panel, enriching each other's meanings: These two modes are not opposite; they exist in a flow (Marks, *Touch* xiii). In figure 3.1, the proximity of the two modes creates the full meaning of the panel. It is against the texture-like background that Neven's face, which itself is built on the sharp contrast of black and white shapes, eventually reveals its own emptiness and artificiality. The whiteness of the face, in contrast to the richness of shaded texture adjacent to it, reinforces the interpretation of this face as a mask that cannot be deciphered. While the story of *The Fixer* is about attempts to see beyond Neven's seamless white mask, the first panel of the second prologue reveals that what is at stake in representation is more than a single revelation: It is the interaction of two bodies, that of the character and that of the drawer. The cartoon body of a character that has a referent in the real world interacts with the body of the drawer, through whose lines we can find out something about the mysterious Neven.

Sacco's style frequently utilizes the surface of crosshatched lines to create backgrounds and shadows. He creates detail that seems to possess a certain quality of aliveness. Sacco's style has been characterized as "dense, virtuosic and often photorealistic" by Hillary Chute (*Disaster* 201) and as crafty and compulsive by Adam Rosenblatt and Andrea A. Lunsford (81). They see compulsion in the abundance of realistic detail in Sacco's comics: in his frequent showing of the quotidian and repetitive actions of life in the war zone[4] and in his "intense graphic attention to landscapes, architecture, and weapons" (Rosenblatt and Lunsford 81). In this way, Chute and Rosenblatt and Lunsford tie compulsion with realism, which, in my opinion, is not quite the whole picture. I also see Sacco's style as compulsive, but I think craft and compulsion are not only characteristic of realism: They are also present in the haptically charged backgrounds. In Sacco's comics, haptic style exists alongside the realistic and figurative images not only to create atmosphere but also to show a form of engagement with the often traumatic and violent subject of drawing.

---

4. The routine of everyday life during war is represented in the double spread showing Goražde in pages 14 and 15. Here realistic detail was drawn based on photo references or Sacco's notes.

When Sacco is controlling the direction of discourse about his own works in interviews or in his manifesto about journalism, just like Chute and Rosenblatt and Lunsford, he also supports interpreting his attention to realistic detail in drawing as a way to guarantee that truth gets conveyed in drawn reportage. Representing a personalized vision of truth is crucial for Sacco: "I'm trying to draw what I've seen. I'm actually not trying to editorialize or put rays of hope" (Sacco and Mitchell 64). To achieve accuracy in drawing the smallest detail, he asks his interviewees to describe, show, or mime visual details of the situations they are talking about (Jenkins, "Interview [Part Two]"), or he elaborates scenes based on photographic records. He also speaks about aiming at visual accuracy in order to convey an atmosphere. He wants the reader to feel the landscape and to feel a given environment as if the reader was there (Sacco and Mitchell 60). In "Preface: A Manifesto, Anyone?" Sacco also argues as follows: "To my mind, anything that *can* be drawn accurately *should* be drawn accurately—by which I mean a drawn thing must be easily recognizable as a real thing it is meant to represent" (x). Realistic detail is thought of here as a means of authenticity, but I would go further and claim that the realistic representation of the often painful details of life is not the only aspect of compulsion present in Sacco's comics.

The meticulously crosshatched surfaces demonstrate that compulsion defines Sacco's relationship to nothing less than drawing itself, while drawing defines his relationship to the people he is creating his journalistic work about. In this way, drawing as an activity introduces an ethical stake: Drawing itself is born out of a compulsion to engage, to spend time with the people and situations of the reportage. Drawing is a means to dwell, and the result is a style of texture-like surfaces created by the repetition of parallel thin lines. These surfaces engage both the reader and the artist differently than figurative realism. They open up toward different kinds of ethically engaged relationships between artist and subject, reader and subject, and artist and reader. These relationships build on the duration of time involved in the activities of the artist: And at this point it becomes significant that crosshatching is a laborious and time-consuming technique requiring embodied attention. Compulsion is present not only in what is shown or how many times a detail is shown, and compulsion is present not only in realism: It is also present in the very labor-intensive style Sacco chooses to work in.

Apart from giving backgrounds and shadows a very tactile quality, crosshatching also transforms almost every panel into a record of Sacco's compulsion to engage with his story and his characters for as long a time as possible. The slow and repetitive work of creating an almost woven surface out of thin lines is the very means by which Sacco's personal engagement with the violated vulnerabilities of his subjects is made manifest on a non-narrative level. On a narrative level, the traumatic stories reveal the cruel ways in which war has preyed upon people's fragility both as a community and individually. The figurative representation reveals broken bodies and broken lives, dead bodies and exhumed bodies. Parallel to this, on the level of style and technique, the laborious representation reveals Sacco's personal answer to what is represented. It is a non-narrative way to acknowledge and give an embodied answer of compassion to their impossibly difficult situations. I interpret this kind of mark making as gestures to dwell with the Bosnians.

The interdependence between people and their environment, which is the very foundation of what Diprose called dwelling, has been broken by war. This is in itself a violation of vulnerability: "We are fundamentally interdependent in such a way that 'injury' involves not being cut or opened to a world, but losing that relatedness or having that openness and exposure exploited," writes Diprose on Butler's definition of "injury" (188). Sacco's artistic engagement through bodily labor and time is expressive of a wish to restore connection with the Goražde community, the severance of which itself is a violation. However, when thinking about Sacco's compulsively drawn surfaces as an embodied expression of an ethical connection with those who have suffered, it is important not to forget that in *every* comic, *each* page bears the marks of the individual who has created it. Any drawing made in an analog way or with a digital pen is always a trace of the body that has made it (Gardner, "Storylines" 56) and is also an indexical sign of drawing (Grennan 15), be it fiction or nonfiction, compulsively drawn or not.[5] Unlike literature, where—in typical cases—the meaning of the text remains the same with the

5. This definition of drawing excludes digital imaging technologies made by software without digital pens as these "can index activities of the body without tracing them" (Grennan 15).

change of, for example, fonts,[6] comics does not efface the traces of the creator's body: The lines of drawing carry meaning that changes if redrawn by another hand. Jared Gardner summarizes the importance of the bodily mark in comics: "The act of inscription remains always visible, and the story of its making remains central to the narrative work of the graphic narrative form" ("Storylines" 57). I believe that Sacco's crosshatched marks offer instances for ethical engagement in two ways: in the artist's already discussed and seemingly unmotivated excessive bodily engagement, and in the peculiar temporality of the haptic surfaces, which interfere with the temporality of the story.

Haptic Surfaces as Indicators of Time and Presence

Haptically charged sections in graphic narratives have been studied by Katalin Orbán, who, in her reading of Jean Philippe Stassen's *Déogratias,* claims that haptic surfaces have a special temporality. Orbán shows that in haptically charged panels, nothing happens "except the passing of time" ("Embodied Reading" 7), and I believe that similarly to the surfaces in *Déogratias,* Sacco's backgrounds and crosshatched surfaces "are on the verge of transforming the image into pure texture" (Orbán, "Embodied Reading" 7). The silent passing of time is key on several levels: on the level of the drawer's embodied engagement with vulnerable bodies; on the level of the represented story, as will be shown shortly (figure 3.2); and finally, on the level of reception as well (to be discussed in chapter 5). Though they can be skipped or disregarded, haptic elements offer immersion and invite the reader to exit from the temporality of action and dwell with both the represented subjects and the artist, whose presence is clearly felt in the materiality of the comics. Haptic elements can but do not necessarily fill whole panels; they also enrich the experience of comics with their contributions to atmosphere and, importantly, offer the temporal dimension of dwelling. In this respect, haptic surfaces function similarly to what Scott Bukatman calls "pillow panels": These panels create atmosphere by showing stills from an aspect of the rep-

6. This is not to deny that layout influences the perception and interpretation of texts, and layout can be used creatively to support the narrative (see Horstkotte, Louvel).

resented story, and they do not bring the action forward (*Hellboy's World,* 168).

Returning to the panel from *The Fixer* that I positioned previously as an introduction to the interplay between figurative and haptic modes in Sacco's drawing (figure 3.1), I now would like to broaden my argument and claim that the panel reveals that the subject of Sacco's work is not exclusively the mysterious Neven—equally prominent topics are the *time* spent with drawing and the performance of the body during drawing. Time and movement, which are prerequisites for the laborious technique Sacco has chosen, are the major means of Sacco's engagement with the Other—apart from the narratives themselves, which are organized around aspects of violence. The time needed to create these comics is prominent via the haptic surfaces, and it is well documented: Sacco signs each page and provides the date of when the given page was finished, recording the chronicle of the embodied production of the pages. This small record of the rhythm of production is a constant reminder of the body and the creative engagement behind each page, in addition to being an indicator of the time needed to finish a reporting project in the medium of comics. The time reveals the extent to which each story and page have stopped being "news" by the time of its publication.[7]

Awareness of the artist's body at work, which Sacco creates by his laborious style, and the intention to explore the connection between bodily movement and conveying meaning, are investigated in a number of contemporary praxis-based doctoral research projects. These projects demonstrate that the meaning of a work of art is born out of the performance of the artist's body and a corresponding performance of the audience's body (Kirk 115), or experiment with ways of bringing back the scale and traces of the human body in digital-image-making contexts (Love). Naturally, the attitudes about whether the artist's bodily work during the creation of a given work of art should be visible, and how this visibility might be interpreted, have their own history. In *Vision and Painting: The Logic of the Gaze* (1983), art historian Norman Bryson reaches back to the tradition of Chi-

7. The dating system has, of course, practical sides during the creative process. Pages that have not been completed for a long time and thus could not be dated serve as personal reminders of the fluctuating rhythm of work or scarce resources. Or, as some pages are more emotionally or technically demanding than others, time stamping helps Sacco keep track of the work that is still to be done (as explained in an interview with Chute, *Outside* 148).

nese landscape painting, where the brush is seen as an extension of the artist's body, and where the temporality of mark making by the brush belongs to the subject of the created work (89). Bryson compares and contrasts the Chinese tradition of attentiveness to the temporality of creation to an approach that is more typical of the West: The Chinese tradition of mark making values and traces the movement of the hand, as opposed to the Western tradition of erasing the traces of the artist's labor, for example, by the materials used, such as oil paint (92). Similarly, the references to the amount of time needed to create the final work are also concealed. Consequently, the work of art is looked at as a completed, finished product: It lacks any traces about its creation and exists in "a temporality outside *duerée*" (93).

In my view, Sacco's comics are characterized by a mentality and attitude toward drawing similar to the Chinese landscape painting tradition in Bryson's example: His pages and surfaces are emphatically and compulsively worked on; the body in the process of leaving traces is a constant presence. This approach invites the reader not only to absorb the figures and surfaces on the page, but also to visualize the cartoonist's body bent over the pages for long hours. The technique Sacco has chosen adds new dimensions to the available repertoire to engage with issues and questions of violence and of the everyday, which are raised by the comics during their plots. Sacco's crosshatching means spending time or dwelling with the stories of abuse and with the people giving testimony. Sacco's style initiates a relationship with the stories and the people that expresses the interrelatedness of bodies (of the locals, of the drawer, and, as will be shown, of the reader) but does not will away the pain that the actual Bosnians had to go through.

Figure 3.2 is another example that shows how Sacco's tactile backgrounds express ethical community or dwelling with the Other. Figure 3.2 shows Sabina, a character from *Safe Area Goražde,* answering Sacco's question about her worst memory of the war. The frames gradually zoom in on her face as she formulates her answer: She is slowly raising a mug to her mouth to take a sip, and after this close-up, the last panel returns to showing her sitting on a chair, looking drained and exhausted (152). The structure of the sequence—the use of same-sized narrow vertical panels—emphasizes Sabina's closed posture and tired face. This page reveals much about Sacco's visualizing the vulnerability of his witnesses. In the panels showing testimonies, the reader is invited to have a closer look and study the faces for minute traces of trauma and post-trauma. In the slow-paced sequence of Sabina's answer, a study of the changes of facial expressions and hand gestures is encouraged.

Sabina has appeared in *Safe Area Goražde* before; she has been represented as a young woman full of life, visiting house parties, having fun, thinking about her boyfriend, displaying a wide scale of emotions ("Silly Girls Part I"). Compared to these images, the impassiveness of her body in this sequence is striking. Before this scene of traumatic recall, she was making a funny mock MTV-style report with one of her friends ("Silly Girls Part II"). In light of the dynamism of the preceding scenes, the sequence in figure 3.2 emphasizes the extent to which Sabina's body is involved in silence, and it highlights that almost invisible gestures tell a lot about one's vulnerable status. The sequence offers the reader a chance to witness the birth of the authentic narrative about a person's experience. The sequence shows Sabina alone, isolated, and aimless. The series of stills, instead of creating a Muybridge-like illusion of motion and progress out of the separated moments of time and action, call attention to the very contrary: the slowness of time and the pointlessness of her gestures. No matter how many stills represent them, these hand gestures do not proceed with a specific aim or direction.

The Sabinas in the pictures seem to be trapped inside the absurd temporality of trauma. Cathy Caruth defines traumatic memory as "a memory that erases" (*Literature* 78): The traumatic event cannot be remembered and cannot be forgotten, and indeed, as a visual indicator of this, the surroundings of Sabina are as bare as if everything had been erased around her. Elsewhere Caruth describes that the sustained presence of the traumatic event is felt precisely in emptiness and vacuum in one's mind, the metaphor of which is the empty background: "Blankness—the space of consciousness—is paradoxically what precisely preserves the event in its literarity" ("Introduction" 8). Sabina's isolation is addressed openly in the last panel, where Riki's enthusiastic and loud singing coming from the side, represented with big, capital letters, intrudes in the panel and interrupts Sabina. In the last panel, the contrast of Riki's loudness, as well as the repetition of almost exactly the same posture as in the first panel, makes the reader revisit the whole page.

Several things become apparent in retrospect: All the panels are so arranged that text is always placed on the top, over Sabina's head, but in fact, Sabina is not saying much. She is mostly silent. There is

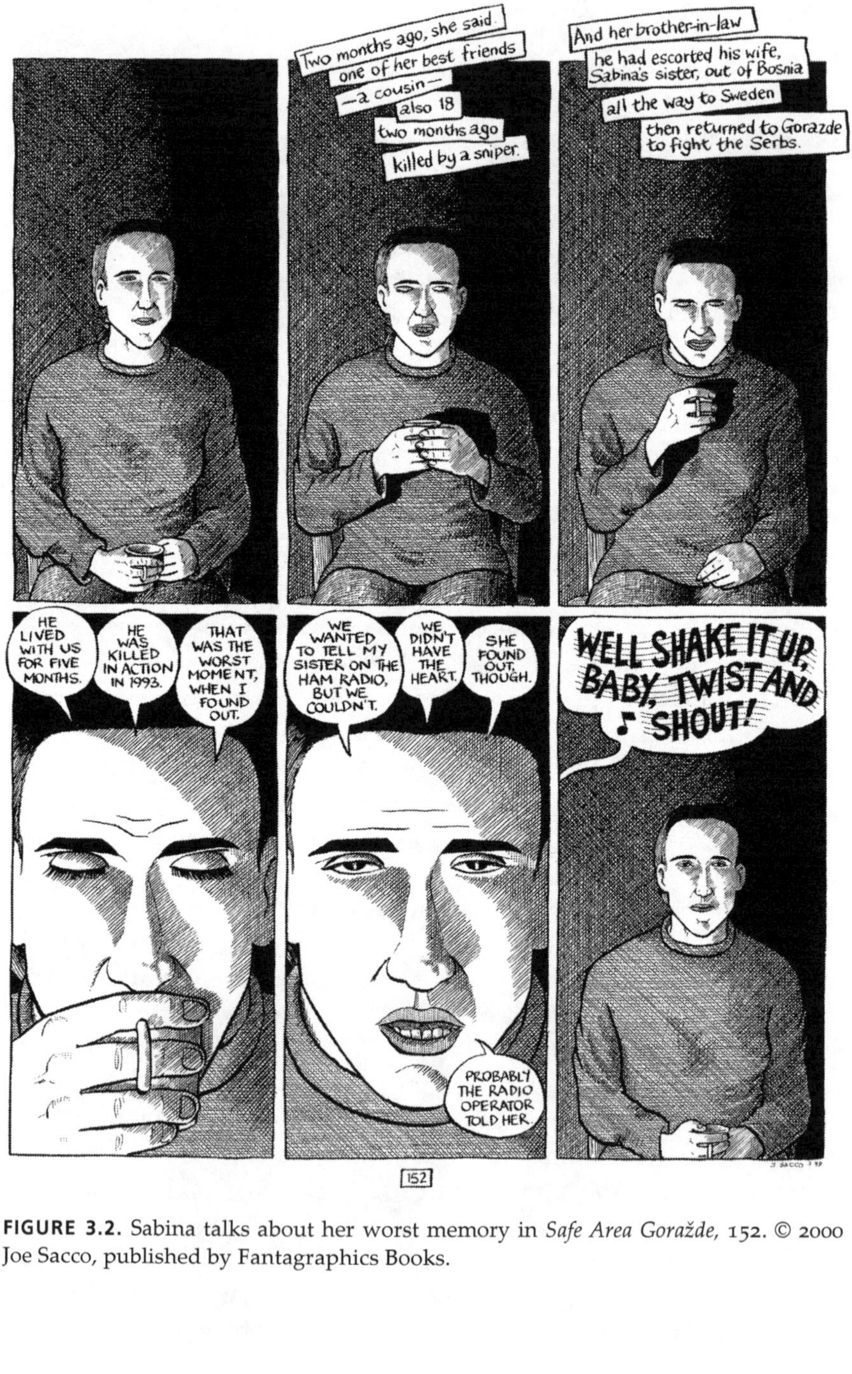

FIGURE 3.2. Sabina talks about her worst memory in *Safe Area Goražde,* 152. © 2000 Joe Sacco, published by Fantagraphics Books.

no text in the first panel; she does not answer the question at once. The next two panels use indirect speech in a series of captions, while the actual character is not saying anything. The first two panels in the second row, the ones that focus on her face, finally show her speaking. The series of small speech balloons—as opposed to using one bigger balloon for all her text—visually expresses the broken rhythm of her sentences. In the final panel, Sabina returns to her silence and looks directly at the journalist and the reader. It becomes apparent that, considering the whole page, the first panel seems to be strangely out of balance. Its top region does not show text, but it is not empty either. Sabina is surrounded by the same rich texture of lines that I have identified as the indicators of the artist's compassionate presence. Though recalling the worst memories isolates her, the presentation in the comics evokes an artistic presence that accompanies her during her account of loss. Sabina is not left alone in her traumatic imprisonment.

Sacco invites the reader to listen to the witness, ponder the haptically charged surfaces, and take time to contemplate the vulnerable subjects of the stories. The traces of compulsive and slow drawing offer opportunities for the reader to engage in what Judith Butler calls an "ethical encounter": "Vulnerability must be perceived and recognized in order to come into play in an ethical encounter, and there is no guarantee this will happen" (43). Haptic surfaces have a potential to facilitate this recognition in the reader: As figure 3.3, the landscape of Sarajevo, demonstrates, haptic surfaces can slow down the narrative and can create pauses in the represented action. Figure 3.1, Neven's portrait, and figure 3.2, a series of Sabina's portraits, show that the haptic surface hints at the attentive presence of the artist and promotes recognition. However, a superficial reader might miss the invitation to contemplate at all. In the conventional reading of comics, which is a reading for action, the pictorial component is normally only looked at in passing. It is not contemplated for long unless another element in the comic encourages the reader to do so. Meanwhile, conventionally, the reader spends the majority of his or her time with reading the textual component of a page, as conventionally the captions and dialogues are responsible for the smooth transitions between adjacent but isolated panels. In Hatfield's words, "words can smooth over transitions and unobtrusively establish a dramatic continuity that belies the discontinuity of the images" (44). The reader does not spend equal time with words and images, and it is all the easier to bypass the seemingly empty surfaces, backgrounds or shadows that I have previously contrasted to figurative drawing. As demonstrated by figure 3.1, it is these surfaces and textures that Sacco has created to arrest the narrative flow and invite the reader to dwell in the world of the characters and contemplate. This way, engaging with the vulnerability of the Other in the form of dwelling becomes not only an activity of the drawer but a kind of engagement by the reader. The temporality of haptic surfaces supports the perception of dwelling as both a place and a process (Diprose 192): The actual physical space between the reader and the comic becomes the site of a dynamic engagement.

The temporal relations between audience and a work of art are defined, at least partly, by how the piece of art (drawing, comics, or painting) frames its own viewing. Parallel to the differences in the way the artist's labor is made visible or is hidden in a painting, Norman Bryson differentiates paintings based on the kind of attention they entice. He calls the two contradictory strategies for framing the audience's attention the painting of the gaze and the painting of the glance (*Vision* 94). Whereas the painting of the gaze, similarly to what Laura U. Marks calls optical visuality, addresses a passive onlooker in a state of "receptive passivity" (Bryson, *Vision* 93) and is met by the frontal contemplation of a finished and perfected painting (often from a predefined fix point), the painting of the glance encourages the mobility of the observing eye to recognize the embodied temporality that the painting carries. The dominant tradition of Western painting, the painting of the gaze, has been described as existing outside *duerée,* because it disregards the time of creation and the time spent with observing it. The opposing tradition of the painting of the glance, in Bryson's words, "addresses vision in the durational temporality of the viewing subject; it does not seek to bracket out the process of viewing, nor in its own techniques does it exclude the traces of the body of labour" (94). I believe Sacco's crosshatched haptic surfaces are drawn along similar ideas about labor, time, and reception, as Sacco makes the traces of his work explicit, and, as far as the reception is concerned, his tactile surfaces build on the "furtive or sideways look" (Bryson, *Vision* 94) of the viewer.

Vision's durational temporality is demonstrated, for example, by a double spread from early on in *The Fixer* (12–13), which, by appealing to the reader's glance, makes the reader not only see but also feel the danger of the situation in Sarajevo and the vulnerability of the

FIGURE 3.3. The journalist approaches the Holiday Inn in Joe Sacco's *The Fixer*, 12–13

people living there (figure 3.3). Sacco explains wordless visual depiction in this double spread in an interview:

> I think in my script I actually did have words. But then part of the process of doing a comic is saying, okay, what words go out? When does the picture speak for itself? And I realized in this case, no words are necessary at all if you want to create that mood. You don't want to talk about that mood. You want the reader to have that mood. (Sacco and Mitchell 57)

The spread showing Sacco's tiny figure arriving at the Holiday Inn hotel in Sarajevo under a sky heavy with ominous clouds establishes Sacco's quest to elicit the logic of the glance. The page slows down time not only due to its irregularly big size—this is the only double spread in the comic—but also due to its expansive tactile surfaces conveying gloom. The patterns of the clouds and the tall buildings with their various arrangements of broken glass and intact windows offer extended surfaces for study. These surfaces are created via the repetition of certain patterns that have the potential to be repeated endlessly. This endless repetition relegates an accidental quality to the actual objects created out of these patterns. Sacco's tiny figure approaching the hotel's gigantic building seems insignificant; his body, bent under the weight of his bags, seems to be suffering to overcome the resistance of not only air but the material actuality of the foreboding clouds looming over him. Sacco's small figure is burdened under a tactile material surface, which, in turn, is expressive of Sacco's artistic presence, concentration, compassion, and traces of his body. Via emphasizing the surface of the double spread, Sacco's compulsive drawing invites the reader to enter the "durational temporality" of the page itself via what Bryson calls the glance, and to take the time to dwell. As a consequence, the reader is also invited to recognize and contemplate the tiny body's relation to its surroundings, the privilege of the body of the Western journalist compared to those of the people living under war, the absence of people, and the vulnerability of the buildings themselves.[8]

Style and technique are artistic and narrative choices, and by the time in Sacco's career when he was reporting on Bosnia, his style has turned realistic and contemplative. His turn to detail and accuracy, as well as the emphasis on the subjectivity of his characters, were preceded by detachment in his first international success, *Palestine* (serialized 1993–1995; collected 2003). *Palestine* builds greatly on visual traits that connect Sacco's comics to the American Underground tradition, such as openness toward the grotesque, caricature, verbal and visual irony, and the frequent alternation of usually wild angles. By *The Fixer* (2003), however, Sacco has abandoned this aesthetic in favor of a greater degree of realism. Parallel to this change, the contours around figures become less important. In the comics on Bosnia, the figures are no longer that radically differentiated from the background. Mark Singer draws a very interesting parallel between Sacco's change of drawing style and a change in Sacco's practice as a journalist: As a journalist and editor of his reportage, Sacco moves away from "he-said she-said journalism" and objectivity, and increasingly invites empathy toward his subjects (79).[9]

Naturally, changes of style are not radical breaks but are continuous processes. *Palestine* is not impersonal as such; it highlights elements of subjective reportage inspired by New Journalism, and occasionally it also features drawings with a haptic charge. Elements similar to the surfaces expressing Sacco's personal commitment have been present in *Palestine,* too, for example, in the "Pilgrimage" chapter. Here the horizontal landscapes of the muddy Jabalia refugee

8. On the importance of the built environment in terms of vulnerability, see Diprose.

9. It must be noted here that Sacco returns to the aesthetics of caricature that characterized his early work in his satire *Bumf Vol. 1.*

camp and the representation of the cloudy sky show traces of the artistic approach of the later works (218–19). Style, however, becomes an indication of an ethical commitment in the Goražde comics in the laboriously cross-hatched surfaces. Tactile surfaces hint at the embodied engagement of the drawer, they convey a presence, and they invite the reader to practice what Bryson has called glance: to spend time with the images and contemplate, and to be part of, together with the drawer, a potentially transformative practice of dwelling with the Other. The next two chapters are going to depart from the study of drawing and practice and will focus on the ways readerly engagement might happen.

Thinking about making a drawing as creating a statement and as creating a visual ontology, as I do in the introduction, has implications on how we can think about the experience of reading drawn nonfiction comics. The visual ontology of graphic narratives invites certain kinds of engagement more easily than others, and comics can guide readers without prescribing specific interpretations and feelings in response. The next chapters focus on responses and interpretations that are rooted in the embodied nature of reading, and in this way the chapters turn from the study of making lines toward receiving them in a dialogue mediated by the comic as object and the bodies of the participants in the dialogue. An important prerequisite of this dialogue is that the parties involved in it are equal parties and see the realness of the Other's vulnerability (see the introduction for a discussion on vulnerability as dialogue).[10]

In the next chapter I will turn to Miriam Katin's graphic memoirs. Both *We Are On Our Own,* which is about Katin's traumatic childhood as a persecuted Jewish toddler in Hungary in the 1940s, and *Letting It Go,* which analyzes how Katin's anxieties, partly resulting from her childhood traumas, manifest in the 2000s, are drawn in Katin's energetic and round lines. The pencil is a fundamental tool for Katin to visualize complex emotional states on paper, regardless of whether she follows a strict grid-like layout, as in the first memoir, or creates free-flowing improvisatory page designs. My analysis focuses on possible ways her lines might be received, and I distinguish the reception of abstract lines from lines used for drawing figures, argu-

10. In the introduction, I argued that vulnerability is a universal condition that is in fact the prerequisite of a moral life. I also showed that vulnerability is structured as a dialogue: One's vulnerability always requires an answer, which is either caring or wounding. Engaging in this dialogue can result in a transformation.

ing that they convey the experience of vulnerability to the reader in different ways. I also study how the sudden and unexpected insertion of abject images can disturb the unreflected and well-rehearsed practices by which readers make progress in comics, and I position this disruption as an opportunity to reflect on both the processes by which comics are read and the respective vulnerability of both the avatar's and the reader's bodies.

FOUR

READING AND THE BODY

Miriam Katin's *We Are On Our Own* and *Letting It Go*

THOUGH THE READER'S engagement with, interpretation of, and performance of a comic cannot be prescribed, every comic guides its readers in how they engage with it during reading. In the introduction of *At the Edges of Vision* (2008), Renée van de Vall records her personal experience of being guided in her interaction with items of an exhibition. Though van de Vall is not talking about comics, she describes an emphatically embodied experience of vulnerability in response to artistic work—an experience I would like to describe and study in relation to comics in this chapter. The installation van de Vall visited was the 1996 exhibition of Alfredo Jaar's *real pictures* in the Museum of Contemporary Art in Antwerp. The installation consisted of columns of boxes in which, according to the captions on top of each box, photographs of the Rwandan genocide were stored. The text provided detailed descriptions of the images in boxes. Here is van de Vall's account of her personal experience:

> As soon as I had entered the room, it seemed as if an invisible hand directed my posture, my movements and my behaviour. It was, for instance, impossible to walk through this room fast or to speak

> loudly. I felt required to shuffle from one column to the next, in an enveloping movement, then to bend over towards the text and to gaze attentively. . . . The whole arrangement called for a discreet, subdued and attentive response, for a kind of attitude proper for the experience and emotion I was supposed to feel. The installation formed a stage where I, as actor, was asked to enact the required experience. (2)

Van de Vall writes about an installation that seemed to influence her movement and posture, and in which the performance of her body influenced, and was indeed part of, her experience and interpretation of the works of art. In a different context, Robin Bernstein examines how things, such as picture books, life-size paper figures, and photographs being taken, can guide how someone is interacting with them, and argues that things can influence cultural practices, such as the performance of race and gender. In "Dances with Things" (2009), Bernstein argues that "agency, intention, and racial subjectivation co-emerge through everyday physical encounters with the material world" (69) and introduces the term "scriptive thing" (69) to describe the object that, via "everyday physical encounters," can "prompt," "inspire," and "structure" (68) the actions of people. Bernstein compares a scriptive thing to a play script, as it "broadly structures a performance while simultaneously allowing for resistance and unleashing original, live variations that may not be individually predictable" (69). I believe that comics can also be scriptive things; they can script both the way they are physically interacted with and can take part in the articulation of broader cultural and political issues without taking away possibilities of improvisation. In fact, Hatfield and Sanders, who also study the performance scripted by a comic book, emphasize the limits of scripts: "People frequently read these texts in ways that do not follow those scripted anticipations. Further, those anticipations are always shaped by local cultural and familial contexts" (461). Bernstein's study of the material relationship between people and objects shows the cultural relevance of thing theory (see Brown). In the rest of the chapter, I do not follow the methodology or vocabulary of thing theory, but I share with Bernstein a curiosity about changes brought about by interactions with objects. Understanding how such changes can come about while reading comics is a major undertaking of this chapter.

Comics definitely call for responses (as van de Vall puts it) and script performances: Comics readers have described their bodies being guided by, or their bodies responding to, certain comics. An example related to my book's focus on vulnerability is the repeated description of Joe Sacco's comics as visceral (Scherr, "Shaking Hands" 20; Singer 79; Rieff). Sacco's comics feature detailed representations of pain, wounding, torture, and death, and readers often interpret this to be close to their own bodies. Mark Singer, for example, writes about the "visceral immediacy" of Sacco's comics (79), and Rebecca Scherr emphasizes that Sacco's works offer instances of "visceral engagement with the pain of others" ("Shaking Hands" 20). Readers interpret images of tortured bodies not only with their eyes, nor exclusively by mentally engaging with the panels and performing closure, but, importantly, also with their bodies. Bodily sensations in readers that influence the experience and performance of reading and that bring the reader closer to a different, renewed understanding of vulnerability will be studied in this chapter.

In this chapter, I show ways in which comics reading can be seen as an embodied performance and describe some ways to make comics reading an activity in which the role of the body in making meaning in general and in experiencing its vulnerability in particular are reflected upon. I will show that moments of reflection are needed for the reader's performance in reading a comic to be part of an embodied dialogue of vulnerability. I argue that calling attention to and making the reader reflect on his or her body's involvement in comics reading can create circumstances for comics reading to become an "ethical encounter" (Butler 43). I do not intend to conduct quantitative studies of measurable bodily responses, such as eye-tracking, nor do I survey readers' verbalized reflections. Instead, relying on observations made by the cognitive sciences, I offer personal readings and reflections on how the body *can* be involved in reading comics and in a discourse of vulnerability. Based on Laura U. Marks's description of "kinaesthetic empathy" ("I Feel" 168–69), I study the reception of abstract lines. I contrast this mode of reception to the way human figures are interpreted in an embodied way: I rely greatly on James Elkins's study of abstract and figurative representations of the human body. Finally, I turn to ways in which the usual, well-rehearsed ways and practices by which one reads a comic are consciously disturbed, and I argue that the interruption of the routine, as well as the practice of interpreting abstract lines and figurative lines in embodied ways, can elicit that comics reading becomes a transformative dialogue among drawer, object, and reader, and can create opportunities for a reflected and/or embodied understanding of one's own and the Other's vulnerability.

My examples come from Miriam Katin's *We Are On Our Own* (2006) and *Letting It Go* (2013), two very different graphic memoirs. *We Are On Our Own* directly deals with the vulnerability of prosecuted minorities, women, children, and civilians during war. *Letting It Go* is a more ironic work on living with the wounds of the past and the necessity to work through and come to terms with one's primordial fears and phobias. The starting point of my investigation of the reading experience is the realization that the body forms the basis of all of our cognitive processes, though we are not aware of our bodily performances. In our everyday activities, as well as in our comics reading practices, the influence of embodiment on experience and thinking is normally hidden from consciousness. In *How the Body Shapes the Mind* (2005), Shaun Gallagher investigates ways in which "the fact of embodiment, the fact that consciousness is embodied, *affect,* and perhaps *effect,* intentional experience" (2). In this chapter, I connect some of Gallagher's findings about an awareness of one's body that enables performing series of actions in order to achieve an aim without paying conscious attention to the action (proprioceptive-kinesthetic awareness; 73), or the intermodal link between vision and this general awareness of one's body (proprioception; 76), to comics reading and to taking part in the transformative dialogue enabled by the experience and the embodied understanding of bodily vulnerability. I also connect concepts of cognitive neuropsychology and the cognitive sciences to performance, sharing Nicola Shaughnessy's enthusiasm that "new paradigms and methodologies are emerging, new vocabularies and registers and new choreographies, as theatre and performance, cognitive and affective science dance together" (24).

The automatic or prenoetic processes and performances of the body are not consciously reflected upon; they are preconscious. For example, the way we read comics is usually given little attention to, as the series of actions required to scan pages, focus, touch, grab, and turn the pages are preconsciously acted out with the aim to read a comic, based on proprioceptive information and proprioceptive awareness. Yet when our bodily performance is defamiliarized, for example, by strategies of foregrounding the materiality of the comic, by building on an element of surprise, or by disturbing the flow of reading, all of which will be elaborated on in this chapter, our bodily performance and the consequences of our embodied consciousness can be reflected upon. The moment of reflection, I argue, is essential for engagement with one's own and the Other's vulnerability.

In my close readings I look for points where Katin guides and invites readers to reflect on the embodied nature of meaning-making mechanisms in order to open up new ways of interpretation and in order to engage with the experience of vulnerability of the Other, which is explored in the comic. I argue that these potential instances, by making readers conscious of their bodily performances while reading, offer new knowledge about the involvement of the body. This new knowledge, as well as the moment of disturbance, in turn, convey a new insight into the experience of vulnerability of all bodies, including that of readers, characters, and the drawer(s). In short, in my emphatically personal readings I explore the readers' possible embodied contributions in the dialogue around the nature and experience of vulnerability, as articulated by the drawer in many ways via the performance of drawing.

The two most important qualities of comics reading from the point of view of my analysis are its performative and embodied nature. It is essential to think about comics reading as an activity that happens in a given context by a particular reader, and not as a normative, standardized, or prescriptive set of expectations: "Embodiment is contextual, enmeshed within specificities of place, time, physiology, and culture, which together compose enactment," explains N. Katherine Hayles (*How We Became Posthuman,* 196). Embodiment, according to Hayles, focuses on the particular. There are, however, frameworks of how our embodiment enables and contributes to our cognitive processes, and comics can have a visceral hold on us because of these frameworks of embodied cognition. However, the interpretations or specific performances of comics reading are always embodied in the sense Hayles speaks about embodiment as "individually articulated" (197).

When I talk about the reader's embodied performance of vulnerability while reading comics, my investigation is influenced by my own experience. As reading is individually, culturally, and contextually embedded, it is impossible to generalize, predict, or prescribe it. To explain my approach, let me quote film theorist Vivian Sobchack from an interview with Scott Bukatman. Sobchack says:

> As a phenomenologist, I very often, although certainly not always, begin with my own specific experience as I start thinking and writing something. And then I generalize these specifics as larger structures of experience. . . . In the end, I don't write about me. I start out from me (even when I write third person mode). But even when I'm in first person mode, I leave "me" (in the egological sense) to look at the structure of the experience I'm writing about, to move into the domain of a more general experiential structure that anybody might inhabit. I start from me but it's not about me. . . . You need to experience and describe before you start interpreting, before you analyze and theorize, before you abstract. (qtd. in Bukatman, "Conversation")

The experience of reading comics is a personal one, as it is based on the actualization of potentialities by an embodied mind and mindful body. The actualization of potentialities establishes reading as a performance, as a unique act of communication. Simon Shepherd writes in his "Closing Note" to *The Cambridge Introduction to Performance Theory* (2016): "Performance is both a practice and a mode of analysis. It is a communicative behavior for which there is no other name. . . . It is a mode of analysis that works by framing, thinking of, its material as if it were performed, which is to say as if it were a deliberate communicative practice" (222–23). The way I understand the term, comics reading can be a performance, because it is a communicative interpretive activity, and it is a unique, unrepeatable, embodied way of creating meaning that manifests in a given environment over a period of time.

In *Comics and the Senses* (2014), Ian Hague also describes comics reading as a performance. This book, starting out from the Aristotelian five senses, lists sense by sense how certain material characteristics of comics can contribute to the reading experience. Hague sees the performative aspect of comics reading in the interaction with the materials of a given comic. He states that "comics are not simply static objects that can be considered from an atemporal perspective. They change and are changed over time, modify the space they occupy as they are being read. The reading of a comic, I argue, constitutes a performance" (5). In this way, he directs attention to the material givens of a comic. This thought is also made explicit when he writes, "For me, conceptualizing the act of 'reading' comics as a performance means explicitly taking up the concept of materiality in reading, but also understanding that the materiality changes over time" (36). For Hague, performance means that comics as objects interact with their surroundings and are therefore slightly changed each time. I agree with Hague that the material aspects of comics form an essential part of interacting with comics: The material nature of a comic is defining when approaching reading as an embodied interpretive performance. However, what is important from my point of view is how material properties are used by the creators and readers of comics in order to create, interpret, and communicate. Therefore, in considering comics reading a performance, I would like to emphasize that performance is a way of communication, a goal-directed activity, which happens by the embodied investment of the reader.

Immersion, Feeling the Line, and Experiencing Vulnerability

Immersion in an activity can obscure the limits of the body and its environment. When immersed in an activity, for example when driving a car, one can feel that the boundaries of one's body include objects—the car—or other people: The car is part of me (Gallagher 36). Dancing with someone is another example by which Gallagher demonstrates immersion: Sometimes one is not entirely sure about where one's body stops and where the other's begins, and one's body has to "take into postural-schematic account the moving extension of [one's] partner" (37). Immersion, and not only sudden disruption, which will be in focus in the next section, are prerequisites for interaction with comics to become, in Barbara Bernstein's words, a "mutual transformative experience" (91). In the introduction of this book, I have already introduced Bernstein's model of art (and not specifically comics) as transformation, which is a concept close to my approach to embodied interaction with comics. Bernstein considers both drawing and looking at drawing an immersive experience that "shifts the *response-ability* of creator and viewer, towards an interfaced, simultaneous, and symbolic relationship of observation *and* participation" (91). In this section, I connect readerly immersion and embodied processes of reading comics, and, based on examples from Katin's comics, I show that immersion and embodied perception are fundamentally linked to an embodied understanding of the vulnerability of the Other as articulated in nonfiction comics.

Miriam Katin's graphic memoirs actively build on the reader's tactile interaction and embodied perception. They use multiple strategies to establish links between the lines of drawing, the represented bodies, and the materiality of the memoir, on the one hand, and the reader's body, on the other, thereby offering possible points of entry for the reader to become part of an interaction of vulnerability. Figure 4.1, showing the first page of *We Are On Our Own* (3), is an instance where tactile interaction with the page and with the materials that make up the comic are utilized to call attention to the bodily processes of reading and to the essentially vulnerable nature of the body. Here the reader's touch of the page, which is usually automatic and not thought of much, is made strange. The page shows a single box of text surrounded by a thick black frame. The blackness is not homogenous; it is made by energetic pencil lines, creating the illusion of a woven texture. The lines carry so much energy that they cannot stop at the boundaries of the frame: They intrude into the caption box and they escape into the white gutter by which the pages in the comic are framed. Though it is part of a printed book, touching the page or tracing any of its lines carries a sense of risk: the risk of making one's hands dirty by touching the intense black lines, and the risk of causing damage to this densely woven surface. As early on as its first page, *We Are On Our Own* invites readers to think about tactility and vulnerability.

The memoir itself is based on Katin's own experience of being a Jewish child in Hungary in 1944 and 1945, and the experience of being vulnerable is a defining one for Katin's avatar. The avatar is called Lisa in the story, and her cosmopolitan family had already broken up when her father was sent to forced labor. Mother and daughter have to leave the capital, Budapest, to go into hiding in the countryside. The mother, Esther, takes on a new identity as a peasant girl with her illegitimate child,[1] but she is helpless when a German officer chooses her as his lover and when Soviet soldiers rape women in the village where they are hiding. The three-year-old Lisa is almost always hungry and does not know how to relate to the people around her. Her vulnerability is a fact she knows well, but she cannot predict if people would abuse it or would respond with care (see Drichel). Her relationships with dogs mirror this unpredictabil-

1. For more on Esther Levy's change of identity and the iconography of how she is represented in *We Are On Our Own*, see my "Graphic Narratives of Women in War."

FIGURE 4.1. The first page of Miriam Katin's *We Are On Our Own,* 3. Copyright Miriam Katin. Image courtesy Drawn & Quarterly.

ity, and she feels a growing inability to relate to God as well as a growing uncertainty about her relationship to her mother.

The memoir is largely based on the stories told to Katin by her own mother, and Katin changed the names of characters at her request (Baskind 240). Despite this name change, the personal nature and authenticity of the graphic memoir are emphasized by several paratextual markers. The cover indicates the book to be a memoir; a photograph of letters written by Katin's mother to her father in 1944 is included at the end (Katin, *We Are* 124), and a long, three-part personal epilogue closes the volume (125–28) together with a photograph of Katin with her mother in 1946 (129). Just like in previous chapters, I would like to repeat that while I think of comics reading

FIGURE 4.2. Mother and daughter arrive at their first hiding place in the countryside in *We Are On Our Own,* 30. Copyright Miriam Katin. Image courtesy Drawn & Quarterly.

in general as an embodied act, I believe that nonfiction comics creates a special link between drawer, reader, and the comic due to the links these narratives claim to have with real bodies.

Katin uses the material nature of her comic to emphasize the bodily vulnerability of her characters, the object of the comic itself, and her readers. As the vulnerability of her characters is more and more exploited, Katin's lines change from neat and controlled to broad and energetic (figures 4.2 and 4.3). The richness of detail in the early scenes showing life in Budapest in 1944, represented with clear pencilwork, is replaced by shades and patches created by lines. The roughness was explained by Katin when, in an interview, she said that certain parts of the drawn narrative were so overwhelming that

FIGURE 4.3. Mother and daughter in a snowstorm of lines in *We Are On Our Own,* 62. Copyright Miriam Katin. Image courtesy Drawn & Quarterly.

she did not correct or rework her initial sketches (Baskind 240). She also used a telling metaphor to describe the process of creation: "This book really sort of spilled out of me, like a vomit or a diarrhea" (Baskind 240). Parallel to the change in the line used for drawing and the darkening of the situations mother and daughter find themselves in, the reader's position also changes.

The fact that the change of the quality of Katin's lines over the graphic memoir, as seen in figures 4.2 and 4.3, can evoke in the reader an understanding of the expressive range of the lines, including an understanding of the possible kinetics and emotional range of the line, hints at two things. First, it indicates that Katin's narrative, which is told by these lines, can evoke an empathetic reaction or identification with the characters. Second, it shows that the visual input of the drawing and the nature of the line are connected to our own bodily experience of what it might feel like to make that specific line. Katin's neat line used at the beginning and also to some extent at the end of her memoir, as well as the energetic lines of more traumatic scenes, are not only visually interpreted by the reader, they are also felt. On the one hand, they can be felt by the reader's hand via touch, as discussed earlier in relation to figure 4.1. On the other hand, they can be felt by the reader's body via having an idea about how that line feels.

The body feels the line. I am not talking about lines used for figurative representation here, as in knowing how to draw a person, and understanding that a specific arrangement of lines makes up a person—interpreting figurative representations of bodies will be studied shortly, in the next section. I am referring here to an embodied knowledge of what drawing a certain line feels like. Philip Rawson, whose theories on drawing as creating an ontology were quoted in the introduction, also says in his *Art of Drawing: An Instructional Guide* (1983) that the experience of mark making influences the interpretation of lines:

> You gather the meaning by reading over the marks to find what they seem to connect with in your own remembered experiences. . . . . You need to learn to follow out the traces the artist made with a special kind of sympathy, a skill best developed by drawing yourself. You can then feel your way into an attitude of mind that encourages your memory to bring up a whole series of responses to marks, to lines, to groups of marks, and to the image that unifies them. The meaning of any drawing can only be a combination of what its marks can mean to you the viewer. (8–9)

It is worth comparing the lines of figure 4.2, from relatively early on in *We Are On Our Own,* and figure 4.3 from the middle. Both pages focus on Lisa and her mother's relationship and on the important presence of dogs in Lisa's life. Placing them next to each other demonstrates that the strong relationship between mother and daughter has loosened, but the remaining link is key to their survival. Their lines, however, evoke very different feelings in the reader's body. In figure 4.3, the multidirectionality of the lines and the uncertainty of the boundaries of Esther's body in the bottom right corner evoke emotional intensity. To represent snow, Katin seems to also have used an eraser in the last panel, making deletion and loss of information a part of the visual makeup of the picture. The empty traces of deleted lines are just as energetic as the lines made by pencil, adding to the reader's knowledge of what these lines feel like.

The line can affect the onlooker and can cause bodily sensations, states Laura U. Marks in "I Feel Like an Abstract Line" (2018), because the body reacts to the aliveness of the line, or, more specifically, to the aliveness of the abstract line. The lines making up the frame in figure 4.1 or the lines of figure 4.3 are abstract in the sense that they carry this vitality: They are living and material (Marks, "I Feel" 161). Marks, whose influential study on the perception of haptic space and haptic surfaces was the foundation of my approach to style and vulnerability in chapter 3, and will be returned to in chapter 5, shows that the abstract line "has its own independent life" (154) and has its own "vitality" (155).

Marks emphasizes the potential of the line to "move" (156) and affect the onlooker and to evoke experiences in the body prior to evoking any emotion, thought, or judgment (159). Feeling like an abstract line means being affected by its sensations without "project[ing] human feelings onto abstract lines" (158). In this way, looking at and experiencing an abstract line is an affective, embodied, and transformative experience: "Something arises in the encounter between our vision and the line that did not exist in our prior experience" (158–59). It is not a coincidence that Marks soon arrives at a conclusion similar to my understanding of embodied responses to comics and my model of establishing an embodied connection based on the experience of vulnerability. She describes the experience of being affected by the line as a communicative situation in which we take part with our embodied cognitive processes when she writes: "Feeling like an abstract line exercises our capacities for extension and connection. Affects put parts of our body in connection with forces beyond it. They unmake and remake the body" (168). This quote also makes it clear that the openness to being transformed is just as important in the experience of feeling like an abstract line as is being moved by it or being affected by it. And this component evokes Butler's description of vulnerability not simply as a basic human experience but as a transformative one. Whereas Marks uses the expression "unmake and remake the body," Butler uses the word "undone"—being "undone" by the Other. In *Precarious Life,* she says:

"Let's face it. We're undone by each other. And if we're not, we're missing something" (23). Feeling like an abstract line and contemporary thinking about vulnerability as a transformative encounter or dialogue share the same basic structure: They are unpredictable relational experiences with the potential to redefine human relationships.

However, there is a significant difference between Marks's description of the onlooker's embodied relationship with the line and mine. I agree with Marks when she says that "we can have empathy *with* abstraction" ("I Feel" 158), and I believe that this is exactly what happens when looking at Katin's lines. However, for Marks the abstract line "embodies a life force that precedes, and is both larger and smaller than, individual bodies. The abstract line participates in a life force anterior to particular life forms" (159). Without contradicting this "vitalist aesthetics" (156), in my analysis I do not focus on a "life force" or "life forms beyond materiality" (161). Instead, in my interpretation, feeling the line in the body and having an embodied idea about the nature and expressive potentialities of that line is what creates the possibility for the birth of an embodied dialogue via the drawn trace. Looking at the line and feeling it can contribute to the dialogue between drawer and reader and can be an immersive transformative experience. In this way, feeling like an abstract line can be a way to experience vulnerability in an embodied way.

I believe that the connection between the embodied reader and the abstract line can happen partly because looking at a line evokes processes of making lines in the brain: The visual perception of lines is connected to the creation of lines, as in the brain visual perception and motor areas are active simultaneously. In "The Production and Perception of Handwritten Traces," two cognitive neuroscientists, Aurélie Lagarrigue and Marieke Longcamp, examine the processes in the brain while writing and perceiving writing, and their findings can explain why readers of Katin's comics can feel empathy with the lines. As Lagarrigue and Longcamp's research is about writing, at this point it is worth evoking Tim Ingold's argument on the lack of difference between hand-drawn and handwritten lines, which was elaborated in the introduction. Ingold argues convincingly in his monograph on the cultural history of writing that writing is a "special case of drawing" (122). According to Lagarrigue and Longcamp,

> the mere visual observation of letters, but not of unknown characters, gave rise to activations of a premotor region of the left

> hemisphere in right-handers, in addition to the typically expected visual cortical activations. This premotor region . . . is considered crucial for the maintenance and retrieval of writing movements in memory. Longcamp et al. (2003) actually observed that this same premotor region was indeed strongly activated when participants were in the course of producing writing. It did not respond when participants observed the unknown characters, because no motor representation could be evoked. (22)

In other words, when we are looking at handmade letters that we ourselves have made (and so their "motor representation could be evoked"), apart from the region responsible for visual perception, the brain also activates the region responsible for making handmade signs, and in this way the line is also felt by our bodies. The study shows that this does not happen if we do not know how to draw a given letter. If we accept that lines used for writing and lines used for drawing are similar, using this study as an analogy can help understand why looking at drawn lines can so strongly connect to the onlooker's body. Looking at lines evokes the movements of the body when making lines, and when looking at Katin's delicate lines with which she elaborates on detail, or her energetic lines by which she renders emotional turmoil, the body has an understanding of these lines because it can rely on memories of movements required to perform lines.

The Body-Schematic Performance of Reading, Interruption, and the Abject

The opening page of *We Are On Our Own* (figure 4.1) is not the only one in Katin's memoir structured around a tiny central angular element and using a thick black frame created by lines with stamina. This structure is used altogether nine times, including two occasions in the epilogue (3, 28, 47, 51, 79, 93, 122, 125, 128). Each iteration brings about a new chance to disrupt the regular rhythm and methods of reading, a chance to foreground the materials this comic has been created with, and a chance to make the reader aware of his or her own body's role in interpretation. This irregular repetition, though it undoubtedly works less and less effectively due to the reader's habituation, evokes the peculiar touch of the first page of the story and repeatedly invites the reader to reflect on the habitual performance of his or her hands. Moments of conscious attention to and reflection on our bodily and mental performances during reading provide occasions for readers to engage in a dialogue initiated by the comic based on the experience of vulnerability.

We are not conscious of most of our bodily performances. We do not need to pay attention to habituated actions, such as the series of minute movements that make up the act of turning the page of a comic. We do not need conscious attention to monitor the details of how the page is turned, because the body has an innate "dynamic, operative performance" (Gallagher 32). This is the body-schema system, which, according to Shaun Gallagher's definition in *How the Body Shapes the Mind,* "prenoetically governs the postures that are taken up by the body in its environments. That a body schema operates in a prenoetic way means that it does not depend on a consciousness that targets or monitors bodily movement" (32). The body schema is an "ongoing pre-reflective proprioceptive awareness" (46) of the body: Under normal circumstances, the body schema is a holistic awareness of the body and its relationship to its surroundings. Body-schematic proprioceptive awareness makes sure that we have information on the positions and sensations of our body parts. Automatically—that is, without conscious awareness or attention—it guides the adjustments of positions, or the performance of actions (36). To return to the example of turning the page in a comic, we know exactly where our hands are and what they are doing; we do not need to monitor them or consciously direct the actions they perform. A consequence of our prenoetic or prereflective awareness of our bodies is that the "body *actively organizes* its sense experience and its movement in relation to pragmatic concerns" (142). This means that when we are reading a comic, we know the distribution of its weight and anticipate the change brought about by our actions. Often, the hand is prepared to turn the page before we have finished reading it.

Gallagher explains that body-schematic performances get noticed, or, in his words, "become apparent to consciousness" when "there is a reflection on my bodily situation brought on by pain, discomfort, fatigue, etc." (34). Normally, our perceptual attention is turned toward the world; it turns toward the body when something is not right. Katin's memoirs provide multiple instances to make us reflect on our body and its performances. The black-framed pages in *We Are On Our Own* (figure 4.1) are reminders of the tactile nature of interpretation and offer instances to bring our bodies to the forefront of our attention, and surprise can also contribute to disrupting the body-schematic set of actions that constitute reading a comic. In the following section, I would like to demonstrate how the element of surprise, together with the closeness of the abject, can contribute to the discourse of vulnerability.

On most pages of *Letting It Go,* Miriam Katin's second graphic memoir, pictures drawn by colorful crayons compete for space with hand-drawn capital letters. Instead of habituating the reader to tightly framed pages, as Katin did in *We Are On Our Own,* the pages of *Letting It Go* offer the reader loosely organized patches of words and images. Most pictures show the face or upper body of Katin's avatar, Miriam, and after a few pages, the reader has a general impression of how this comic operates in terms of its storytelling, visual ontology, design, and materiality, and the reader has an idea about what to expect. Katin explores controversial and difficult topics in *Letting It Go,* but instead of directly representing them, traumatic memories, prejudices, and fears are mostly displayed on Miriam's bespectacled face. We see Miriam shocked by the thought of her adult son moving to the country that she still associates with Nazism, Germany. She is worried and anxious about having to deal with a buried part of her past; she is confused about her place in the world. Miriam's emotional state and face, the irregular page layouts, and color crayons as well as the texture and weight of the paper contribute to the set of automated repertoires of action that the reader will repeat without reflection while reading.

This habituated performance of reading is disrupted when, two-thirds into the narrative, Katin unexpectedly inserts a three-page sequence revealing the vulnerability of her avatar in multiple ways. Miriam is first shown to defecate herself, then she is shown naked, trying to wash the poop off herself (figure 4.4). This sequence, naturally, has its own dramatical significance in the narrative: Preceding this scene, Miriam and her husband arrived in Berlin to visit their son and his partner, and the experience of visiting the country that she has been avoiding all her life causes Miriam serious anxieties. Upon arriving in Germany, a disillusioned Miriam comments on a seemingly neutral smartphone advertisement featuring an athlete ready to run, with the slogan "Ultraschnelle Performance": "Ok. Ok. I get the picture. Now I feel a whole lot more comfortable." Every detail convinces Miriam that little has changed since her war-torn childhood in

Europe and strengthens her stereotypes that were introduced with irony in the first part of the comic. Miriam tries in vain to comfort herself with an illusion of safety: "Great food. Great wine. Great mattress." She cannot rest, and tension is eased only via Miriam's accidental defecation, a scene bordering on the abject and the taboo.

The sequence might as well be regarded as a scene of elongated purification, but there is nothing cathartic about it. The visit to Germany will continue to be emotionally distressing for Miriam, though she does start to notice and appreciate ways in which the people killed in the Holocaust are remembered in the streets of Berlin. This sequence, however, is of importance to my study of readerly engagement because it is an unexpected break with the returning visual themes, and for me at least, it is a disruption in the prenoetic bodily performances I use to read this comic. Turning the page is not that easy and automatic with this scene: I am suddenly aware of my hand touching the naked body of an elderly woman who has been anxious about the thought of Germany and who is shown to be covered in poop (figure 4.4).

Abject images are not often used in *Letting It Go,* so surprise and a sense of transgression contribute to making me aware of my habituated performance. I am cautious with my touch and with turning this specific page. I am aware of the vulnerable situation that the character is in, and the idea of touching something as abject as these pages makes me hesitate. This touch seems to be different from the previous ones; it has the potentiality to link my body to that of the avatar. Katin has not only made me conscious of the performance of my body, but the habituated bodily interaction with the comic is turned into a provocation. The abject topic of defecation interferes with my reading of *Letting It Go,* and through the creation of a moment of self-reflection, it offers a point of entry into the discourse of vulnerability.

Katin does not hide the vulnerability of her comics avatar but exposes it in detail. The first nine pictures fit in the most often used way of drawing Katin's avatar: They zoom in on Miriam's head. The long exposure of the scene uses an unusual color palette of browns and reds to frame Miriam's portrait. To appreciate this choice of visually building up the page toward the climatic act of showing defecation, we need to remember that Katin rarely represents backgrounds in *Letting It Go,* and if she does, she usually draws recognizable settings or, in the case of abstract backgrounds, shades of green seem to dominate. The last tier of the page changes from a focus on the face

FIGURE 4.4. The first page of the purification sequence in *Letting It Go.* Copyright Miriam Katin. Image courtesy Drawn & Quarterly.

to a focus on the whole body. Miriam's body, covered in excrement, is revealed to the look and the touch of readers. The last-but-one picture of the twelve-panel page shows Miriam in a position of extreme defenselessness: In an act of self-examination and diagnosis, she raises her gown, exposing her open legs and the excrement covering her lower body (figure 4.4). Touching the page can cause unease, as the abjection of excrement comes close. This unease as a response to Miriam's much greater existential and physical ordeal can create a not-at-all automatic engagement with her vulnerability. This engagement is not simply emotional or mental but is rooted in bodily experience. Julia Kristeva writes that abjection is a liminal state, where "I am at the border of my condition as a living being" (3)—with this page, both the autobiographical avatar and the reader are suddenly brought to a threshold that is understood best by their bodies.

Kristeva continues to define the abject as "something rejected from which one does not part, from which one does not protect oneself as from an object. Imaginary uncanniness and real threat, it beckons to us and ends up engulfing us" (4). The abject is repulsive and desirable at the same time—it belongs to the self, but it is rejected; it is radically other. "Not at all an other with whom I identify and incorporate, but an Other who precedes and possesses me, and through such possession causes me to be" (Kristeva 10). The provocative disruption of the reading process by this page is not without risk: The abject can widen the distance between avatar, comic, and reader, but it can also be a key scene to interact with the vulnerability of the Other.

Abject images evoke real fears. Tina Helbig, in her essay on horror comics, talks about an invasion of the barrier between the reader's reality and the world of the comic by abject images (195). Surprise, touch, and vision all contribute to the reader's liminal experience and fear that abject images can "invade the reality of their own real bodies in their own real world" (Helbig 199). For Helbig, the reader is quite passive, and the relationship between abject image and reader is like a war where the reader is losing. The reader's world might be invaded ("invade" is used four times), or the gutter between panels can be "infest[ed]" by "[u]ncanny objects" (196), while "uncanny and frightening pictures in comics always *prey on* your mind, even when we rationally know that they are only pictures" (193; emphasis added). I believe that Helbig's study of touch and fear in horror comics contributes to an understanding of the abject in other genres, and it is largely due to a difference in our focus that I do not agree with Helbig's metaphors. For me, abject images do not simply threaten but also offer a chance to engage. I see visual and tactile interaction with abject images, as well as the element of the unexpected in nonfiction comics as possibilities to engage not simply with our own dehabituated reading processes, but with the vulnerability of the Other.

In this section, I have focused on the first page of this scene of defecation and cleaning, but Katin devotes two more pages to the details of how her avatar washes herself and her bedsheets. No details are left out; the attention and narrative space given to the scene give time to the reader to contemplate the performance of his or her own body. As Shaun Gallagher reminds us, "conscious attention can focus on only one part or area of the body at a time" (57), and the conscious attention is guided by the various body parts featured in Katin's drawings. Similarly to the way Lynda Barry is guiding attention to the *drawer's* body in performing the movements that lead to the birth of the line on paper in figure 1.3, Katin is guiding the *reader's* attention to parts of her body in interpretation. The practical steps of washing Miriam's body are interpreted by establishing a relationship between the represented body and the reader's own body; and the abject topic of excrement maintains the focus on helplessness and vulnerability.

Visceral Seeing and Vulnerability

So far, I have related immersion, surprise, touch, and abjection to the experience of vulnerability in reading. I would like to emphasize again that these offer possibilities to connect the reader and the Other via an embodied understanding of vulnerability. This way, in the case of nonfiction comics, the reader's performance of reading can be an answer to the drawer's articulation of the experience of vulnerability. In this last section, after studying the body's response to abstract lines and abject topics, I examine the body's possible responses to drawn bodies. When looking at drawn bodies, the visual stimulus is felt in our bodies—our visual perception seems to be connected to the way we feel touch and to the way we feel our own bodies. The relationship between tactility and vision has been explored in chapter 3, and will be central to chapter 5, but now I would like to work with the link between vision and proprioceptive sensations. Proprioception is "the body's internal sense of itself" (Elkins, *Pictures* 23); it is an awareness of the body's position and movement. In this section I will connect the involuntary sharing of bodily sensations when looking at representations of bodies—a phenomenon James Elkins termed "visceral seeing" in *Pictures of the Body: Pain and Metamorphosis* (viii)—to possibilities to engage with the vulnerability articulated in a comic.

In the discussion of visceral seeing, Elkins shows that "it can be difficult to maintain the traditional distinctions between viewer and viewed, and depicted bodies may be understood as opportunities for a peculiar kind of response that can be difficult to name" (*Pictures* vii–viii). As part of this response, onlookers understand the experience of a drawn body as their own bodies respond to seeing more or less realistically drawn bodies. This connection is not felt by the body, however, when looking at abstracted bodies or metaphorical representations,[2] for example the human figures of Cubism, which are perceived as a puzzle for the mind to figure out.

The study of the onlooker's bodily reaction started in nineteenth-century German aesthetics: Robert Vischer's term *Einfühlung* (92), translated into English as "empathy,"[3] described what was perceived to be an automatic mirroring of sensations and a vital aspect of affect. Elkins defines empathy as the "involuntary sharing of sensation between our bodies and something or someone we see" (*Object* 137). Empathy has a key role in interpretation, because the body does not simply mirror or share the sensations of other bodies; the body also takes part in *making* meaning. Elkins calls this "thoughtful embodiedness" (*Pictures* vii–viii), and Mark Johnson summarizes the connection between the body and thinking: "Via our embodied understanding we learn how to go on with our thinking" (101).

In Katin's three-page scene of defecation and purification, the "ethical provocation" (Murphy's term: 66) caused by the multiply exposed vulnerability of Katin's autobiographical avatar can be unsettling for multiple reasons: the element of surprise, the disturbance in the habituated body-schematic performance of how the comic is read, or in having to look at and/or touch something abject. However, the vulnerability of the character is provocative because

2. Elkins calls this kind of representation metamorphosis, explaining that these metamorphic distractions are also responded by the body to some degree, but primarily, they "exist *as an idea*" (*Pictures* 26).

3. This approach of empathy is not the same as empathy as "emotional responsiveness" studied by Suzanne Keen (vii).

the scene is interpreted by "visceral seeing": Certain sensations are shared by the reader's actual body. Knowledge and understanding can be achieved because vision is not an isolated sense but is linked to other senses and to the proprioceptive awareness of the body: Intermodal connections in the brain play a crucial role in being able to engage imaginatively with the comic being read as well as being able to engage with the vulnerability of the Other. The intermodal connections of the brain are studied by neuroscientist Jamie Ward, who focuses on the visual perception of pain in "The Vicarious Perception of Touch and Pain: Embodied Empathy" and points out that "observing pain activates many of the same regions involved in physically perceiving pain" (60). This means that in neurotypical people, the same brain regions are active when they are touched and when they look at a painful touch to somebody else. Ward also states that this is true not only for pain but also for touch in a broader sense: "Vicarious pain and touch (from observing others) use many of the same mechanisms in the brain as physical sensations of pain and touch" (61).

This link between the seen body of the Other and the felt body of the self was also studied in infants—and I believe the conclusions of these experiments can help understand the interpretation of represented bodies in comics. Shaun Gallagher shows that neonates and young babies respond to and copy facial gestures they see: Their visual input is linked to their awareness of their bodies and to movement (82). Without having an idea about the image of their bodies, neonates respond to the "*action* and *expression* of the other" (83): Vision creates a link between bodies. I believe that this visual, proprioceptive, and sensory-motor link to the other influences the interpretation of represented bodies in comics and can, in the case of nonfiction comics, constitute a basis of an acknowledgment of and an engagement with the vulnerability of the Other articulated in the comic.

Vision is linked to proprioception: In Ward's words, "a purely visual stimulus elicits a matching embodied response, even in non-synaesthetes [that is, in the neurotypical control group of Ward's experiments]" (58). Ward's research focuses on synesthetes, and neurotypical people constitute a control group whose answers the answers of synesthetes can be compared to. I will return to the possibilities of considering neuroatypical perception and a model for interaction with comics based on synesthesia in the conclusion. For now,

I use the link between looking at bodies and becoming proprioceptively aware of our bodies in neurotypical people: When neurotypical people see other bodies, they understand the positions, actions, and sensations of these bodies because they have proprioceptive information about and awareness of their own bodies.

A response in the reader's body, naturally, does not only happen with Katin's comics. This link between vision and proprioception is behind the already mentioned adjective by which Joe Sacco's comics reportage is described: They are visceral. They connect the reader's body to representations of bodies in pain. Whereas some of the most critically acclaimed nonfiction comics (as collected by Beaty and Woo 7–8), such as Marjane Satrapi in *Persepolis,* tend to use nonrealistic styles to represent pain, Sacco represents physical pain and the inside of the body in raw and uncompromising ways. Another way to create distance between represented bodies and readers' bodies is drawing hybrid bodies, as Art Spiegelman does in *Maus.* Sacco and Katin are more realistic than the above strategies in representing details of scenes of death, wounding, or medical operations. Realism, as Elkins argues, facilitates visceral seeing, and based on this embodied understanding, a dialogue of vulnerability can be started.[4]

The scene of defecation is in fact not the first occasion in which Katin draws on the embodied link between avatar and reader to invite the reader to understand the experience of vulnerability. Figure 4.5 is a page from the beginning of *Letting It Go,* representing a little talked about and liminal experience: giving birth by Cesarean section.

Whereas the purification scene started with Miriam's face and zoomed out to reveal the body of the character, here the representation zooms in on her belly in the moments when it is cut open. The inside of the body, which was a taboo to represent in a realistic way for much of the history of art, and was either transformed into metaphors of food and liquids or was excluded altogether (Elkins, *Pictures* 126), is now drawn multiple times on this single page. Miriam's belly is drawn in a simplified way, and the naïveté of the representation is emphasized by the tools she is using in the whole graphic memoir: colorful crayons. Nevertheless, Miriam's body is clearly shown as a piece of flesh that is acted upon and is transgressed. Her belly is

4. Naturally, realism is not a prerequisite of such a transformative engagement with comics.

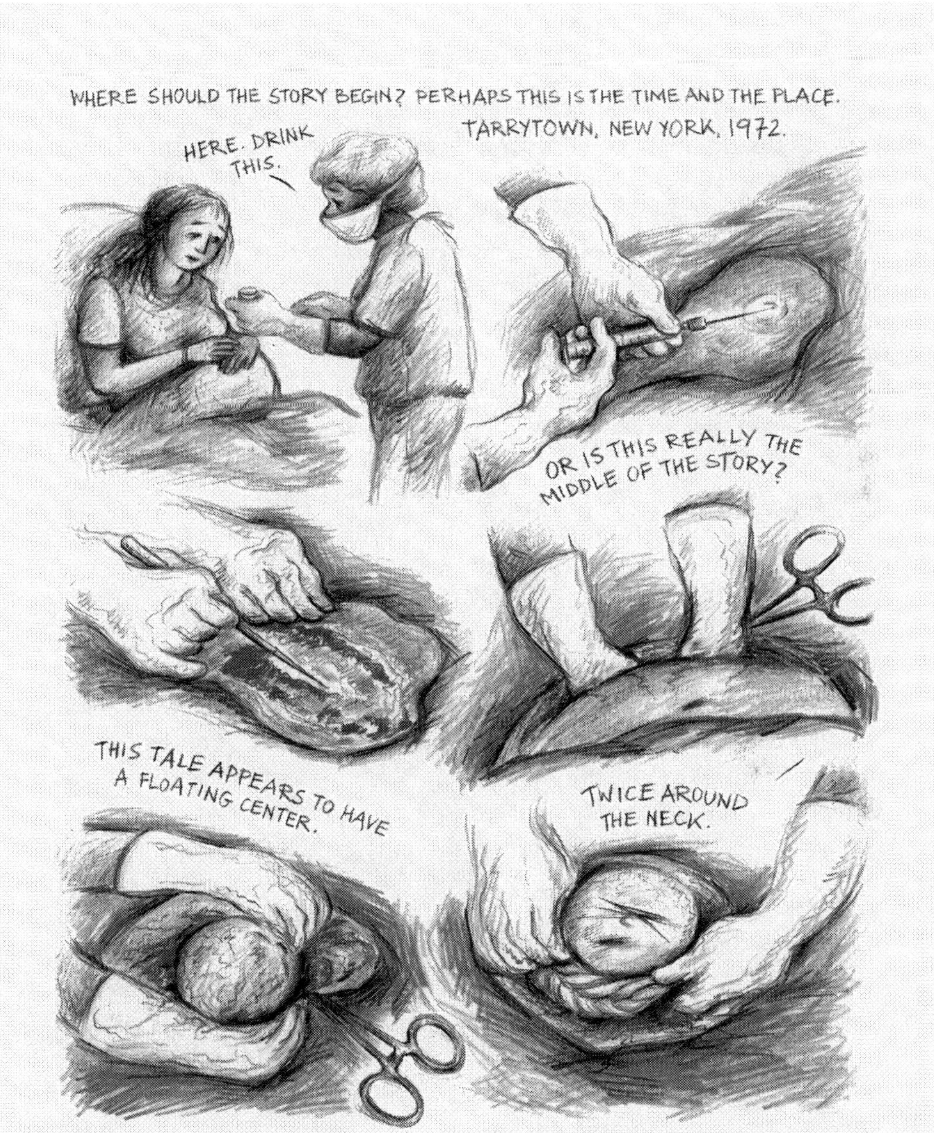

FIGURE 4.5. Giving birth by Cesarean section in Miriam Katin's *Letting It Go.* Copyright Miriam Katin. Image courtesy Drawn & Quarterly.

isolated from the rest of her body by the color green surrounding it, possibly a green sheet. The active gloved hands of the doctor and the sharp instruments by which the operation is performed emphasize Miriam's helplessness.

The scene is visceral. Katin applies a narrow focus on pain: It is not only the doctor who is cutting up the female body, but so is Katin herself when she chose to draw only her avatar's belly, and nothing else of her body, five times. The narrator's text reveals that this liminal scene is linked to the creation of the narrative of *Letting It Go*: "Where should the story begin? Perhaps this is the time and the place. Tarrytown, New York, 1972." After several pages of procrastination (being annoyed by music, making coffee, cleaning glasses, looking out of the window, getting rid of cockroaches) and unsuccessful attempts to start narrating the actual story of letting go of lifelong traumas, this scene of birth is chosen as a point of departure. The birth of her son helps Miriam start telling and showing her story.[5] The starting point is of extreme vulnerability, yet the doctor's hands are helping her, and are not there to harm, when they perform the C-section: In this case, the doctor's caring response to the character's vulnerability is not without risk and danger.

The reader, as I have demonstrated, does not respond to the situation of the character only by empathy or character identification. Because comics uses images as well as words, and because images are not simply processed in a monosensory, visual way but are linked to tactile perception as well as the reader's information about and awareness of his or her own body, the reader responds to the represented character with his or her body. I do not mean here an actual physical response, such as sudden and involuntary movement. Rather, the reader processes this page (and similar pages) and can understand it because our cognitive processes are embodied.

In this chapter, using comics by Miriam Katin, I have explored three ways in which the body takes part in the performance of comics reading: immersion and understanding the kinetics of the abstract line, the body-schematic performance of reading and the role of abjection in eliciting reflection, and visceral seeing. With acknowledging that each performance is unique, I argue that becoming conscious of the involvement of the body in cognition can either help read-

5. The maternal body in the moments of giving birth is conceptualized as the starting point of a narrative of learning to deal with the past in another recent graphic memoir as well, in Thi Bui's *The Best We Could Do* (2017).

ers reconsider the vulnerability of their own bodies or help form an embodied understanding of the vulnerability of the Other, or both. The embodied nature of comics reading is the foundation of my considering comics reading as a possibility to engage with the experience of vulnerability and be transformed by this dialogue.

I believe that in the study of the embodied performance of reading, the complexity of comics allows for *not* separating immersive experiences elicited by lines and haptic surfaces (and also, naturally, by the flow of the narratives) and interpreting the figurative representations of bodies. In this vein, the next chapter is going to investigate the embodied performance of reading as a possibility to engage in a dialogue of vulnerability with the Other by further exploring immersion and reflection in the reader's interaction with the material characteristics of a publication, in engagement with haptically visual surfaces.

FIVE

EMBODIED INTERACTION

Katie Green's *Lighter Than My Shadow* and Joe Sacco's *The Great War*

READING ANY COMIC is an encounter with the dimension, weight, materials, fragility, and all the physical characteristics of the published object or of the device on which the comic is read in a given environment. The significance of physical form is stereotypically emphasized when comics, especially the comic book, is approached as a collector's item; however, the material characteristics influence the ways readers interpret any comic. Material characteristics, which include the complexities of page design as well as the physical characteristics of the pages and of the actual object, are interpreted together with the content of the comics in the performance of reading. In fact, they cannot be separated in processes of meaning making: Each feature becomes part of the performance of comics reading.

It is easier to examine the ways material characteristics shape reading and take part in creating meaning in nontypical comics, as here the well-rehearsed ways one reads a comic are suspended, and new strategies of interaction are required. As described in chapter 4, the physical act of comics reading, such as turning the pages or holding a comic in hand, is a prereflective and body-schematic performance, meaning that the reader does not need to pay conscious attention to the coordination of the set of minute movements required to read a typical comic. The body schema governs adjustments in the performance of the body by relying on a constant, not conscious awareness of one's own body (called proprioceptive awareness). Body-schematic performances are always ongoing, because, as Shaun Gallagher explains, they "enable us to find our way in space; to walk without bumping into things; to run without tripping and falling; to locate targets; to perceive depth, distance and direction; to throw and to catch a ball with accuracy" (141). Comics reading as a body-schematic performance is governed, on the one hand, by the awareness of one's body and one's surrounding, and on the other hand, by the aim of turning the page in order to proceed with reading. Comics that are not typical in their size, materials, or publication format make it easier to reflect on both the set of actions performed during reading and the important ways material characteristics are part of the meaning of a comic.

Chris Ware's *Building Stories,* a box containing fourteen pieces of comics of various sizes, shapes, and materials, is possibly the most famous comic that showcases the inevitability of its own material presence and openly invites reflected interaction. Aaron Jacob Kashtan chooses a photo of *Building Stories* to introduce his comics essay on materiality in comics (figure 5.1). In *Building Stories,* "each reader's engagement . . . is a distinct event that brings into being a new assemblage," as Dittmer says (485), and each engagement also creates new physical relations between the elements of *Building Stories* and the reader. The material objects in the box are "handled, manipulated, reshuffled" (Crucifix 12) during the performance of reading, making *Building Stories* a dynamic archive that forever exists in motion and is in a "constant condition of becoming" (Shildrick 1), if you wish. *Building Stories* foregrounds its own thingness; it showcases the variety of ways by which it can structure the actions of people and can prompt open-ended creative performances. Here, I return to Robin Bernstein's notion of the "scriptive thing" (69), introduced in the previous chapter, because I believe that this idea allows us to consider comics not simply as three-dimensional objects but as things with agency or even as partners.

The comics I read in this chapter are published in unusual formats, and this strangeness invites us to think about the ways in which guided or scripted interactions, acted out by the reader's bodily ges-

FIGURE 5.1. Aaron Jacob Kashtan demonstrates the "physicality of the reading experience" with Chris Ware's *Building Stories* in "Materiality Comics," an academic comic published in *Digital Humanities Quarterly*, vol. 9, no. 4, p. 2. Licensed under Creative Commons.

tures, can shape interpretations and can also shape the articulation and understanding of vulnerability in a given comic. The first comic I analyze is Katie Green's *Lighter Than My Shadow* (2013), which is an unusually heavy and thick memoir on a body disappearing due to anorexia, and it is also a brutally honest account of sexual abuse and a long, nonlinear healing process. In the second section, I read Joe Sacco's *The Great War: July 1, 1916: The First Day of the Battle of the Somme* (2013), which is an accordion-shaped visual narrative on one of the bloodiest battles of the First World War. These graphic narratives are very different: Green's work is a personal memoir and Sacco's work is a wordless printed panorama that lacks a single protagonist. I do not offer comparative readings; rather, I read both comics with the same technique: I offer holistic interpretations in which what is on the page is connected to the comic as a thing. I chose these narratives because both center on the experience of abused vulnerability in nonfiction settings, though in radically different ways. I show that the graphic narratives of both Green and Sacco imbue the actual object of reading with a special presence and connect the material object with the represented bodies. This presence carries "an ethical scene fraught with possibilities" (Gilmore 106). I show that both authors utilize the fact that dominantly figurative representations of the body and dominantly haptic visual styles are interpreted differently (see chapter 4 or later sections of this chapter for details), and I also argue that the materiality and thingness of *Lighter Than*

My Shadow and *The Great War* contribute to the articulation of bodily pain and abused vulnerability. I am aware that Ware's, Green's, and Sacco's works are atypical, and I offer these readings as steps in a direction to what I call holistic readings of comics: exploring how a comic as an object can be interacted with, exploring how attention to the thingness of comics can broaden the possibilities of both making and reading.

Whereas so far in this book I have kept the focus narrowly on the drawn line as it is reproduced in print, arguing that the drawn line can be read as an initiation of a dialogue of vulnerability, this chapter's focus on comics as things means considering the work of not only the drawer, but of different people who take part in designing the material characteristics of a given comic. Talking about memoirs, Leigh Gilmore emphasizes how the work of others contributes to the authenticity of first-person narratives: "A memoir is . . . an autobiographical scene . . . where multiple meaning makers, including publisher, marketing team, and graphic designer influence what readers understand about the identity of an author" (107). Gilmore calls attention to the fact that authenticity, identity, and authorial presence are negotiated by many professionals, and this can result in gaps between the text of the memoir and, in Gilmore's examples, the book covers these memoirs were given. While I am not conducting paratextual analysis here, I take Gilmore's article as a warning not to attribute too much authorial control over how comics as objects exist. Interestingly, whereas comics scholarship has separate words for the graphiateur, the narrator, and the avatar, for example, we cannot really name teams of people who facilitate a piece of nonfiction comic getting material form. Gilmore calls them "meaning makers," by which she emphasizes the collaborative nature of meaning if comics is studied as an object (which has the potential to become a thing).

The Body in Three Dimensions

Katie Green's graphic memoir, *Lighter Than My Shadow,* is a story of Green's avatar, whom I will call Katie: She is diagnosed anorexic as a teenager, and when she is sexually harassed by her therapist, she denies even to herself that it has happened. The memoir reveals the mental state of living with an eating disorder, the experience of being touched against her will, and the very long process of recovery with a new therapist. Katie's wish to disappear, hinted in the title of the memoir, is visualized multiple times (e.g., 124–25). The very opening introduces thoughts, fears, and anxieties as a material presence: A shadow created out of dynamic and multidirectional black lines is hovering over a very skinny Katie standing on the scales (1). I will call this formation "scribble," and I will show that apart from being related to thoughts, it also connects to Katie's body and transforms the layout of the comic.

The way the opening sequence continues calls attention to the scribble's connection to Katie's body: Multiple images of her naked body float in a current of abstract black scribble. Her body is getting smaller and smaller until it disappears, but the scribble flows on, and after turning the page once more, we find out that the scribble is coming from the pen of Katie the grown-up artist, sitting at her desk, drawing (1–9). This rather abstract introduction points to the very topic that I would like to explore in this section, namely that though the comic offers the utter vulnerability of the female body as spectacle by multiple figurative representations where Katie's vulnerability is abused, Green uses the scribble to visualize the subjective experience of how that body feels, and gradually Green connects Katie's body to the structure of the comic. I will also show that Green literally breaks up the body of her protagonist and re-creates the comic out of it (see figure 5.3). Green connects Katie's body and the body of the comic, and interaction with *Lighter Than My Shadow* becomes a different performance and different spatial relations are established once the reader understands this embodied connection. Although it might seem a paradox that a comic on the experience of having an extremely thin body is one of the heaviest graphic narratives on the market, I would like to show that the link between the avatar's body and the material body of the comic as a scriptive thing is more nuanced. The substantial and thick body of the comic the reader is interacting with constitutes a material presence essentially linked to Katie's disappearing body.

The scribble has three major functions. In its most basic use, it represents Katie's anxiety: It is floating as a cloud over Katie's head in moments of distress. In its second function, as hinted above, the scribble is an environment where the sensations of Katie's body are visualized and where fears and memories are represented figuratively. The scribble seems to be an environment of thought. By creating greater surfaces, the scribble can elicit a different kind of look, a

FIGURE 5.2. A double spread showing the scribble as an indicator of anxiety, material presence, and structural element in Katie Green's *Lighter Than My Shadow,* 172–73

slower one that "moves on the surface plane of the screen [here: the page] for some time" (Marks, *Skin* 162–63) and "pull[s] the viewer in close" (163). The haptic presence of the scribble is perceived differently than the figurative bodies of the comic, and Green basically keeps the visual repertoire of her memoir to these things: the scribble and bodies. Backgrounds are very rarely articulated; distraction is rarely provided. When covering larger surfaces, the scribble creates a material presence of lines that exists outside time. The tactile presence of the scribble functions very differently than the tactile surfaces created by Joe Sacco and analyzed in chapter 3. Looking at this surface is menacing, whereas earlier I showed that tactile surfaces in Sacco's comics on Bosnia indicate compassion and dwelling with the subjects of his reportage.

The black scribble is not merely an abstraction that contrasts to the whiteness of Katie's body: It can break her body open in painful ways. For example, pages 105 through 108 show the scribble coming directly from Katie's body: Her feeling of guilt over eating a biscuit is expressed by an ever-growing mass of scribble in her throat, slowly reaching her stomach. Then the scribble inside her literally tears her body apart. On a double spread that shows Katie four times (106–7), first Katie is choking, then her body is torn into two pieces along

FIGURE 5.3. The scribble interferes with the regular grid structure in Katie Green, *Lighter Than My Shadow*, 198–99.

the waist. Finally, she reaches down inside her own throat through the mouth, grabbing what is inside, trying to tear it out. These three figures of Katie's body in moments of extreme pain are represented against a background of scribble. The scribble violates the wholeness of Katie's body on multiple occasions. Figure 5.2 shows one such painful sequence, and in this figure the scribble also functions as an indicator of her anxiety, as an environment for alternative and imaginary bodies, and also as a material presence (172–73).

This sequence is significant for a second reason: It shows the scribble interfering with the basic layout of the comic. In fact, figure 5.2 also hints at the triple orientation of the scribble to some extent: The scribble is linked to Katie's thoughts, to representing experiences of her body, and to the layout. Figure 5.3 is a revealing example for the scribble taking over governing the layout of the double-spread page (198–99). The standard way to divide up the page into panels in *Lighter Than My Shadow* is by gutters resembling three-dimensional paper-tears, which give the impression that the complete page is made of individual panels glued together. Now the scribble starts filling the gutters, separating and connecting individual panels; however, by the bottom of the second page of figure 5.3, the regular gutter is reinstated. After being an emotional marker and an environment to

FIGURE 5.4. In traumatic moments, the scribble takes over structuring the page in Katie Green, *Lighter Than My Shadow*, 148–49

represent subjective bodily experience, the scribble is seen here in its third function: It has become a structural element of page layout. It is important to note that this sequence is not the first time this happens; I chose this scene as it shows most clearly the link of the scribble to the gutter.

The scribble interferes with the layout mostly in traumatic moments: On the one hand, it serves as a gutter in pages where the geometry of the grid is still followed (185, 196, 198), and on the other hand, it has the capacity to leave the angular structure of the grid behind, as seen in figure 5.4. In such cases, bits of action flash up in isolated bubbles, their position suggesting discontinuity and distance between the figurative elements. For example, the scene when Katie is diagnosed as anorexic is represented by a page structurally defined by the scribble (147–48), and the scribble defines the structure of the page when Green shows the therapist touching Katie in a tent (308), Katie burying the realization that she has been touched by the therapist (314), and Katie remembering that she has been touched against her will (366–67).

The link between the experience of Katie's body and the scribble as an element of comics structure is taken to the extreme by a double spread covered in black scribble (142–43). These pages are followed by a plain black double spread (144–45). At this relatively early point in the narrative, Katie collapses due to lack of eating, and the spread pages represent her blackout. The reader, who has learned to connect the scribble and Katie's body, is presented pages where the figurative representation of this body is absent, yet the body and Katie are present in the scribble. As I have connected the scribble to the gutter, I propose thinking of these pages as consisting of nothing but gutter. These pages are a hiatus in figurative representation, yet they convey the emotional and bodily experience of the vulnerability of the body. Green uses the scribble as gutter to link the abused vulnerability of her avatar to the way the page and the comic are structured.

There is a change in density and texture between the double page filled with scribble and the plain black pages. These haptic surfaces reference Katie's body in different ways, and they require different readerly interpretative strategies. The plain black surface can equally be read as a lack of sensation or as the intensity of the experience of the starving body. In these pages, without offering it as a figurative spectacle, a liminal bodily experience is given a material presence on paper. When the scribble takes over the in-between space, it influences the way the reader connects the represented moments of action. The reader's performance of closure is influenced by the haptic scribble of the gutter and by its associations with emotional anxiety and with Katie's body. Skimming the surface of scribble becomes a way to spend time with Katie's pain and abused vulnerability.

The representation of girls' precarity, particularly of sexual violence against girls, is studied, for example, by Marshall and Gilmore in the article "Girlhood in the Gutter." The authors are very critical of visual cultural practices, pointing out that way too often representations make it easier for the audience to look away and not to notice. They write that "visual culture is invested in hiding the sexual precarity of girls in plain sight through techniques of omission and oblique references that groom audiences to overlook the social fact of sexual violence against girls" (95). I find *Lighter Than My Shadow* particularly important in this regard, as Green makes looking away difficult by making the vulnerable body the subject of her comic on so many levels. So far I have studied the scribble's complicated relationship to Katie's body and it becoming a structural element, the gutter.

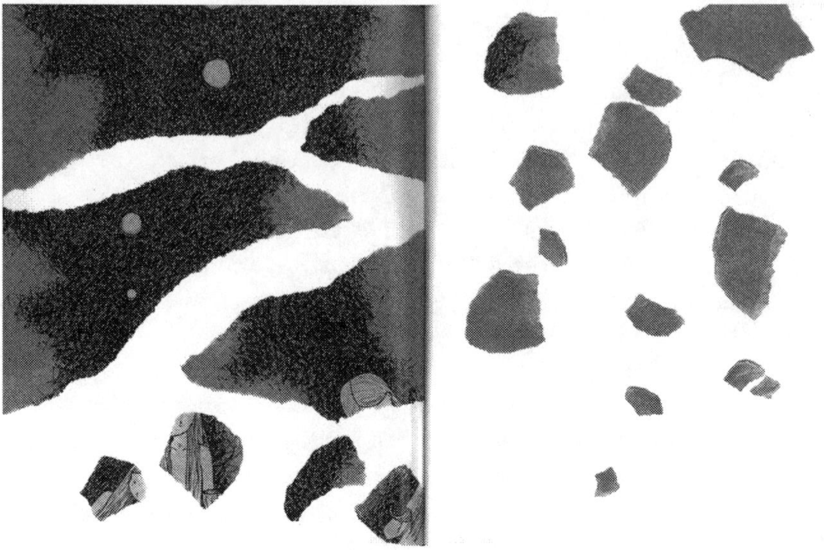

FIGURE 5.5. Green connects the body of her avatar to the materiality of the published comic in *Lighter Than My Shadow*, 382–83

There is a further level, however: A material link is created between Katie's exposed and abused vulnerable body and the actual object of the comic made out of paper.

The connection between Katie's body and the book-format comic is made apparent in the sequence where Katie contemplates suicide (380–403). Katie is shown with a handful of pills and a glass of water in hand; a column of black scribble is behind and above her; in the scribble five empty bubbles, equally resembling tablets, thought bubbles, and air, point toward Katie's head (381). The structural and visual innovation of this page, however, is that it is damaged: Two white scars of tearing run from the sides of the page toward its center. One white tear reaches toward Katie's ear, scarring her body. When the page is turned, we find the same image completely torn up (figure 5.5) and the pieces scattered (382–83). It is impossible to harm Katie's body in the act of suicide without harming the book, and this double spread with her body torn up together with the paper makes the tie between Katie's body and the object so strong that the opposite of the above statement is equally true: It is impossible to harm the book without harming Katie's body.

This heavy, oversized book-shaped object is not simply an object (or a scriptive thing); from now on, it is a metaphor-object standing for Katie's body. Holding it, turning its pages, and closing it are more than acts of physical interaction with a thing; the spatial relationship between a copy of *Lighter Than My Shadow* and the reader is more complicated than a spatial relationship between a comic and its reader. Interaction is now imbued with presence; Katie's body is present in the pages. Having seen how her body and the page have been torn into pieces gives a new significance to the tears that are the standard ways to represent the gutter. The assemblages of panels and the scarring presence of lines created out of tears at the borders of these panels also get connected to Katie's body.

Emphasizing the material connection to Katie is a possibility to reflect on the distance between the comic and the reader, even to change the way the comic is read and interacted with. When this connection is realized by the reader, the space of reading is transformed: Vulnerability is articulated in material ways by the narrative and by the body of the comic, and the scene of reading becomes an ethical scene. *Lighter Than My Shadow,* the three-dimensional thing that is tied to the body of the avatar, connects the embodied work of the drawer and the embodied work of the reader: The interaction between these three agents can be what artist and filmmaker Daria Martin called a "subtle" (13) encounter that has the potential to become a scene where vulnerabilities are articulated by all parties involved, and where the relationships between these agents can be changed: "Such a relationship to an artwork—in which we make it and it, in turn, makes us through the medium of our embodied sense—can be subtle" (13).

The Object and the Reader's Body

Lighter Than My Shadow links the character's body to the three-dimensional object of the comic and emphasizes that the object of the comic can be an important and semantically charged presence in the space of reading, taking part in the discourse of vulnerability. Joe Sacco's *The Great War,* analyzed in this section, has similar interests: Figurative and haptic representation, as well as its unusual format, facilitate (or script) unusual interaction and reflected reading practices. These can, in turn, encourage an embodied understanding of the experience of the trenches in the battle of the Somme. Visually, this twenty-four-foot-long narrative shows uninterrupted images of countless soldiers marching from left to right: First they prepare for war, then they are squeezing in the trenches, are blown up, fall, die, and the survivors bury other bodies. *The Great War* is unusual because it does not have an autobiographical avatar or a protagonist at the center of its narrative; no character is singled out as a possible bearer of readerly empathy or identification or as the agent of vulnerability. Instead, it shows countless almost identical bodies and repeats situations in which the body can be harmed multiple times.

The Great War is a wordless drawn narrative printed on a long ribbon of paper, folded between two thick cardboard covers, and packaged in a box together with a booklet containing Sacco's "Author's Note" and a guide to identifying certain people or events in the narrative, as well as a contextualizing historical essay, "July 1, 1916," by Adam Hochschild. The box promises the content to be "An Illustrated Panorama," invoking nineteenth-century panoramic traditions. Yet this work works with radically different spatial and material relations between the object of looking and the body of the onlooker. Panoramas were one of the most popular forms of entertainment in the nineteenth century: Stephan Oettermann writes in *The Panorama: History of a Mass Medium* (1997) that

> the basic aim of a panorama was to reproduce the real world so skillfully that spectators could believe what they were seeing was genuine. . . . The painting had to surround observers and envelop them completely, so as to exclude any glimpse of their real whereabouts. An entire pictorial environment was created for visitors to pass through. (49)

The nineteenth-century panorama offers a world of representation that is on the same scale as the onlooker's reality, with the goal of creating the illusion of a genuine elsewhere. It belongs to the tradition of simulation: The panorama "aims to blend virtual and physical spaces rather than to separate them" (Manovich 112); it deemphasizes boundaries and invites the onlooker to move around in this space (Gunning 38). By creating a book-sized panorama, Sacco reverses the relationship between the panorama and the onlooker's body. It works on a scale far smaller than reality: Instead of enveloping the onlooker, it invites the reader to bend closer, examine, touch, smell, and interact with *The Great War* and be engaged in an unpredictable material interaction with the "pages" when turning them.

FIGURE 5.6. The plates of Joe Sacco's *The Great War*

The reader can choose to bend closer or to move on: It is the reader who controls the distance from the world of this printed panorama. The movement of the onlooker was an important element in the appreciation of the nineteenth-century panorama, but a degree of distance had to be maintained between the moving observer and the spectacle, otherwise the illusion of simulation would have perished. A contrary process takes place when reading *The Great War*: The distance between the object and the reader can be reduced endlessly by the reader's interaction, and the printed panorama does not lose its meaning. On the contrary, this active management of the space of reading by the material and visual features of the work is one of the ways in which *The Great War* engages in the discourse of vulnerability.

During reading, the materiality of the support of this printed panorama is constantly drawn attention to—an aspect that was to be hidden in the nineteenth century. The ribbon of the narrative does not have a spine; it is folded and packaged as an accordion (figure 5.6). The accompanying booklet calls the page-like units defined by the folds "plates." When the reader attempts to proceed in the narrative, *The Great War* responds to his or her touch in unexpected ways: The folds sometimes help, sometimes hinder progress. A way to read *The*

Great War is to completely unfold the accordion-fold book in order to perceive the graphic narrative in its full length. Alternatively, the reader tries turning the pages, but the paper is hard and resists; one always touches two pages connected at their outer edges, and the spine is painfully missing: The imitation will be poor. A desk or table can lend some improvised support, but reading it in an armchair is doomed to failure: The accordion unfolds, and it becomes very difficult to turn the plates along their folds. The instability of the material support can change the reader's touch: Touching to trace Sacco's lines in gestures of interpretation can easily turn into touching the page to discipline the behavior of the publication. This physical interaction is very much related to the ways in which *The Great War* mobilizes the concept of vulnerability.

Furthermore, as the plates are not separated by margins, the seamlessness of the narrative constantly questions what should be considered as a unit of interpretation. Readers frequently bridge the disruption of the folds by connecting the images on adjacent plates. By looking at the scenes as if they were not separated by the folds, readers reorganize the units predefined by packaging and engage with the represented action and the materiality of the work simultaneously. Awareness of the materiality of *The Great War* is linked both to the topic of representing bodies in war and to the reader's awareness and experience of his or her body taking part in unusual performances when interpreting *The Great War*.

Though the very materiality and format of *The Great War* make immersion difficult, the drawings invite it. The dominant direction of represented action is from left to right, and this creates a horizontal drive and a possibility to immerse oneself in the flow of the progress of the battle. Simultaneously, each plate creates possibilities for immersion by studying minute details, a strategy *The Great War* has in common with the Bayeux Tapestry. In the "Author's Note," Sacco mentions the Bayeux Tapestry as a visual and narrative influence on the undisturbed pictorial narrative in *The Great War* (Sacco and Hochschild 1). The Bayeux Tapestry is a 68.38 meter- (224 foot)-long handcrafted embroidery made a little after the Battle of Hastings in 1066. As its size indicates, it was meant to be a work for public display (Pastan and White 1). It shows "627 human figures, 190 horses or mules, 35 dogs, 32 ships, 33 buildings, and 37 trees" (Pastan and White 1), and Sacco's panorama shares not only the Bayeux Tapestry's format but also its interest in the human figure and in the details of battle: Sacco represents countless human figures, a great number of modern war instruments, and also the landscape of war.[1]

The soldiers resemble each other even despite their individualized gestures: Everyone is engaged in different activities, yet none of these activities or people is deemed more important than the others. The soldiers are not shown from up close; representation always keeps a certain distance from them. This visual reserve, the multitude of bodies, and the lack of a named central character influence the way the reader positions him- or herself in relation to the text. Instead of focusing on the story of an individual as he does in his journalism, in *The Great War* Sacco emphasizes that humans are part of social structures, in this case the military. In the first part of the narrative, repeated rows of bodies and repetitive actions become the major motifs by detailing ordinary and very physical experiences of eating, sleeping, doing physical work, and going to the latrines.

I would like to show that the reader's interaction with *The Great War* as a physical three-dimensional object establishes a connection between the reader's body and the bodies of the represented soldiers. This connection also allows me to introduce vulnerability in the performance of reading. While attempting to proceed in the narrative, the reader follows the marching of thousands of tiny soldiers from spacious locations to narrow trenches. The dynamism of this movement slows down as the soldiers' march becomes less goal-oriented in the maze of trenches. The depth of the plates gets mobilized when the soldiers crawl out of the trenches and start to attack the allies: Instead of moving from left to right, they attempt to move "up" on the surface of the page as they run toward a quickly diminishing horizon (13–16). However, they cannot proceed because of explosions and smoke, and on plates 16 and 17 the illusion of a space in which the body could move is annihilated by the shells directly hitting the trenches. The bodies of the soldiers are tiny compared to the massive extension of smoke. After the various military formations the

1. Another feature the Bayeux Tapestry and *The Great War* have in common is that both visual narratives call attention to their material nature. The Bayeux Tapestry "thematizes its own materiality" (Pastan 9) by paying detailed attention to the representation of textiles, in this way emphasizing the very stitches by which the story of the Norman conquest is narrated. A way for Sacco to thematize the materiality of *The Great War,* as a drawn product in print, is to change the amount of ink used and to create tactile surfaces out of lines that appeal to the interconnected nature of our senses to a greater degree than usual.

soldiers are now represented in their individual helplessness. The narrative shows the experience of war as a wounding response to vulnerability. The condition of vulnerability always elicits a response, and here wounding manifests not only in the injured and dead bodies but in the isolated living ones: Separated from each other, soldiers are shown crawling, bending, or making futile efforts to move (e.g., plates 15 and 16).

On plates 13 and 14, the soldiers' bodies are represented as individual units: They start their attack as no longer united by a tight and complex system. Smoke of exploding shells gradually takes over, and an increasing percentage of the surface of the plates is devoted to intricately curving lines, groups of dots creating waves, and the seemingly empty white surfaces complicating the pattern (e.g., plates 17 and 18). Reading "for" the bodies and focusing on the figures and movement of the soldiers, which has been facilitated by the representational strategies so far and will be the prompted way of reading after these scenes, is no longer possible. Instead, the reading process slows down as the haptically visual surfaces created out of smoke, explosions, and bodies are contemplated. The plates appeal to a more sensual reading experience as the texture-like nature of these plates does not reveal depth or perspective (e.g., plates 17 and 18), nor do they offer any highlighted elements (e.g., 15 and 16). These plates invite skimming the pages and reading for pattern. In this way, the topic of the tension between the individual and bigger structures, such as the military, and the tension between looking for identifiable bodies as individual units and perceiving masses created out of bodies are expressed by the alternation between two representational strategies. On the one hand, readers can focus on the drawn bodies, all of which are elaborated in equal detail. The mode of visceral seeing is active: The realistically represented bodies are observed in detail and are understood partly in terms of our own bodies, bodily sensations, and body schema and by "that mode of awareness that listens to the body and is aware of its feeling" (Elkins, *Pictures* 23). On the other hand, these bodies and other elements of the battle create very tactile surfaces in which the soldiers are no longer seen as individual bodies but as parts of a pattern. The haptically inviting textural surfaces of plate 15 (figure 5.7) and plate 16 create haptic input out of smoke and bodies. These bodies, however, are no longer those of healthy soldiers; they are wounded, broken, or dead bodies. Our look grazes aimlessly and

FIGURE 5.7. The haptically most charged plates also show the body as injured, broken, or dead in Joe Sacco's *The Great War*, plate 15

the surface "pull[s] the viewer in close" (Marks, *Skin* 163). These two modes go together. Switching between them, together with the unusual material characteristics and spatial features of *The Great War* already discussed, directs awareness to the reader's own body and its performance. In this way, the reader's embodied engagement with the graphic narrative can become an embodied engagement with the abuse of vulnerability by war.

It is not a coincidence that the haptically most charged plates (14–18) introduce the body as injured and broken (figure 5.7). These plates appeal to the reader's body in all possible channels: via visceral seeing, via haptic vision, and via the bodily interaction with the accordion. At the heart of these images we find the experience of vulnerability: It has been an underlying motive of the narrative of *The Great War,* but these plates showing the chaos of the battle articulate it most clearly. Vulnerability can also be experienced in acts of interaction during reading, particularly if we unfold the accordion to get an overview of the narrative. Caution is needed to balance the massive cover and the fragile ribbon of paper, and a lot of space is also required. When *The Great War* is displayed in a public space, it is frequently flattened out and its ribbonlike structure is emphasized. This is not possible in the privacy of a room. Once *The Great War* is unfolded without being flattened out, the spatial experience is shocking: One is encircled and entrenched by and within the work. The spatial experience evokes a metonymical similarity to the rows of trenches represented in such great numbers on the plates. Thus, the story entrenches the reader, surrounds the reader with its own materiality. When reading in this way, the position of the reader's body evokes the soldiers lying or squatting behind endless and fragile shelters. This very peculiar spatial relationship and physical interaction between book and reader can elicit an embodied understanding via a bodily realization of vulnerability.

The trench becomes more than a returning element on the drawings. If we unfold *The Great War,* our position will be very similar to those of the soldiers hiding behind walls. At the climax of the narrative, the reader's physical position resembles the physical position of the soldiers minutes before being sent to certain death. The explosions, smoke, and dead bodies on plates 16 through 19 activate the reader's performance of bodily empathy and haptic reading most strongly; these are possibly the most disturbing and chaotic parts of the panorama. The array of limbs and helmets is swarming in the trenches and ditches without any hope of escape. In the meantime, the reader is painfully aware of his or her own body, as the narrative and the materiality of the accordion never allow him or her to take reading and the actions of the body for granted, but the reader is also aware of the fundamental difference between how vulnerabilities are experienced. At this point, and in this position, a dialogue based on the mutual nature of vulnerability takes place: an understanding based on an embodied reading experience and an embodied understanding of the Other's position. However, the end of the narrative of *The Great War* does not bring any bodily consolation: Trench scenes are followed by scenes of medical help and burial. The site of the labyrinth of trenches is left behind, but their structure of geometrically organized rows is repeated. Trenches are replaced by the rows of beds that the injured are placed on, while the rows of mass graves being dug on the last plate finalize the feeling that there is no escape.

The form, dimensions, and material features of *The Great War* never let the reader forget what is held in hand or what is interacted with, yet these characteristics also evoke a bodily experience that raises questions of vulnerability in a different way than figures and haptically visual surfaces. Just like in Green's work, the materiality of the comic adds an extra channel in which the discourse of vulnerability can manifest: The invitation to understand the realness of the vulnerability of the Other is articulated on the plates and also in three dimensions, and the reader can reflect on these articulations and can be transformed by the changed relationship between object and self, as well as between Other and self, in multiple material ways.

CONCLUSION

COMICS AND THE BODY

Lining Things Up

A COMIC BY THE AUTHOR

WRITTEN & DRAWN BY ESZTER SZÉP, 2019.

IN THIS DIALOG THE BODY IS ACTIVE IN MAKING LINES AND IN UNDERSTANDING THEM.
TO FIND OUT HOW DRAWERS TAKE PART IN THE DIALOG GO TO
LYNDA BARRY
TO FIND OUT HOW READERS TAKE PART IN THE DIALOG GO TO
JAMES ELKINS
CARTOONIST LYNDA BARRY SAYS THAT ONE'S LINE IS PERSONAL & THAT IT IS BORN OUT OF THE MOVEMENT OF THE BODY IN A CERTAIN STATE OF MIND
THE PRACTICE IS TO KEEP OUR HAND IN MOTION AND TO STAY OPEN TO THE IMAGE IT IS LEAVING FOR US
THE LINE HAS BEEN THOUGHT OF AS THE DRAWER'S MARK OR AS THE TRACE OF THE DRAWER'S MOVEMENT. BUT THE LINE IS ALSO A PARTNER OF THE DRAWER. THEY EXPLORE AND EXPRESS TOGETHER.
Where shall we go next?
THE LINES USED TO DRAW & REDRAW ARTISTS' AVATARS ALSO TAKE PART IN THE DIALOG.
THEY ALSO HAVE TRANSFORMATIVE POWER.
DRAWING IS A KIND OF THINKING AND A PERSONAL & EMBODIED WAY OF UNDERSTANDING THE WORLD, OTHERS, OR OURSELVES. DURING AND BY MAKING MARKS ON A SURFACE.
THIS IS WHY JOE SACCO SAYS
YOU KIND OF INHABIT EVERYTHING YOU DRAW.
LINES ARE AT THE HEART OF SOMETIMES UNSETTLING PROCESSES.

I BELIEVE THE LINK BETWEEN THE LINE AND THE BODY CONTRIBUTES TO COMICS NARRATIVES AND TO THE DRAWER-READER DIALOG MORE THAN WE THINK!
ESZTER SZEP
THERE IS A SIMPLE STATEMENT BY JAMES ELKINS THAT GREATLY INFLUENCED HOW I THINK ABOUT COMICS AND THE BODY.
EVERY PICTURE IS A PICTURE OF THE BODY.
READERS UNDERSTAND LINES WITH THEIR BODIES IN WAYS THAT RARELY BECOME CONSCIOUS.
OUR BODIES ARE ACTIVE IN MAKING SENSE OF IMAGES.
"IT CAN BE DIFFICULT TO MAINTAIN TRADITIONAL DISTINCTIONS BETWEEN VIEWER AND VIEWED." JAMES ELKINS
READERS DO NOT SIMPLY FOLLOW PLOTLINES IN COMICS, NOR DO THEY SIMPLY IDENTIFY OR EMPATHIZE WITH CERTAIN CHARACTERS.
FOR EXAMPLE, READERS MOVE TOGETHER WITH ABSTRACT LINES AND ARE ALSO MOVED BY THEM. LAURA U. MARKS CALLS THIS KINAESTHETIC EMPATHY.
READERS MAKE SENSE OF DRAWN BODIES IN TERMS OF THEIR OWN BODY'S SENSE OF ITSELF. ELKINS CALLS THIS VISCERAL SEEING.

A NOTE ON NAVIGATING THIS COMIC:
IF YOU HAVEN'T READ ABOUT THE DRAWER-LINE RELATIONSHIP YET → NOW IS A GOOD TIME TO GO BACK & FIND LYNDA BARRY
GREAT!
WE ARE NOW ON THE SAME PAGE & CAN START TO CONSIDER FURTHER IMPLICATIONS!
THE BODY IS ACTIVELY INVOLVED IN COMMUNICATION WITH AND BY DRAWN LINES. AND THE BODY IS ALSO
VULNERABLE
WE NEED OTHERS
WITHOUT OTHER PEOPLE CARING FOR US WE COULD DIE
VULNERABILITY IS A PREREQUISITE OF EXPERIENCING PLEASURE
ASK FREUD
ASK ME!
PAIN AND WOUNDING
ARE ALSO RESPONSES TO ONE'S VULNERABILITY.
BOTH VULNERABILITY AND COMICS
ARE PERFORMED AS INTERACTION AND AS DIALOG
AND BOTH ARE EXPERIENCED IN PERFORMANCES OF THE BODY.
DUE TO THEIR DRAWN NATURE,
COMICS CAN GIVE OPPORTUNITIES
TO EXPRESS & TO STUDY THE VULNERABILITY OF THE BODY
TO UNDERSTAND DIFFERENTLY
(WITH THE BODY)
AND TO RESPOND TO THE VULNERABILITY
OF THE SELF & OF THE OTHER.

Annotation

Some of the sources and references in the four-page scholarly comic "Comics and the Body: Lining Things Up" are the following:

Page 184: The bathtub picture hints at Frida Kahlo's *What the Water Gave Me.*

Page 185: The source of the Lynda Barry quote is *Syllabus* 22. In the panel explaining that the line can be a partner to the drawer, which is a central topic of chapter 1, the image hints at Paul Klee's drawing *Was Fehlt Ihm?* (*What Is He Missing?*). The source of the Joe Sacco quote is Sacco and Mitchell 60.

Page 186: Katie Green's avatar in *Lighter Than My Shadow* is referred to in the background of the first panel and is a central character in the last panel. The James Elkins quotes come from *Pictures of the Body: Pain and Metamorphosis.* The quote in panel 2 is on page 32. As it is part of a longer argument, it is worth quoting it at length so that some of its original context is known:

> Yet if every picture is a picture of the body, and if "distortion" is an adequate word for the means of representation, then pictures are continuous refusals and repressions of the body: they are ways of controlling the body by fixing an image of what it is not.

The quotation by Elkins in panel 4 is in *Pictures of the Body* vii–viii, and visceral seeing is explained on page viii in the same book. Laura U. Marks explains kinesthetic empathy in "I Feel Like an Abstract Line" 168–69. A part from Katie Green's avatar in the last panel on this page evokes Miriam Katin's avatar from *Letting It Go.*

Page 187: The aspects of vulnerability represented here are based on Simone Drichel's "Introduction: Reframing Vulnerability: 'So Obviously the Problem . . .'?" In this introduction, she also connects vulnerability to Freud's notion of "original helplessness." The last image on this page shows my avatar reading Joe Sacco's *The Great War.*

WORKS CITED

Archer, Dan. "Nisoor Square Shootings." *The Cartoon Movement,* 20 June 2011.

Archer, Michael. "Introduction: What Is to Come." Winter, pp. 6–8.

Axe, David, and Matt Bors. *War Is Boring.* New American Library, 2010.

B, David. *Epileptic.* Translated by Kim Thompson, Pantheon Books, 2005.

Baetens, Jan. "Guest Editor's Introduction: Theorising Photography as a Social and Artistic Practice." *Visual Studies,* vol. 24, no. 2, 2009, pp. 93–96. *tandfonline.com,* doi: 10.1080/14725860903106096. Accessed 31 Oct. 2014.

———. "Revealing Traces: A New Theory of Graphic Enunciation." *The Language of Comics: Word and Image,* edited by Robin Varnum and Christina T. Gibbons, University Press of Mississippi, 2001, pp. 145–55.

Baetens, Jan, and Hugo Frey. *The Graphic Novel: An Introduction.* Cambridge University Press, 2015.

Ball, David M., and Martha B. Kuhlman. *The Comics of Chris Ware: Drawing Is a Way of Thinking.* University Press of Mississippi, 2010.

Barry, Lynda. "Car and Batman." *Critical Inquiry,* vol. 40, no. 3, 2014, pp. 11–19.

———. *One! Hundred! Demons!* Sasquatch Books, 2002.

———. *Picture This: The Near-Sighted Monkey Book.* Drawn and Quarterly, 2010.

———. *Syllabus.* Drawn & Quarterly, 2014.

———. *What It Is.* Drawn & Quarterly, 2008.

Baskind, Samantha. "A Conversation with Miriam Katin." *The Jewish Graphic Novel: Critical Approaches,* edited by Samantha Baskind and Ranen Omer-Sherman, Rutgers University Press, 2008, pp. 237–43.

Beaty, Bart. *Comics versus Art.* University of Toronto Press, 2012.

Beaty, Bart, and Benjamin Woo. *The Greatest Comic Book of All Time: Symbolic Capital and the Field of American Comic Books.* Palgrave Macmillan, 2016.

Bennett, Jill. *Empathic Vision: Affect, Trauma, and Contemporary Art.* Stanford University Press, 2005.

Bernstein, Barbara. "Drawing a Breath." Pegram, pp. 91–99.

Bernstein, Robin. "Dances with Things: Material Culture and the Performance of Race." *Social Text,* vol. 27, no. 4, 2009, pp. 67–94.

Borkin, Michelle. "Visualization Recognition and Recall." *YouTube,* uploaded by TapestryConference, 13 Mar. 2017, http://www.youtube.com/watch?v=k7141r6QQ2A.

Brillenburg Wurth, Kiene, Sara Rosa Espi, and Inge van de Ven. "Visual Text and Media Divergence." *European Journal of English Studies,* vol. 17, no. 1, 2013, pp. 92–108.

Brown, Bill. "Thing Theory." *Critical Inquiry,* vol. 28, no. 1, 2001, pp. 1–22.

Bryson, Norman. *Vision and Painting: The Logic of the Gaze.* Macmillan, 1983.

Bui, Thi. *The Best We Could Do: An Illustrated Memoir.* Abrams Comicarts, 2017.

Bukatman, Scott. *Hellboy's World: Comics and Monsters on the Margins.* University of California Press, 2016.

———. *The Poetics of Slumberland: Animated Spirits and the Animating Spirit.* University of California Press, 2012.

———. "Vivian Sobchack in Conversation with Scott Bukatman." e-*Media Studies,* vol. 2, no. 1, 2009, doi:10.1349/PS1.1938–6060.A.338 journals.dartmouth.edu/cgi-bin/WebObjects/Journals.woa/1/xmlpage/4/article/338. Accessed 10 Feb. 2017.

Butler, Judith. *Precarious Life: The Powers of Mourning and Violence.* London, Verso, 2004.

Campbell, David. "Cultural Governance and Pictorial Resistance: Reflections on the Imaging of War." *Review of International Studies,* 2003, vol. 29, pp. 57–73.

Caruth, Cathy. "Introduction." *Trauma. Explorations in Memory,* edited by Cathy Caruth, The John Hopkins University Press, 1995, pp. 3–11.

———. *Literature in the Ashes of History.* The John Hopkins University Press, 2013.

Chaney, Michael. *Reading Lessons in Seeing: Mirrors, Masks, and Mazes in the Autobiographical Graphic Novel.* University Press of Mississippi, 2016.

Chappatte, Patrick. "Inside Death Row." *The New York Times,* 4 May 2016, http://www.nytimes.com/interactive/2016/05/04/opinion/the-last-phone-call.html.

———. "Revealing the Humanity Behind the News." *TEDx Talks,* 13 Dec. 2011, http://www.youtube.com/watch?v=4N5NopQUFbI.

Chute, Hillary. "Comics Form and Narrating Lives." *Profession,* 2011, pp. 107–17.

———. *Disaster Drawn: Visual Witness, Comics, and Documentary Form.* Harvard University Press, 2016.

———. *Graphic Women: Life Narrative and Contemporary Comics.* Columbia University Press, 2010.

——. *Outside the Box: Interviews with Contemporary Cartoonists.* The University of Chicago Press, 2014.

——. "Review of *Our Cancer Year* by Harvey Pekar, Joyce Brabner and Frank Stack, *Janet and Me: An Illustrated Story of Love and Loss* by Stan Mack, *Cancer Vixen: A True Story* by Maria Acocella Marcetto, *Mom's Cancer* by Brian Fies, *Blue Pills: A Positive Love Story* by Frederik Peeters, *Epileptic* by David B, *Black Hole* by Charles Burns." *Literature and Medicine,* vol. 26, no. 2, 2007, pp. 413–29. *Project Muse,* doi:10.1353/lm.0.0005. Accessed 21 Oct. 2013.

——. "The Texture of Retracing in Marjane Satrapi's *Persepolis.*" *Women's Studies Quarterly,* vol. 36, no. 1–2, 2008, pp. 92–110.

Chute, Hillary, and Marianne DeKoven. "Introduction: Graphic Narrative." *Modern Fiction Studies,* vol. 52, no. 4, 2006, pp. 767–82. *Project Muse,* doi:10.1353/mfs.2007.0002. Accessed 14 Nov. 2012.

Clowes, Daniel. "Just Another Day." *The Daniel Clowes Reader,* edited by Ken Parille, Fantagraphics Books, 2013, pp. 279–85.

Crucifix, Benoît. "From Loose to Boxed Fragments and Back Again: Seriality and Archive in Chris Ware's *Building Stories.*" *Journal of Graphic Novels and Comics,* vol. 9, no 1, 2018, pp. 3–22.

Crumb, A., and R. Crumb. *Drawn Together.* Liveright, 2012.

Dahl, Ken. *Monsters.* Secret Acres, 2009.

Davis, Vanessa. *Make Me a Woman.* Drawn & Quarterly, 2010.

de Jesus, Melinda. "Of Monsters and Mothers: Filipina American Identity and Maternal Legacies in Lynda J. Barry's *One Hundred Demons.*" *Meridians: Feminism, Race, Transnationalism,* vol. 5, no. 1, 2004, pp. 1–26.

Diprose, Rosalyn. "Corporeal Interdependence: From Vulnerability to Dwelling in Ethical Community." *SubStance,* vol. 42, no. 3, 2013, pp. 185–204.

Dittmer, Jason. "Narrating Urban Assamblages: Chris Ware and *Building Stories.*" *Social and Cultural Geography,* vol. 15, no. 5, 2014, pp. 477–503.

Dong, Lan. "Inside and Outside the Frame: Joe Sacco's *Safe Area Goražde.*" Worden, pp. 39–53.

Dony, Christophe L. "Trauma, Identity and Memory: The Individual/Collective Dialectic in 9/11-Related Comics." *IJOCA,* vol. 9, no. 2, 2007, pp. 340–72.

Doucet, Julie. *My Most Secret Desire.* Drawn & Quarterly, 2006.

Drichel, Simone. "Introduction: Reframing Vulnerability: 'So Obviously the Problem . . . '?" *SubStance,* vol. 42, no. 3, 2013, pp. 3–27. *Project Muse,* doi:10.1353/sub.2013.0030. Accessed 27 Dec. 2016.

Duncan, Randy, Michael Ray Taylor, and David Stoddard. *Creating Comics as Journalism, Memoir & Nonfiction.* Routledge, 2015.

Dunn, Kevin. C. "Teaching World Politics: *Safe Area Goražde* in the Classroom." Worden, pp. 256–71.

Earle, Harriet E. H. *Comics, Trauma, and the New Art of War.* University Press of Mississippi, 2017.

Elkins, James. *The Object Stares Back: On the Nature of Seeing.* Harvest, 1996.

——. *Pictures of the Body: Pain and Metamorphosis.* Stanford University Press, 1999.

El Refaie, Elisabeth. *Autobiographical Comics: Life Writing in Pictures.* University of Mississippi Press, 2012.

Elsaesser, Thomas, and Malte Hagener. *Film Theory: An Introduction through the Senses.* Routledge, 2010.

Engelberg, Miriam. *Cancer Made Me a Shallower Person: A Memoir in Comics.* Harper Perennial, 2006.

Fies, Brian. *Mom's Cancer.* Harry N. Abrams, 2009.

Findley, Laura. "*In the Shadow of No Towers*: The Anxiety of Expression and Images of Past Trauma in Art Spiegelman's Graphic Novel." *Studies in Comics,* vol. 5. no. 1, 2014, pp. 187–203.

Fischer, Craig, and Charles Hatfield. "Teeth, Sticks, and Bricks: Calligraphy, Graphic Focalization, and Narrative Braiding in Eddie Campbell's *Alec.*" *SubStance,* vol. 40, no. 1, 2011, pp. 70–93.

Galison, Peter, and Trevor Paglen. "The Lives of Images: Peter Galison in Conversation with Trevor Paglen." *Aperture,* no. 211, 2013, pp. 32–39.

Gallagher, Shaun. *How the Body Shapes the Mind.* Clarendon Press, 2006.

Gardner, Jared. "Autography's Biography, 1972–2007." *Biography,* vol. 31, no. 1, 2008, pp. 1–26. *Project Muse,* doi:10.1353/bio.0.0003. Accessed 19 Feb. 2015.

———. *Projections: Comics and the History of Twenty-First-Century Storytelling.* Stanford University Press, 2012.

———. "Storylines." *SubStance,* vol. 40, no. 1, 2011, pp. 53–69.

———. "Time under Siege." Worden, pp. 21–38.

Gauthier, Tim. *9/11 Fiction, Empathy, and Otherness.* Lexington Books, 2015.

Gilmore, Leigh. "Covering Pain: Pain Memoirs and Sequential Reading as an Ethical Practice." *Biography,* vol. 38, no. 1, 2015, pp. 104–17.

Gloeckner, Phoebe. *A Child's Life and Other Stories.* North Atlantic Books, 2001.

Gloeckner, Phoebe, Justin Green, Aline Kominsky-Crumb, and Carol Tyler. "Panel: Comics and Autobiography." *Critical Inquiry,* vol. 40, no. 3, 2014, pp. 86–103.

Green, Justin. *Binky Brown Meets the Holy Virgin Mary. Justin Green's Binky Brown Sampler,* Last Gasp, 1995, pp. 9–52.

Green, Katie. *Lighter Than My Shadow.* Jonathan Cape, 2013.

Grennan, Simon. *A Theory of Narrative Drawing.* Palgrave Macmillan, 2017.

Groeger, Lena. "When the Storyteller Shows Up in the Story." *YouTube,* uploaded by TapestryConference, 13 Mar. 2017, http://www.youtube.com/watch?v=TvJYDz8849g&t=1419s.

Groensteen, Thierry. *The System of Comics.* Translated by Bart Beaty and Nick Nguyen, University Press of Mississippi, 2007.

Gunning, Tom. "The Art of Succession: Reading, Writing, and Watching Comics." *Critical Inquiry,* vol. 40, no. 3, 2014, pp. 36–51.

Hague, Ian. *Comics and the Senses: A Multisensory Approach to Comics and Graphic Novels.* Routledge, 2014.

Hatfield, Charles. *Alternative Comics: An Emerging Literature.* University Press of Mississippi, 2005.

Hatfield, Charles, and Joe Sutliff Sanders. "Bonding Time or Solo Flight? Picture Books, Comics, and the Independent Reader." *Children's Literature Association Quarterly*, vol. 42, no. 4, 2017, pp. 459–86.

Hayles, Katherine N. *How We Became Posthuman: Virtual Bodies in Cybernetics, Literature, and Informatics.* The University of Chicago Press, 1999.

Helbig, Tina. "Beware the Living Dead: The Corpo-Reality of Comics." *Studies in Comics*, vol. 8, no. 2, 2017, pp. 187–203, doi:10.1386/stic.8.2.187_1.

Hewish, Andrew. "Introduction to the Special Edition on the Line." *Journal of Visual Art Practice*, vol. 14, no 1. 2015, pp. 1–2.

———. "A Line from Klee." *Journal of Visual Art Practice*, vol. 14, no 1. 2015, pp. 3–15.

Higgie, Jennifer. "lips become leaves." Winter, pp. 40–41.

Hirsch, Marianne. "The Generation of Postmemory." *Poetics Today*, vol. 29, no. 1, 2008, pp. 103–28, doi:10.1215/03335372-2007-019.

———. "Marked by Memory: Feminist Reflections on Trauma and Transmission." *Extremities: Trauma, Testimony, Community*, edited by Nancy K. Miller and Jason Tougaw, University of Illinois, 2002, pp. 71–91.

Horstkotte, Inge. "Photo-Text Topographies: Photography and the Representation of Space in W. G. Sebald and Monika Maron." *Poetics Today*, vol. 29, no. 1, 2008, pp. 49–78.

Horstkotte, Silke, and Pedri, Nancy. "Focalization in Graphic Narrative." *Narrative*, vol. 19, no. 3, 2011, pp. 330–57.

Ingold, Tim. *Lines: A Brief History.* Routledge, 2007.

Jenkins, Henry. "An Interview with Comics Journalist Joe Sacco (Part Two)" *Confessions of an Aca-Fan: The Official Weblog of Henry Jenkins*, 15 Mar. 2007, http://www.henryjenkins.org/2007/03/an_interview_with_comics_journ_2.html. Accessed 4 Mar. 2012.

———. "Photoshop for Democracy: The New Relationship between Politics and Popular Culture." *Convergence Culture: Where Old and New Media Collide*, New York University Press, 2006, pp. 206–39.

Johnson, Mark. "'The Stone That Was Cast Out Shall Become the Cornerstone': The Bodily Aesthetics of Human Meaning." *Journal of Visual Art Practice*, vol. 6, no. 2, 2007, pp. 89–103.

Karasik, Paul, and Mark Newgarden. *How to Read Nancy: The Elements of Comics in Three Easy Panels.* Fantagraphics Books, 2017.

Kashtan, Aaron Jacob. "Materiality Comics." *Digital Humanities Quarterly*, vol. 9, no. 4, 2015, http://www.digitalhumanities.org/dhq/vol/9/4/000212/000212.html.

Katin, Miriam. *Letting It Go.* Drawn and Quarterly, 2013.

———. *We Are On Our Own.* Drawn & Quarterly, 2006.

Keen, Suzanne. "A Theory of Narrative Empathy.' *Narrative*, vol. 14, no. 3, 2006, pp. 207–36.

———. *Empathy and the Novel.* Oxford University Press, 2007.

Kirk, Carole. "'Painting' as Emergent Knowledge: A Practice-led Case Study of Contemporary Artistic Labour." *Journal of Visual Art Practice*, vol. 13, no. 2, 2014, pp. 114–29.

Klee, Paul. *Pedagogical Sketchbook.* Translated by Sybil Moholy-Nagy, Praeger Publishers, 1953.

Koch, Christina Maria. "Comic-Grotesque Metamorphoses: Boundaries between Illness and Health in Ken Dahl's *Monsters.*" *Comics an der Grenze: Sub/Versionen von Form und Inhalt,* edited by Matthias Harbech, Linda-Rabea Heyden, and Marie Schröer, Ch. A. Bachmann Verlag, 2017, pp. 149–64.

Kominsky-Crumb, Aline. *Need More Love.* Spruce, 2007.

Kristeva, Julia. *The Powers of Horror.* Translated by Leon S. Roudiez, Columbia University Press, 1982.

Kübler-Ross, Elisabeth, and David Kessler. *On Grief and Grieving: Finding the Meaning of Grief through the Five Stages of Loss.* Scribner, 2014.

Kukonnen, Karin. *Studying Comics and Graphic Novels.* Wiley Blackwell, 2013.

Kurczynski, Karen. "Drawing Is the New Painting." *Art Journal,* vol. 70, no. 1, 2011, pp. 92–110.

Lagarrigue, Aurélie, and Marieke Longcamp. "The Production and Perception of Handwritten Traces." *The Materiality of Writing: A Trace-Making Perspective,* edited by Christian Mosbæk Johannessen and Theo van Leeuwen, Routledge, 2018, pp. 15–29.

Lahner, Elsy. "Die Zeichnung und ihr Potenzial / Drawing and Its Potential." Schröder and Lahner, 12–23.

Lakoff, George, and Mark Johnson. *Metaphors We Live By.* University of Chicago Press, 1980.

———. *Philosophy in the Flesh: The Embodied Mind and Its Challenge to Western Thought.* Basic Books, 1999.

Lefèvre, Pascal. "Some Medium-Specific Qualities of Graphic Sequences." *SubStance,* vol. 40, no. 1, 2011, pp. 14–33.

Linthout, Willy. *Years of the Elephant.* Fanfare, 2009.

Louvel, Liliane. "Photography as Critical Idiom and Intermedial Criticism." *Poetics Today,* vol. 29, no. 1, 2008, pp. 31–48.

Love, Johanna. "Somewhere between Printmaking, Photography and Drawing: Viewing Contradictions within the Printed Image." *Journal of Visual Art Practice,* vol. 14, no. 3, 2015, pp. 214–23.

Lunsford, Andrea A., and Adam Rosenblatt. "'Down a Road and into an Awful Silence': Graphic Listening in Joe Sacco's Comics Journalism." *Silence and Listening as Rhetorical Arts,* edited by Cheryl Glenn and Krista Ratcliffe, Southern Illinois University Press, 2011, pp. 130–46.

Macdonald, Isabel. "Drawing on the Facts: Comics Journalism and the Critique of Objectivity." Worden, pp. 54–66.

Mackenzie, Catriona, Wendy Rogers, and Susan Dodds, editors. *Vulnerability: New Essays in Ethics and Feminist Philosophy.* Oxford University Press, 2014.

Manovich, Lev. *The Language of New Media.* The MIT Press, 2001.

Marks, Laura U. "I Feel Like an Abstract Line." Martin, pp. 151–76.

———. *The Skin of the Film: Intercultural Cinema, Embodiment, and the Senses.* Duke University Press, 2000.

———. *Touch: Sensuous Theory and Multisensory Media.* University of Minnesota Press, 2002.

Marshall, Elizabeth, and Leigh Gilmore. "Girlhood in the Gutter: Feminist Graphic Knowledge and the Visualization of Sexual Precarity." *WSQ: Women's Studies Quarterly,* vol. 42, no. 1–2, 2015, pp. 95–114.

Martin, Daria, editor. *Mirror-Touch Synaesthesia.* Oxford University Press, 2017.

Massumi, Brian. "The Art of the Relational Body: From Mirror-Touch to the Virtual Body." Martin, pp. 191–209.

McCloud, Scott. *Understanding Comics: The Invisible Art.* Harper Perennial, 1994.

Mickwitz, Nina. *Documentary Comics: Graphic Truth-Telling in a Sceptical Age.* Palgrave Macmillan, 2016.

Miodrag, Hannah. *Comics and Language: Reimagining Critical Discourse on the Form.* University Press of Mississippi, 2013.

Mitchell, W. J. T. *What Do Pictures Want? The Lives and Loves of Images.* University of Chicago Press, 2005.

Möller, Frank. "Witnessing Violence through Photography." *Global Discourse,* vol. 7, no. 2–3, 2017, pp. 264–81, doi:10.1080/23269995.2017.1339979.

Murphy, Ann. *Violence and the Philosophical Imaginary.* State University of New York Press, 2012.

Ndula, Victor. "50 Years On, Still Hungry." *The Cartoon Movement,* 2013, https://www.cartoonmovement.com/icomic/52. Accessed 29 June 2019.

Nussbaumer Knaflic, Cole. "Where's Larry? Bringing Data To Life through Story." *YouTube,* uploaded by TapestryConference, 13 Mar. 2017, https://www.youtube.com/watch?v=TWASJxLVdYo.

Oettermann, Stephan. *The Panorama: History of a Mass Medium.* Zone Books, 1997.

Orbán, Katalin. "Embodied Reading: The Graphic Novel, Perception, and Memory." *The International Journal of the Humanities: Annual Review,* vol. 11, 2013, pp. 1–11, *orbankati.net.* Accessed 2 Apr. 2014.

———. "A Language of Scratches and Stitches: The Graphic Novel between Hyperreading and Print." *Critical Inquiry,* vol. 40, no. 3, 2014, pp. 169–81.

———. "Mediating Distant Violence: Reports on Non-Photographic Reporting in *The Fixer* and *The Photographer.*" *Journal of Graphic Novels and Comics,* vol. 6, no. 2, 2015, pp. 122–37.

———. "Trauma and Visuality: Art Spiegelman's *Maus* and *In the Shadow of No Towers.*" *Representations,* vol. 97, no. 1, 2007, pp. 57–89.

Pastan, Elizabeth Carson. "The Material Context of the Bayeux Embroidery: Manufacture, Display, and Literary References." *The Bayeux Tapestry and Its Contexts: A Reassessment,* edited by Elizabeth Carson Pastan and Stephen D. White, The Boydell Press, 2014, pp. 9–32.

Pastan, Elizabeth Carson, and Stephen D. White. "Introduction." *The Bayeux Tapestry and Its Contexts: A Reassessment,* edited by Elizabeth Carson Pastan and Stephen D. White, The Boydell Press, 2014, pp. 1–7.

Pegram, Elizabeth A., editor. *Drawing in the Twenty-First Century: The Politics and Poetics of Contemporary Practice.* Ashgate, 2015.

Pekar, Harvey, Joyce Brabner, and Frank Stack. *Our Cancer Year.* Running Press, 1994.

Pines, Davida. "History, Memory, and Trauma: Confronting Dominant Interpretations of 9/11 in Alissa Torres's *American Widow* and Art Spiegelman's *In the Shadow of No Towers.* Tolmie, pp. 185–206.

Polak, Kate. *Ethics in the Gutter: Empathy and Historical Fiction in Comics.* The Ohio State University Press, 2017.

Precup, Mihaela. *The American Graphic Memoir: An Introduction.* University of Bucharest, 2013.

Presenti, Allegra. "The Binding Line": A Conversation with Allegra Presenti, Curator at Large, The Menil Drawing Institute, The Menil Collection." Pegram, pp. 141–57.

Rawson, Philip. *Drawing.* University of Pennsylvania Press, 1987.

——. *The Art of Drawing: An Instructional Guide.* Macdonald & Co, 1983.

Rieff, David. "Bosnia beyond Words." *The New York Times,* 24 Dec. 2000, https://www.nytimes.com/2000/12/24/books/bosnia-beyond-words.html. Accessed 12 Oct. 2018.

Ritchin, Fred. *After Photography.* W. W. Norton & Company, 2009.

——. *Bending the Frame: Photojournalism, Documentary, and the Citizen.* Aperture, 2013.

Romero-Jódar, Andrés. *The Trauma Graphic Novel.* Routledge, 2017.

Rosenblatt, Adam, and Andrea A. Lunsford. "Critique, Caricature and Compulsion in Joe Sacco's Comics Journalism." *The Rise of the American Comics Artist: Cartoons and Contexts,* edited by Paul Williams and James Lyons, University of Mississippi, 2010, pp. 68–87.

Sabin, Roger. *Adult Comics: An Introduction.* Routledge, 1993.

Sacco, Joe. *Bumf Vol. 1.* Jonathan Cape, 2014.

——. "Complacency Kills." *The Guardian Weekend,* 26 Feb. 2005.

——. *The Fixer: A Story from Sarajevo*. Jonathan Cape, 2004.

——. *The Great War: July 1, 1916: The First Day of the Battle of the Somme*. Jonathan Cape, 2013.

——. *Journalism.* Jonathan Cape, 2012.

——. *Palestine.* Jonathan Cape, 2003.

——. "Preface: A Manifesto, Anyone?" *Journalism,* Jonathan Cape, 2012, pp. ix–xii.

——. *Safe Area Goražde.* Fantagraphics Books, 2000.

Sacco, Joe, and Adam Hochschild. *On the Great War.* Jonathan Cape, 2013.

Sacco, Joe, and W. J. T. Mitchell. "Public Conversation." *Critical Inquiry,* vol. 40, no. 3, 2014, pp. 53–70.

Sacco, Joe, and Chris Ware. "Joe Sacco and Chris Ware at the Edinburgh International Book Festival." *YouTube,* uploaded by ebookfest, 18 Aug. 2013, https://www.youtube.com/watch?v=LBGWfLzNNFg&t=1111s.

Sassoon, Rosemary. *Handwriting of the Twentieth Century.* Routledge, 1999.

Satrapi, Marjane. *Persepolis: The Story of a Childhood and The Story of a Return.* Translated by Anjali Singh, Vintage Books, 2006.

Scherr, Rebecca. "Framing Human Rights: Comics Form and the Politics of Recognition in Joe Sacco's *Footnotes in Gaza*." *Textual Practice*, vol. 29, no. 1, 2015, pp. 111–31.

———. "Joe Sacco's Comics of Performance." Worden, pp. 184–200.

———. "Shaking Hands with Other People's Pain: Joe Sacco's *Palestine*." *Mosaic: A Journal for the Interdisciplinary Study of Literature*, vol. 46, no. 1, 2013, pp. 19–36. *Project Muse*, doi:10.1353/mos.2013.0004. Accessed 6 Mar. 2015.

Schlick, Yaël. "What Is an Experience? Selves and Texts in the Comic Autobiographies of Alison Bechdel and Lynda Barry." Tolmie, pp. 26–43.

Schröder, Klaus Albrecht, "Vorwort / Preface." Schröder and Lahner, 6–11.

Schröder, Klaus Albrecht and Elsy Lahner, editors. *Drawing Now 2015*. Hirmer, 2015.

Shaughnessy, Nicola, editor. *Affective Performance and Cognitive Science: Body, Brain and Being*. Bloomsbury, 2013.

Shepherd, Simon. *The Cambridge Introduction to Performance Theory*. Cambridge University Press, 2016.

Shildrick, Margrit. *Embodying the Monster: Encounters with the Vulnerable Self*. Sage, 2002.

Singer, Marc. "Views from Nowhere: Journalistic Detachment in *Palestine*." Worden, pp. 67–81.

Small, David. *Stitches: A Memoir*. W. W. Norton & Company, 2009.

Smiciklas, Mark. *The Power of Infographics: Using Pictures to Communicate and Connect with Your Audiences*. Que, 2012.

Sobchack, Vivian. *The Address of the Eye: A Phenomenology of Film Experience*. Princeton University Press, 1992.

Sontag, Susan. *AIDS and Its Metaphors*. Farrar, Straus & Giroux, 1989.

———. *Regarding the Pain of Others*. Penguin, 2003.

Sousanis, Nick. *Unflattening*. Harvard University Press, 2015.

Spiegelman, Art. *In the Shadow of No Towers*. Pantheon, 2004.

———. *Maus I*. Pantheon Books, 1986.

———. *Maus II*. Pantheon Books, 1991.

Stafford, Richard Todd. "The Politics of Space in Joe Sacco's Representations of the Appalachian Coalfields." Worden, pp. 123–38.

Stout, Katherine. *Contemporary Drawing: From the 1960s to Now*. Tate Publishing, 2014.

Szép, Eszter. "Graphic Narratives of Women in War: Identity Construction in the Works of Zeina Abirached, Miriam Katin, and Marjane Satrapi." *International Studies: Interdisciplinary Political and Cultural Journal*, vol. 16, no. 1, 2014, pp. 21–33.

Tolmie, Jane, editor. *Drawing from Life: Memory and Subjectivity in Comic Art*. University Press of Mississippi, 2013.

Tribble, Evelyn B., and John Sutton. "Introduction: Interdisciplinarity and Cognitive Approaches to Performance." Shaughnessy, pp. 27–37.

Una. *Becoming Unbecoming*. Myriad Editions, 2015.

Vågnes, Øyvind. "John's Story: Joe Sacco's Depiction of 'Bare Life.'" Worden, pp. 158–67.

van de Vall, Renée. *At the Edges of Vision: A Phenomenological Aesthetics of Contemporary Spectatorship.* Ashgate, 2008.

Versaci, Rocco. *This Book Contains Graphic Language: Comics as Literature.* Continuum International Publishing Group, 2007.

Versluys, Kristiaan. "Art Spiegelman's *In the Shadow of No Towers*: 9–11 and the Representation of Trauma." *MFS Modern Fiction Studies,* vol. 52, no. 4, 2006, pp. 980–1003.

Vischer, Robert. "On the Optical Sense of Form: A Contribution to Aesthetics." *Empathy, Form, and Space: Problems in German Aesthetics, 1873–1893,* The Getty Center for the History of Art and the Humanities, 1994, pp. 89–123.

Ward, Jamie. "The Vicarious Perception of Touch and Pain: Embodied Empathy." *Mirror-Touch Synaesthesia,* edited by Daria Martin, Oxford University Press, 2017, pp. 55–70.

Ware, Chris. *Building Stories.* Pantheon Graphic Library, 2012.

——. *Monograph.* Rizzoli, 2017.

Weber, Wibke, and Hans-Martin Rall. "Authenticity in Comics Journalism: Visual Strategies for Reporting Facts." *Journal of Graphic Novels and Comics,* vol. 8, no. 4, 2017, pp. 376–97, doi:10.1080/21504857.2017.1299020.

Whitlock, Gillian. "Autographics: The Seeing 'I' of the Comics." *MFS Modern Fiction Studies,* vol. 52, no. 4, 2006, pp. 965–79.

Williams, Ian. "Graphic Medicine: Comics as Medical Narrative." *Medical Humanities,* no. 38, 2012, pp. 21–27, doi:10.1136/medhum-2011-010093. Accessed 12 Jan. 2015.

——. "Monsters: Review." *Graphic Medicine,* 23 July 2012, http://www.graphicmedicine.org/comic-reviews/monsters. Accessed 12 Jan. 2017.

——. "Years of the Elephant: Review." *Graphic Medicine,* 20 Aug. 2009, http://www.graphicmedicine.org/comic-reviews/years-of-the-elephant. Accessed 29 Sep. 2017.

Winter, Judith, editor. *Draw: Conversations around the Legacy of Drawing.* Middlesborough Institute of Modern Art, 2007.

Woo, Benjamin. "Reconsidering Comics Journalism: Information and Experience in Joe Sacco's *Palestine.*" *The Rise and Reason of Comics and Graphic Literature: Critical Essays on the Form,* edited by Joyce Goggin and Dan Hassler-Forest, McFarland, 2010, pp. 166–77.

Worden, Daniel, editor. *The Comics of Joe Sacco: Journalism in a Visual World.* University Press of Mississippi, 2015.

INDEX

STUDIES IN COMICS AND CARTOONS

Jared Gardner and Charles Hatfield, Series Editors
Lucy Shelton Caswell, Founding Editor Emerita

Books published in Studies in Comics and Cartoons focus exclusively on comics and graphic literature, highlighting their relation to literary studies. The series includes monographs and edited collections that cover the history of comics and cartoons from the editorial cartoon and early sequential comics of the nineteenth century through webcomics of the twenty-first. Studies that focus on international comics are also considered.

Comics and the Body: Drawing, Reading, and Vulnerability
Eszter Szép

Producing Mass Entertainment: The Serial Life of the Yellow Kid
Christina Meyer

The Goat-Getters: Jack Johnson, the Fight of the Century, and How a Bunch of Raucous Cartoonists Reinvented Comics
Eddie Campbell

Between Pen and Pixel: Comics, Materiality, and the Book of the Future
Aaron Kashtan

Ethics in the Gutter: Empathy and Historical Fiction in Comics
Kate Polak

Drawing the Line: Comics Studies and INKS, 1994–1997
Edited by Lucy Shelton Caswell and Jared Gardner

The Humours of Parliament: Harry Furniss's View of Late-Victorian Political Culture
Edited and with an Introduction by Gareth Cordery and Joseph S. Meisel

Redrawing French Empire in Comics
Mark McKinney